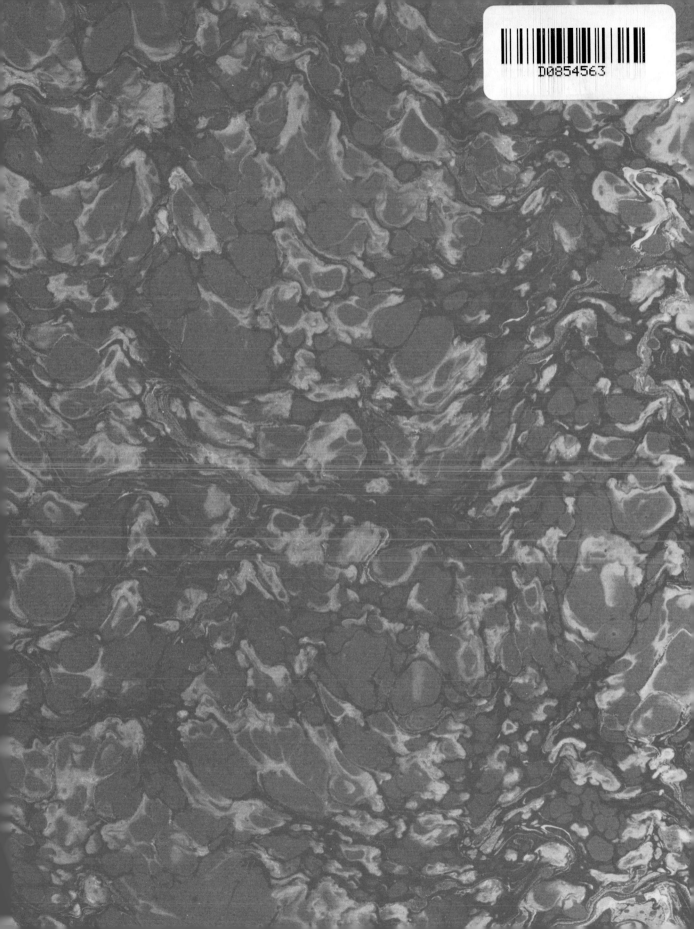

THE ROUX BROTHERS ON
· *PATISSERIE* ·

THE ROUX BROTHERS ON
· PATISSERIE ·

MICHEL &
ALBERT ROUX

PHOTOGRAPHS BY ANTHONY BLAKE

· Macdonald ·

A Macdonald Book

Copyright © 1986 QED Publishing Ltd
Text Copyright © 1986   Michel and Albert Roux

First published in Great Britain in 1986
Published by Macdonald & Co (Publishers) Ltd
London & Sydney
A Member of BPCC plc

British Cataloguing in Publication Data
Roux, Albert
    The Roux brothers on patisserie.
    1. Pastry   2. Cookery, French
    I. Title   II. Roux, Michel
    641.8'65   TX773

ISBN 0 356 12379 0

This book was designed and produced by
QED Publishing Ltd
The Old Brewery, 6 Blundell Street, London N7 9BH

Project Director Alastair Campbell
Translated by Kate Whiteman
Editors Carolyn King and Tessa Rose
Art Editor Moira Clinch

Editorial Director Jim Miles

Illustrations Liza Adamczewski

Typeset by QV Typesetting, London
Manufactured in Hong Kong by
Regent Publishing Services Limited
Printed by Leefung Asco Printers Limited, Hong Kong

Macdonald & Co (Publishers) Ltd
Greater London House, Hampstead Road,
London NW1 7QX

The Publishers would like to thank the many people who have helped in the preparation of this book, especially the following: Laura Beck of QV Typesetting; Mr Maghbroda for the use of his orchard; Osborne & Little and Falkiner Fine Papers for supplying background papers used in the book; Sarah Campbell; Dickins & Jones for supplying picnic hampers. Thanks also go to Suzannah Smith of The Conran Shop, Colin Harris of Wedgwood, Camilla Adams of General Trading Company (Mayfair) Ltd., Caroline Franklin of Reject China Shops, Abbie Sinclair of Elizabeth David Ltd., and Lynne Stephenson and Jeanette Galbraith of Rosenthal for lending the chinaware used in the photographs. All the kitchen equipment illustrated in this book can be obtained from **Maison Mora**, specialist suppliers of utensils for patisserie, 13 Rue Montmartre, B.P.273, 75024 Paris Cedex 01.

To Jean-Louis Berthelot
(1951-1979)

The craftsman, the artist, the friend, whose death was so untimely; in only a few short years, he brought and bestowed more knowledge to our craft than most men could have achieved in fifty years.

Coupe Grand Prix Charles Proust 1971
Médaille d'Or Arpajon 1971
Premier Commis de France 'Cusenier' 1971
Médaille d'Or Académie Culinaire Française 1971
International Gold Medal, Vienna 1974
1st prize: Sèvres vase, given by President Valéry Giscard d'Estaing, 1974
Meilleur Ouvrier de France 1976
Compagnon du Tour de France 1976
Chevalier des Arts, Sciences et Lettres 1977
Culinary Trophy of New York (Chef of the Year 1977)
Chevalier Côteaux de Champagne 1977
Chevaliers Cuiseurs du Sucre 1978

With profound respect, Michel and Albert pay homage to Jean-Louis

*T*he authors would like to express special thanks to all the people listed here, without whose help this book could never have been written: Robyn Roux, for her invaluable good sense and loyal support; John Hubert, senior lecturer at the Slough College of Higher Education, winner of numerous gold and silver medals in international competitions for patisserie work, chief examiner for advanced pastry courses (City & Guilds), member of the Académie Culinaire de France, U.K., who read all the recipes for us; Guy Barbé, chef de partie at The Waterside Inn, who tested most of the recipes and took part in almost all the photographic sessions; Geneviève Barbé for typing the manuscript; Moira Clinch and Carolyn King for their dedication and diligence in designing and editing the book; and finally Kate Whiteman for her excellent and sympathetic translation.

· FOREWORD ·

· INTRODUCTION ·

USING THIS BOOK

· CHAPTER ONE ·
· BASIC MATERIALS ·

· CHAPTER TWO ·
· BASIC RECIPES ·

PASTRY & DOUGH

BREAD

SPONGE & DESSERT BASES

CREAMS, SAUCES, FRUIT COULIS AND JELLY

· CHAPTER THREE ·
· DESSERTS ·

TARTS

CONFÉDÉRATION NATIONALE
DE LA
PÂTISSERIE-CONFISERIE-GLACERIE

For many years I have had the very highest regard for the Roux brothers — how could it be otherwise? Here are two men who, throughout their professional lives, have given the best possible service to their employers. Their courage, taste and attention to detail, combined with a love of their craft and hard work, have brought them to the very pinnacle of gastronomic achievement.

Albert is regarded by his peers as one of the greatest chefs in the world, while Michel is recognised as not only a very great chef, but also a master pâtissier — one of the Meilleurs Ouvriers de France in patisserie.

Here are two brothers, as inseparable in private life as they are professionally, who are prepared to face up to any situation, however difficult — look how they left their native land and came to London, speaking not a word of English, to snatch six Michelin stars for their two restaurants.

But they will not stop at that. Aware that honours demand duties, they have decided to share their knowledge and skill by writing two books — the enormously successful New Classic Cuisine, and now The Roux Brothers on Patisserie. You may be sure that professionals and beginners alike will find this book is the definitive guide to the art of patisserie.

I can confirm that this is a book full of riches, both in content and presentation. Its readers will find it an inspiration and from it will learn all there is to know about the noble craft of patisserie.

I offer Albert and Michel my congratulations and thanks on behalf of our profession.

Jean Millet M.O.F.
President

INTRODUCTION

*I*n this book, you will find many recipes, hints and tricks of the trade, gleaned from years of experience, right back to our earliest years in the profession. Our inspiration has come from the exercise books we kept as apprentices, when day after day we scribbled down tips and notes on pages besmeared by our buttery fingers.

Although most of our recipes are classic, we have adapted them to our own taste and to conform with modern ideas. Many of these dishes were once served in the private houses where we worked as chefs; today they appear on the menu at our restaurants, Le Gavroche and The Waterside Inn. We have given the most detailed instructions possible for all the dishes, so that, however simple or complex the recipe may be, it will be easy to follow. To ensure that each recipe is produced to the highest standard, we have limited the number presented in this volume and chosen to omit certain chapters like confectionery, chocolates and fresh, glazed or candied petits fours.

PATISSERIE: PAST AND PRESENT

From time immemorial, children have been attracted to the sweet scents of vanilla, lemon and sugar which their grandmothers and mothers used in their baking.

Waffles, pale, golden brown, topped with whipped cream, *crêpes* filled with jam, warm mirabelle tarts — these fragrant images remain firmly embedded in our memory.

The patisserie of yesterday has not disappeared; all the recipes of our heritage are founded upon it. But perhaps it is time to update it to conform to today's culinary ideas. Certain desserts, like those filled with buttercream or frangipane (mocha and *mascotte* cakes and *mille-feuilles*, for example) are less popular than they used to be. We no longer have the same passion for choux buns, eclairs, *réligieuses* or *Paris-Brest*. Elaborate piped decorations, silver balls and mimosa have declined in popularity, as have gateaus with fondant icing. Pastries and portions of cake, which were often far too large, have become smaller and more delicate. Even ice creams are making way for fresh fruit sorbets.

A *pâtissier* sells a little happiness to children, young people and adults alike, but nowadays he dispenses a healthier bounty. His confections contain less

*Michel Roux's apprenticeship was served under the searching gaze of M Camille Loyal,
pictured here with his wife outside his patisserie in the Paris district of Belleville in 1956.*

butter and sugar and fewer eggs than they did twenty years ago and, as a result,
his cakes are so light that we can enjoy them at any time of day, even when we
aren't particularly hungry. There is no doubt that, eaten in moderation, butter,
sugar and eggs are vital to our well-being.

The past few years have seen a very important change in our approach to
desserts; elaborate decorations, too, have been much simplified and, indeed,
have almost disappeared. Now, charlottes with fruit *coulis* abound — what is
more divine than a pear charlotte? Bitter chocolate is often the main ingredient
in a pudding, and in patisserie fruits (often exotic) reign supreme; they are pure
and natural and offer an endless range of possibilities — *bavaroises, bombes,*
charlottes, mousses, ice creams and tarts. It is a pity, though, that the ubiquitous
kiwi fruit has become somewhat over-used, both in savoury dishes and in
patisserie.

Fruit sorbets, too, are much in demand, adding a magical, refreshing note to
the end of a meal. Mousses, alas, are now so commonplace that many people are
becoming bored with them.

Obviously, it is easier to create really original patisserie at home or in a
restaurant than in a shop. The restaurateur is fortunate because he can prepare
the most delicate and fragile desserts which have only to be carried from
kitchen to dining room and not from shop to home. Thus he can offer his

famous *assiette du chef* — a plateful of tiny portions of his most sumptuous desserts — and set it all before a dumbfounded and amazed gourmet, who can scarcely take in such a feast for eye and palate.

THE SEMINAR FOR THE MAITRES PATISSIERS OF FRANCE

Every year, Michel takes part in the seminar of the *Maîtres Pâtissiers de France.* Sixty or so master *pâtissiers*, aged between 30 and 65, gather together for this gastronomic happening with its three days of culinary demonstrations. Among their number are found the most famous *pâtissiers* of France and between them they own the finest patisseries in the land.

From six o'clock in the morning till six at night, they assemble in groups of six to eight, and for two to three hours each *pâtissier* demonstrates his art to the rest of the assembled company.

The last morning of this seminar is spent discussing and debating the ground covered during the first two days. New ideas and methods are approved or rejected; problems are aired and solutions suggested. Thus, the whole future of patisserie in France is shaped. Our profession can only evolve for the better if experts like these are prepared to share all their secrets.

BECOMING A MEILLEUR OUVRIER DE FRANCE

France's most prestigious competition is organised by the state every three years. It brings together representatives from 217 professions, assembled in 17 groups, including mosaics, ironmongery, sculpture, floral art, culinary art — all trades where hand and mind combine.

The title of 'Meilleur Ouvrier' was officially recognized by a decree which appeared in the official trades journal no. 194 on 21 August 1980. It was classed as equivalent to Level 4 in education: Technical *Baccalauréat*, Certificate of Mastership, etc. In other words, it entitles the holder to teach at the highest technical level.

Once the participants have enrolled for the competition, they are given the subject matter and size of the piece they must create. The general commissioner or his deputies oversee and control the work in progress. First, a departmental jury judges the quality of the work; if it meets with their

MEILLEUR OUVRIER
DE FRANCE

My body trembles as though I have been beaten, my throat is tight with emotion, my eyes brim with tears — they have just announced my name; my work as a pâtissier-confiseur has received the ultimate recognition and I have been honoured with the title of 'un des Meilleurs Ouvriers de France 1976, Pâtissier-Confiseur'; in other words, I am considered to be one of France's finest craftsmen in pâtisserie. Drained by the physical effort of the hundreds of hours of work and the nervous tension of the past few weeks, I hardly dare believe it. All I know is that I am here and I have succeeded. I stagger, I lurch forward as though in a dream to collect that gold medal on its red, white and blue ribbon, the first to be presented by the President of the French Republic, Monsieur Valéry Giscard d'Estaing.

I am burning hot. I am consumed by that fire which burns in every craftsman who cares passionately about his work. This is the strongest emotion I have ever felt in all my thirty-five years. I feel intoxicated. My mind flashes back, as in a film, to the master whose apprentice I was, who awoke in the adolescent I was then that most precious love for this work. I can see the craftsmen who guided me, my colleagues and my friends, the MOFs who gave me good advice — I see everyone who has helped to teach me my wonderful craft. To them I give my joy, my pride and my gratitude.

THE GLITTERING PRIZE

After many years of sheer hard work and single-minded dedication came public recognition with the award of the gold medal and the title 'Meilleur Ouvrier de France'. Some of the pieces, made in the course of the competition, that won Michel Roux the coveted title include:

ABOVE *Chocolate presentation, made completely out of chocolate — both dark and white — and accompanied by six varieties of chocolates, has a contemporary flavour.*

ABOVE *The pièce de résistance — 'A window opening onto Spring'. The view through the open window is in pastillage, hand-painted with edible food colouring, as are the balcony and window frame. The window glazing is formed from Sucre coulé. The exuberant vine with its glossy flowers and leaves is made from Sucre tiré. It took more than 70 hours to create this particular piece.*

LEFT *Six different petits fours frais, presented on individual hand-painted pastillage bases.*

approval, it is then presented to the national juries. But now let Michel take up the story.

'On Monday 6 September 1976, I came to the final in which I was participating. Only twenty candidates had been short-listed. They came from everywhere — Paris, the provinces, even, like me, from abroad. The theme for our artistic presentation was "Spring"; I decided to christen mine "A window opening onto Spring". First there was to be a dessert designed for a baptism, then six sorts of glazed petits fours and six kinds of chocolates. We also had to model from sugar any flowers, fruits or animals of our choice. Our aim was to surpass ourselves, to scale new heights of excellence in pastry-making, dessert-creating, in preparing little cakes and vast cakes for catering — in short, in every aspect of the craft, we aimed to be complete masters of our art. To crown it all, we had to create pieces for special occasions and ceremonies, designed to titillate the palate and satisfy the most demanding of clients.

'Obviously, it is not possible to classify all the various crafts in the competition all together. That is why every three years a total of 400 craftsmen, representing every trade, are chosen from tens of thousands of hopeful competitors to become MOFs. In my year, seven *pâtissiers-confiseurs* were awarded the title of "un des Meilleurs Ouvriers de France" and I am happy to give you all their names. They are, from left to right: M Jean-Louis Berthelot, from La Celle-Saint-Cloud; M Gérard Hee, from Paris; M Michel Foussard, from Paris; M Gérard Moyne-Bressand, from Nîmes; M G. Marzet (President); M Yves Thuries, from Gaillac; M René Fontaine, from Langeac; and myself.'

USING THIS BOOK

*T*his most important part of the book can and should be consulted at all times. It is intended to teach and give simple guidance, and to remind you of certain facts and guidelines which you may have forgotten.

It is easy enough for a *pâtissier* to divulge his recipes, but a great deal harder to teach his skills and techniques in a book, for they have become second nature to him. It is these techniques which make all the difference to a creative piece of patisserie, which raise it from attractive to stunning, from good to excellent, and make it a source of pride.

· THE GOLDEN RULES ·

There are three vital ground rules for following a recipe successfully:

1 Have ready to hand all the equipment you will need for the recipe.

2 Weigh out and measure all the ingredients before commencing the recipe.

3 Preheat the oven to the desired temperature.

By following these golden rules you will find you can produce desserts and pastries easily and quickly.

Before embarking on the recipes in this book, there are some important points you should note.

· MEASUREMENTS ·

All our recipes have been tested using metric measurements and, if possible, you should use these precise measurements. For perfect results it is worth investing in a set of metric measuring spoons, jug and scales. If you feel you have to use the imperial system, bear in mind that these quantities can not be as specific as the metric scale. Imperial measurements in this book have been rounded up or down to the nearest half-ounce and half-fluid ounce. Whichever system you choose, stick to it; do not mix metric and imperial measures in one recipe. Conversion tables are given on page 245.

· INGREDIENTS ·

In order to achieve a perfect result in patisserie, basic ingredients such as butter, eggs and cream must be ultra-fresh and of the finest quality.

One or two ingredients can be difficult to find in local shops and alternatives may be substituted. For example, we use gelatine leaves each weighing 3 g/$\frac{1}{10}$ oz approximately, but these can be replaced by the same weight of powdered gelatine; *couverture* can be replaced by best quality, plain chocolate cake covering. Unless otherwise specified, all butter in the recipes is unsalted; sugar is caster sugar; flour is sifted plain flour.

The preparation time given for each recipe begins after all the ingredients have been weighed and measured, and all the necessary equipment is ready to hand.

Recommended storage times are for food kept in an airtight container or wrapped or covered in clingfilm.

· EQUIPMENT ·

The flan ring and mould sizes given in the recipes are ideal dimensions. Your own existing equipment should, if used, approximate the specified measurements.

Where a copper pan or casserole is given, you can use a heavy, copper-bottomed stainless steel pan instead.

· OVEN TEMPERATURES ·

These tend to vary from oven to oven so we suggest you use an oven thermometer. The results achieved in baking can vary according to the oven. On the whole, domestic gas ovens do not reach such high temperatures as commercial ovens and for this reason we have quoted slightly higher gas conversions than those generally given.

It is very important to watch cakes carefully during baking and not to place too much faith in the temperature indicated by the thermostat but rely instead on a cooking thermometer.

°C	°F	Gas	°C	°F	Gas
100	200	¼	180	350	5
110	225	¼	190	375	6
120	240	½	200	400	7
130	250	1	220	425	8
140	275	2	230	450	9
150	300	3	240	475	10
170	325	4	250	500	10

· SERVING TEMPERATURE ·

All patisserie must be served at the temperature which best suits its flavour and texture. This is why we have never used a sweet trolley at Le Gavroche and The Waterside Inn. All our desserts are kept in the kitchen at the correct temperature and are served to order, with no risk of being spoilt through careless cutting or inept serving by a waiter who is not a highly qualified *pâtissier*.

Chocolate-based desserts: mousses, *ganaches*, etc.	6°-8°C/42°-48°F
Fruit mousse-based desserts: charlottes, etc.	8°-12°C/48°-52°F
Warm puddings, such as tarts and some *feuilletés*.	35°-45°C/95°-104°F
Hot puddings, mainly soufflés.	Between 70° and 80°C/158° and 176°F

PRACTICAL ADVICE ON
· METHODS AND TECHNIQUES ·

Almond paste or marzipan: If it is crumbly or too firm, soften with fondant or glucose.
Coffee: Ground coffee will keep its flavour if it is stored in an airtight container in the fridge.
Fondant: When you warm it, add some 30° Baumé sorbet syrup and a little nut of glucose to soften the

fondant and make it glossy. Never add uncooked egg whites, as they might cause the fondant to ferment; health regulations forbid the addition of raw egg whites.

To beat: Always do this with a whisk.
To grease or butter: Use softened, clarified or melted butter as appropriate. It is important to use precisely the right quantity of butter for greasing moulds, flan rings, baking sheets, etc. Too much butter may crinkle the pastry; not enough may cause the food to stick. You can also buy a silicone spray, which eliminates the need for greasing.
To incorporate: Fold in with a flat slotted spoon, spatula or whisk.

To line: Do this with flour, sugar, ice cream or jelly etc, always using the exact quantity — neither too much nor too little.
To mix: Always do this with a spatula, paddle or whisk.
Sifting: This is necessary to get rid of any foreign particles and lumps in powdery ingredients such as flour, baking powder, ground almonds, cocoa, etc. It also aerates them. Flour must always be sifted for all pastry work.
Flouring: This prevents the dough from sticking to the marble or wooden surface and makes rolling out

easier. Sprinkle the flour in a fine cloud, a very little at a time, and brush away any excess before lining a dish with the pastry or placing it on a baking sheet.

Working with dough: Dough taken from the freezer must be left at 5°C/41°F for several hours to allow it to thaw gradually before using.

Maximum kneading of leavened dough or puff pastry: The dough is sufficiently kneaded when all the ingredients are incorporated and, after the dough has been kneaded for some time, the ball of dough comes cleanly away from the sides of the bowl or work surface. By this time, the flour will have absorbed all the moisture, and the dough will be elastic.

Rising of doughs leavened with yeast: If you are kneading dough in a warm temperature, chill the liquid ingredients (eggs, milk and water) before using. The temperature of the dough after kneading should never exceed 24°C/75°F.

After rich yeast-leavened doughs (eg, croissants, *brioches*, Viennese pastries, etc) have fermented in a warm place, it is best to leave them to 'relax' at room temperature for a further 15 minutes before baking so that they develop a full, even spring and puff up as much as possible during cooking.

Storing all types of uncooked dough: Before placing in the fridge, wrap the dough in polythene to prevent it from drying out and forming a crust.

Refrigerating puff pastry: Puff pastry must be brought to room temperature before using, so that the fat content has time to soften. If the pastry is too cold, the layers of fat might break during rolling and the dough will not develop and rise fully.

Rolled-out pastry: Move this by rolling it loosely onto a rolling pin, so as not to spoil the shape or break it. This applies to puff pastry, almond paste, etc.

Lining: To prevent the pastry from shrinking during cooking, line the mould the day before if possible and

keep in the fridge or freezer. In any event, the pastry must be left to rest for at least an hour before baking.

Allow about 50 g/2 oz pastry per person when making a tart or flan case.

Puff pastry: Place the rolled-out dough on a baking sheet dampened with water. This will prevent the pastry from slipping when you glaze it and stops it from shrinking during cooking, which would spoil the shape.

Staggered rows: Always arrange all pastry tins, tartlet and *brioche* moulds, etc. in staggered rows on the baking sheet to ensure more even cooking.

Glazing with eggwash: For a really shiny finish, it is best to give two light coats of glaze. A single, heavier glaze is more likely to run.

To make a durable glaze for puff pastry desserts (eg, Pithiviers,): Sprinkle with icing sugar at the end of cooking, and place in a very hot oven for a few moments to obtain a subtle, varnish-like glaze. If you use a 30° Baumé sorbet syrup to glaze, it may become dull and whitish after several hours, as the sugar recrystallises.

Egg yolks: These 'burn' when they come into contact with sugar or salt, so they must be beaten immediately with a whisk or spatula until completely homogenous. If this is not done, hard little granules of yolk will form, and it is impossible to get rid of them.

Stiffly beaten egg whites: To ensure that egg whites rise perfectly, all utensils must be scrupulously clean. Rinse them in cold water and allow to dry thoroughly before using.

Make sure that there is no trace of yolk left in the whites.

If they are very fresh, add a pinch of salt to break them down. Start by beating the whites at medium speed to make them frothy, and stretch them as much as possible, then increase the speed to high to firm them up.

When flecks of beaten egg white appear at the edges of the bowl, add a little sugar to prevent them from becoming grainy. They will be firmer and easier to mix and handle. This is very important in both savoury and sweet soufflés.

Weighing eggs:

Size 1	at least 70 g/2½ oz.
Size 2	65–70 g/2¼–2½ oz.
Size 3	60–65 g/2–2¼ oz.
Size 4	55–60 g/2 oz approx.
Size 5	50–55 g/1 ¾ oz approx.
Size 6	45–50 g/1½–1¾ oz.
Size 7	under 45 g/1½ oz.

A medium egg weighing about 60 g/2 oz contains approximately 30 g/1 oz white; 20 g/¾ oz yolk; 10 g/¼ oz shell.

20 whole eggs = 1 L/1 ¾ pts
32 egg whites = 1 L/1¾ pts
52 egg yolks = 1 L/1¾ pts

Freezing egg whites: Freeze them just as they are; they will keep very well for several weeks.

Freezing yolks: Beat them lightly with 5–10 per cent sugar, then freeze at –25°C/–13°F for not more than four weeks.

Cold storage: Modern methods of cold storage have opened up new horizons and make for more efficient methods of working.

Fridge: 5°C/41°F.
'Holding' freezer: 18°C/0°F.
Freezer: –25°C/–13°F.
Blast freezer: –35°C/–31°F. (Ideally, you should freeze food for 30 minutes at this temperature before transferring it to the 'holding' freezer.)

Making nougatine: In humid weather, add 50 g/2 oz butter or fat for each 1 kg/2 lb 2 oz as soon as you have mixed in the almonds; this will prevent the *nougatine* from attracting surface moisture.

Hygiene: One final general observation; we strongly recommend that you wear neither a watch nor jewellery when making patisserie. They can cause allergies and, because there is a tendency for flour and icing to get into the crevices, they are unhygienic.

CHAPTER
· 1 ·

THE BASIC
MATERIALS

Nowadays we tend to forget that the basic ingredients for patisserie were once produced by the *pâtissiers* themselves in the slack periods between the festive seasons. Only thirty years ago, one *pâtissier* in two in every town (more in country areas) skinned the almonds himself and from them made his own *tant pour tant, praliné* and marzipan. He would also make simple fondant icing and maybe prepare his own apple fillings.

Nothing can be nicer for an apprentice (as we were in those days) than to help in the making of hazelnut or almond *praliné*. How greedily we enjoyed watching and smelling the pounding of the nuts!

Today, all these basic ingredients are manufactured in factories; this ensures tighter health controls, consistently high quality and better keeping qualities. Professional and amateur *pâtissiers* can now obtain at any time of year whatever ingredients they need for every conceivable type of patisserie.

Kitchen equipment must be chosen with care and should always be top quality. Buy it from long-established specialist suppliers; their research departments consult professional chefs about their needs before launching new products on the market, so you can be assured that the equipment they sell will be useful, efficient and durable.

Good quality equipment is essential if you are to produce successful dishes. Quantity is far less important and this is why we have classified the equipment in three categories. The first short but adequate list allows the beginner to take his first faltering steps without spending a fortune or making expensive mistakes; this equipment will suffice for most of our recipes.

The second is a complementary list for the more experienced cook, and the third list is intended for professional chefs and amateur patisserie fanatics.

We have used non-stick baking parchment or silicone paper for several years now; it is easy to peel off and does away with the need for greasing. Metal flan rings ensure more even cooking and lift off neatly for easy unmoulding. Bake tarts or flans directly on a baking sheet inside a flan ring. These flan rings are also useful for Genoise sponges, sponge biscuits etc.

If you do not possess a flan ring, you can easily make one from a strip of cardboard cut to the desired length and depth. Stick the ends with sellotape and cover the ring with strips of greaseproof paper or foil. This type of ring is fine for assembling desserts, but not, of course, for cooking them!

Soufflés will rise best if you cook them in a bain-marie or on a baking sheet which has been preheated for ten minutes.

Brioches too will develop much better during cooking if baked on a preheated baking sheet.

Always soak a new pastry brush in lukewarm water for twenty-four hours before using it to prevent it from shedding its hairs. Small kitchen utensils should be washed in hot water and detergent but rinsed in cold; this will achieve a form of sterilization.

When sizes for flan rings, cake boards and other equipment are specified in a recipe, these are only approximate; there is no need to abandon a recipe because you do not possess a utensil of the precise size given!

A GRAIN OF SALT, A GRAIN OF SUGAR

Fundamentally, these two ingredients are diametrically opposed, both in their basic properties and in the way we use them. And yet, they stand together in the dock, each accused of the same crime — that of 'endangering health'.

Faddishness, snobbery, defenders of the steady march towards healthy living, be they dieticians or even cooks — they have all found not one, but both of them, guilty.

Used in moderation, however, these ingredients are essential to a balanced diet and our physical well-being. For generations, they have been a means of survival in times when food was in short supply. They are natural agents which highlight flavours, sweeten dishes and heighten colours, as well as preserving and conserving foodstuffs. Patisserie, like all cookery, would be lost without them; they are essential to life the world over, no matter what the climate, race, religion or lifestyle.

As for us, nothing will change our natural tastes and needs, so let us all cherish 'a grain of salt, a grain of sugar'.

· ESSENTIAL EQUIPMENT ·

1 *Plastic scraper*
2 *Pastry crimper*
3 *Dough scissors*
4 *Vegetable peeler*
5 *Apple corer*
6 *Small sharp knife*
7 *Filleting knife*
8 *Serrated knife*
9 *Three sizes of flexible knife with supple, stainless steel blade. Buy the best quality knives for the best*

result and the longest lifespan. Always dry the knife blade as soon as it is washed.
10 *Flat, wooden-handled pastry brush.*
11 *Two wooden spatulas. Remember not to leave these in any cooking preparation as they will absorb the flavour and then impart this taste to the next sauce or cream that you prepare. Use*

them for stirring and then rest them on top of the saucepan.

<u>RIGHT</u>
1 *A family-sized, electric ice cream machine is a worthwhile investment which will pay for itself in any ice cream- or sorbet-loving family. Ice creams and sorbets are inexpensive to make, particularly*

if seasonal fruits are incorporated.
2 *Balloon whisk*
3 *Dough hook*
4 *Electric mixer with plastic paddle. This is indispensible. Choose the best quality and the most dependable make; it should last a lifetime.*
5 *A splash-guard prevents dry ingredients such as icing sugar from blowing about.*

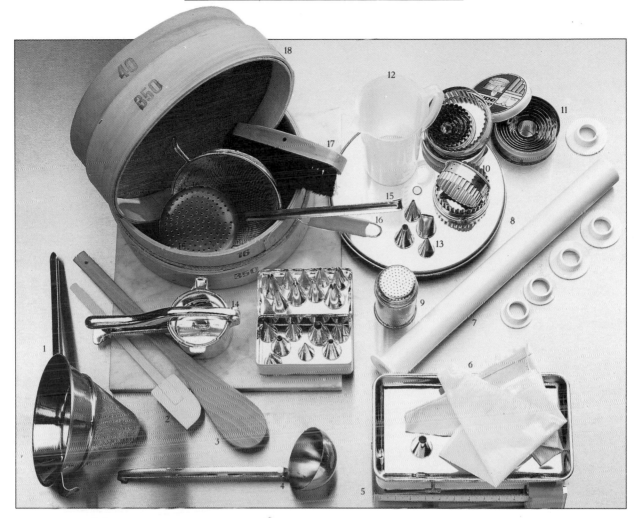

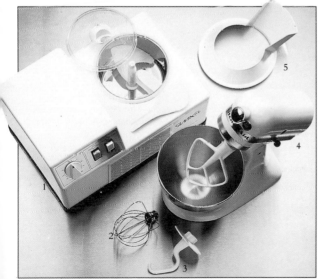

<u>ABOVE</u>
1 *Conical strainer*
2 *Rubber scraper*
3 *Wooden spatula*
4 *Ladle*
5 *Automatic weighing scales*
6 *Piping bag*
7 *A variable-gauge rolling pin. By changing the end rings you can control the thickness of the pastry — an invention which makes rolling pastry to a predetermined thickness foolproof.*
8 *A revolving turntable makes decorating a large cake with a piping bag or paper cornet easy.*
9 *Flour or sugar dredger*
10 *Set of fluted pastry cutters*
11 *Set of plain round pastry cutters*
12 *Measuring jug*
13 *Piping nozzles*
14 *Fruit press*

15 *Skimmer or flat slotted spoon*
16 *Fine mesh metal strainer*
17 *Flouring brush*
18 *Double mesh wooden sieves, size 40 for icing sugar, size 25 for flour, size 16 for ground almonds. It is best to avoid washing these sieves; dust with a dry brush after each use.*

· ESSENTIAL EQUIPMENT ·

1 Round-bottomed stainless steel mixing bowl is an ideal shape for any process involving a whisk.
2 Wire whisk for sauces and creams
3 Tray for small madeleines
4 Large fluted brioche mould
5 Tuile-shaper tray
6 Flat-bottomed stainless steel mixing bowl
7 Flan ring
8 Round sponge biscuit rings are available in sizes from about 5–30 cm/2–12 in and in rectangular and square shapes as well. It is more popular than any other sponge or biscuit mould.
9 Plain round tartlet tin
10 Small fluted brioche mould

<u>RIGHT</u>
Essences are very useful to give a boost of flavour to a natural ingredient. The best quality essence is made from the natural extract. The flavour must be discreet and not overpower the taste of the preparation so use sparingly. Once opened, the essence will last 6-12 months and will lose some of its strength.
1 Vanilla, 2 Coffee, 3 Orange blossom water, 4 Lemon zest, 5 Pistachio, 6 Bitter almond, 7 Orange.

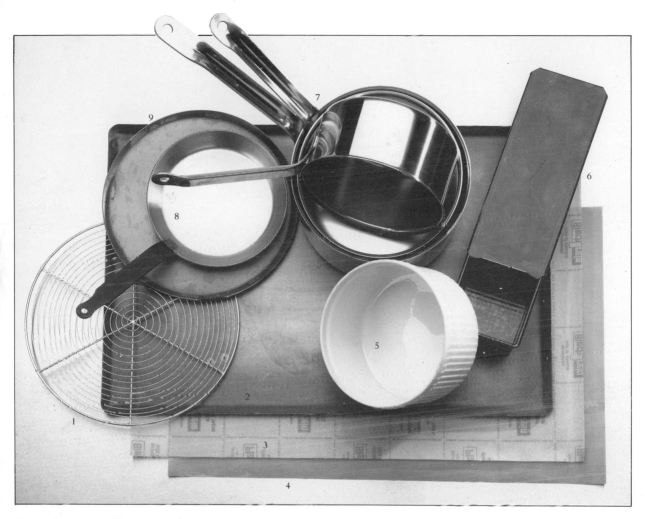

1 Wire rack
2 Baking sheet
3 Non-stick baking parchment
4 Silicone paper for baking can be re-used about 30 times. It is one of the most important new introductions to small equipment in pastry. The surface is extremely smooth, giving a perfect finish to cake, dough or pastry. No ingredient will stick to it.
5 Soufflé dish
6 Rectangular tin with sliding lid
7 Saucepans
8 Crêpe or pancake pan
9 Black metal baking sheet — an ideal shape and size for cooking a single tart.

· ADVANCED EQUIPMENT ·

1 A rigid conical strainer is mainly for draining fruits in syrup, and for straining sauces or fruit coulis which are quite thick.
2 Large plain savarin mould
3 Baking mould for büche de Noël or tuile shaper
4 Small baba mould with a rim
5 Small savarin mould
6 Small plain barquette tin
7 Blinis pan
8 Large round brioche or mousseline mould which could be substituted by a small, high–sided, -ovenproof saucepan.
9 Stainless steel wire rack
10 Stainless steel baba drainer
11 Large lined copper Tart Tatin mould. Without a handle, it takes up less room in the oven.
12 Round colander with feet
13 Icing tray with grill

<u>RIGHT</u>
Basic food colourings are used primarily for decorating marzipan, royal icing, pastillage, etc. The decorative elements are, of course, more for visual effect and are certainly not consumed in any quantity. For pastry preparation they are not essential; it is better to retain the colour of the natural ingredients. It is not necessary to buy the entire range of colourings. You can blend your own with a selection of primary and secondary colours: **1** Green, **2** Blue, **3** Yellow, **4** Black, and **5** Red. Powdered food colourings are much stronger than liquid, dissolving easily in a few drops of water. For colouring sugar, dissolve it in 90° proof alcohol or Cognac which will evaporate during cooking.

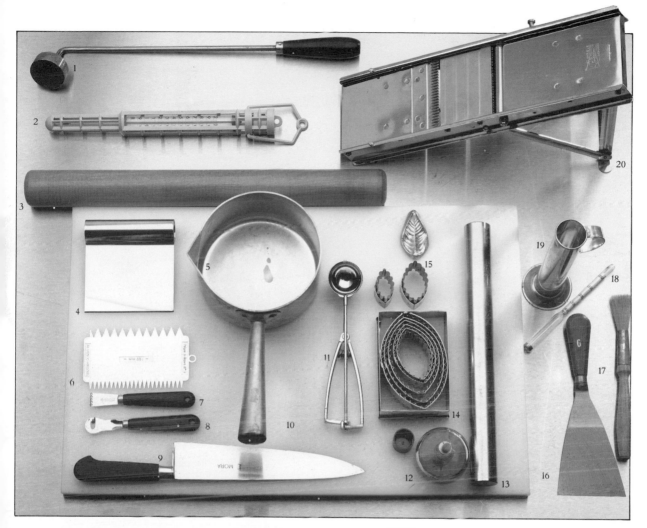

ABOVE

1 Glazing iron for Crème brulée, Crème Chiboust, etc must be heated to very hot in either a gas flame or the coals of a fire. A more sophisticated electric model is available.

2 Sugar thermometer

3 Wooden rolling pin for pastry

4 Metal pastry scraper and cutter

5 Copper sugar pan

6 This small decorating comb is very effective for mixing dark and white couverture for making 2-tone chocolate curls (see page 242). It can also be used to decorate buttercream on the top of a cake.

7 Citrus zester

8 Cannelizing knife

9 Cook's knife

10 Plastic chopping board

11 Ice cream scoop

12 Spirit lamp

13 Rolling pin for nougatine

14 Set of oval fluted pastry cutters

15 Leaf mould for Sucre tiré

16 Painter's broad palette knife

17 Round-ended pastry brush for glazing

18 Beaumé scale or density saccharometer for measuring the density of the sugar in sorbet syrup or sorbet preparation. If the reading is too high, the sorbet will not set; if too low, the mixture will become icy and heavy. The correct reading is 16°Beaumé/1.1247 density. Sorbet syrup should be 30° Beaumé/1.2624 density.

19 Density measuring cup.

20 Mandoline

· PROFESSIONAL EQUIPMENT ·

1 Tray for large madeleines
Pastry cutters: **2** Holly leaf,
3 Pig, **4** Cat, **5** Duck, **6** Sitting
rabbit, **7** Heart, **8** Fish, **9**
Butterfly.
10 Assorted small pastry cutters
11 Assorted petits fours moulds
12 Supple, right-angled,
steel-bladed palette knife
13 Aluminium baking beans are
used for blind-baking tarts. They
are cleaner and heavier than the
dried beans; these are often too
light and let the pastry on the

bottom of the shell rise during
cooking, and they also tend to
burn, producing an unpleasant
smell.
14 Bakers' blades are the best
implement for slashing the bread
dough.
15 Skewers for fruits déguisés.
With a fruit déguisé on each end of
the skewer, dip each fruit into hard
crack sugar. Rest the skewer on a
rectangular mould set in a tray to
collect the drips, and allow the
sugar to cool. Large strawberries

and grapes are also delicious
dipped in sugar.
16 Rulers for fondant or Sucre
coulé (poured sugar)
17 Expanding sponge ring
18 Set of graduated pastry cutters
for vol-au-vents and Pithiviers
19 Large Croquembouche mould
20 Fondant saucepan
21 Small rectangular cake tin
22 Spiked plastic roller
23 Basketwork rolling pin. After
rolling marzipan to the desired
thickness and shape, use this

decorative rolling pin to roll over
the marzipan in one continuous
motion. Marked like this, the
marzipan should then be used
immediately to cover a whole cake
before it dries out.
24 Patisserie tray with raised edges
25 Plastic rolling pin achieves
smoothness on marzipan or
pastillage. It has a good weight.
26 Aluminium scoop for flour or
sugar
27 Rectangular straight-sided
cake tin

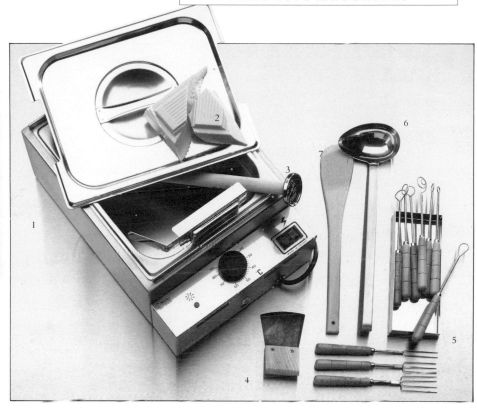

1 A chocolate warmer is an ideal piece of equipment for tempering and moulding when working with chocolate. It will melt and hold the chocolate at a constant temperature of between 30° and 35°C, depending on the couverture and the work to be done.

2 White chocolate

3 A chocolate thermometer, an essential tool which measures the chocolate temperature when using a bain-marie, rather than a chocolate warmer.

4 Scraper for making chocolate curls

5 Various sizes and shapes of chocolate holders and forks are employed for lifting the interior fillings out of the melted couverture and placing them on aluminium foil. The top of the chocolate can also be decorated with them before it sets.

6 Pouring ladle

7 Wooden spatula

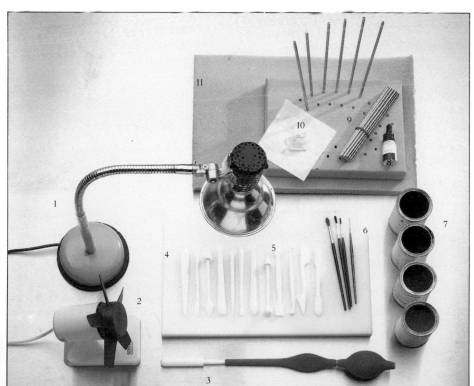

1 A sugar lamp can be either a reflective lamp mounted with an electric element (illustrated) or a warming lamp.

2 Electric fan

3 Sugar pump

4 Plastic sugar board

5 Sculpting tools for marzipan, chocolate or lard sculpture

6 Assorted paintbrushes for decorating

7 Powdered food colourings: blue, green, red and yellow

8 Acetic acid

9 Mandrin for weaving a basket in sugar. This one allows you to weave a basket in 2 different sizes. When the weaving is finished, remove the metal prongs and replace them with strips of Sucre tiré, placing the basket on a Sucre coulé base.

10 Cream of tartar

11 Foam pad

CHAPTER
· 2 ·

THE
BASIC RECIPES

*T*hese are the recipes which form the basis for all patisserie. From these are fashioned the tarts and flans, breads and croissants — all the delectable patisserie which *pâtissiers* love to display in their shop windows.

The various sponges are used as the base for charlottes, *bavaroises* and *délices* and are often brushed with a mixture of syrup and alcohol or fruit purée to enhance the flavour of the dessert. They are then topped or filled with mousses or custards made from meringue and cream mixtures and the resulting desserts are often served with a cream or fruit *coulis*.

PASTRY AND DOUGH

*T*he job of the *tourrier*, the person responsible for making dough, all pastes and dough products, is one of the most important in the art of patisserie. He is the point of departure for all the other pastry-cooks and his dough and pastes provide the foundation and guarantee of quality for all patisserie.

His job is fairly unrewarding compared to those who prepare the desserts and cakes; unlike him, they have the satisfaction of seeing the finished product. At the crack of dawn, and sometimes earlier, the *tourrier* is the first to arrive at the patisserie to prepare and shape his croissants and *brioches*. Then he cuts out his *mille-feuilles* and shapes his flans and tartlets.

Even uncooked dough gives off a delicious smell; the very texture and colour awaken the tastebuds. It is not unusual to see a *tourrier* who loves his work nibbling at his raw dough.

All dough keeps very well in the fridge for several days. It should be wrapped in clingfilm or polythene to prevent it from drying out and forming a crust. Dough can also be frozen successfully for several days.

PATE BRISEE
(Shortcrust)

· INGREDIENTS ·

250 g/9 oz flour
160 g/5½ oz butter, slightly softened
1 egg
Pinch of sugar
5 g/¾ tsp salt
1 tbsp milk

Makes about 475 g/1 lb 1 oz
Preparation time: 15 minutes

This light, crumbly, delicate shortcrust can be used as a substitute for puff pastry; it is particularly good for meat or fish *en croûte*. It can also be used as the crust for *pâté en croûte*, in place of the traditional pastry. It is always used to make classic flan and tartlet cases.

· PREPARATION ·

Place the flour on the work surface and make a well in the centre. Cut the butter into small pieces and place them in the well, together with the egg, sugar and salt. Rub in all these ingredients with the fingertips of your right hand, then, with your left hand, draw in the flour a little at a time. When all the ingredients are almost amalgamated, add the cold milk. Knead the dough with the palm of your hand 2 or 3 times

· EQUIPMENT ·

Marble or *wooden pastry board*

Greaseproof paper or *polythene*

until completely homogenous. Wrap in greaseproof paper or polythene and chill in the fridge for several hours before using.

· STORAGE ·

Wrapped in greaseproof paper or polythene, shortcrust will keep for several days in the fridge, or can be frozen for several weeks.

BRIOCHE

· INGREDIENTS ·

| 15 g/½ oz fresh yeast |
| 70 ml/3 fl oz warm milk |
| 15 g/2 tsp salt |
| 500 g/1 lb 1 oz flour |
| 6 eggs |
| 350 g/12 oz butter, softened |
| 30 g/1 oz sugar |
| 1 egg yolk, lightly beaten with 1 tbsp milk |

Serves 16

Preparation time: 20 minutes in an electric mixer, 35 minutes by hand

Rising and resting time: about 6 hours

Cooking time: 8 minutes for the small brioche *(60 g/2 oz) 40-45 minutes for the large* brioche

Weight: 1.2 kg/2 lb 10 oz

The essence of a perfect *brioche* is that it should have a delicious, rich, buttery flavour, yet leave no trace of butter on your fingers or aftertaste on the palate.

· PREPARATION ·

Place the yeast and warm milk in the mixer bowl and beat lightly with a wire whisk, then add the salt.

Add the flour and eggs and knead the dough with the dough hook or a spatula until it is smooth and elastic; this will take about 10 minutes in an electric mixer or 20 minutes by hand.

Beat the softened butter and sugar together, then, at low speed, add this mixture to the dough, a little at a time, making sure that it is completely amalgamated each time. Continue to mix for about 5 minutes in the mixer or 15 minutes by hand, until the dough is perfectly smooth. It should be glossy and shiny and fairly elastic.

Cover the bowl with a tea towel and leave in a warm place (about 24°C/75°F) for about 2 hours, until the dough has doubled in bulk.

Knocking back: Knock back the dough by flipping it over quickly with your fingertips not more than 2 or 3 times. Cover with a tea towel and place in the fridge for several hours (but not more than 24 hours).

Moulding and shaping: Place the dough on a lightly floured work surface and shape it into a large ball. If you are using a saucepan, line it with a sheet of buttered greaseproof paper twice the height of the pan. Place the dough in the saucepan.

If you are making the *brioche* in a mould, follow the step-by-step instructions opposite.

Lightly glaze the top of the *brioche* with eggwash, working from the outside inwards and taking care not to let any run into the cracks in the dough or onto the edges of the mould; this will prevent the dough from rising properly.

· EQUIPMENT ·

Electric mixer, or a large earthenware bowl

1 brioche *mould for 16 people, 24 cm/9½ in diameter at the top, 11 cm/4½ in at the base or 1 18 cm/7 in copper saucepan or 20 small* brioche *moulds 8 cm/3¼ in diameter at the top, 4 cm/1½ in at the base*

PICTURE PAGES 36-7

1

For a moulded brioche, cut off one-third of the dough to make the 'head'. Shape the larger piece into a ball and place in the mould. Press a hole in the centre with your fingertips.

2

With your hand at an angle, roll the 'head' into an elongated egg shape. Gently press the narrow end into the hole in the centre of the large ball with lightly floured fingertips.

1

3

After rising, glaze the top with eggwash, brushing from the outside inwards. Snip all around the edges of the large brioche with scissors dipped in cold water.

2

3

4

Bake immediately, then unmould on to a wire rack and leave to cool.

4

Rising: Leave to rise in a warm draught-free place until the dough has almost doubled in bulk (about 20 minutes for the small *brioches* and 1½ hours for a large one).

· TO COOK ·

Preheat the oven to 220°C/425°F/gas 8.

Lightly glaze the top of the *brioche* again, then snip all round the edges of the large *brioche* with scissors or a razor blade dipped in cold water. Do not snip the edges of the small *brioches*.

Bake immediately in the preheated oven for 40-45 minutes for the large *brioche*, 8 minutes for small ones.

Unmould immediately and place on a wire rack to cool.

Brioche looks very impressive if plaited or formed into a crown shape. For a real treat, cut it into slices, sprinkle with icing sugar and glaze under a very hot grill. Serve by itself for breakfast or, as a monstrous indulgence, warm with chocolate mousse.

· STORAGE ·

Brioche dough can be frozen, wrapped in polythene, after the knocking back stage. To bake, leave the dough to thaw gradually in the fridge for 4-5 hours, then proceed as above.

PATE A SAVARIN
(Savarin dough)

· INGREDIENTS ·

15 g/½ oz fresh yeast

200 ml/7 fl oz warm milk

15 g/2 tsp salt

500 g/1 lb 1 oz flour

6 eggs

150 g/5 oz butter, softened

15 g/½ oz sugar

Makes about 1.1 kg/2½ lb

Preparation time: 30 minutes in an electric mixer, 40 minutes by hand

· PREPARATION ·

Proceed exactly as for a *Brioche* (see page 32), but place only half the milk in the bowl with the yeast; reserve the other half and add it when the dough has become smooth and glossy and is fairly elastic. Add the milk, a little at a time, until the dough is more supple than for a *brioche*: it should not break when you stretch it between your fingers.

Cover the dough with a baking sheet or cloth and leave it to rise for 1 hour in a warm place (24°C/75°F). The dough should double in volume. Knock back the dough by flipping it once or twice with your hand. It is now ready to mould.

· NOTES ·

It is important not to let the dough rise too much, or the *savarins* will break when you soak them.

This dough will not keep, even in the fridge. It must be used within half an hour.

· EQUIPMENT ·

Electric mixer or a large earthenware bowl

1 saucepan

PATE A BLINIS
(Batter for blinis)

· INGREDIENTS ·

THE LEAVENING:

15 g/½ oz fresh yeast

250 ml/9 fl oz lukewarm milk

25 g/1 oz plain *or* wholemeal flour

THE BATTER:

125 g/4 oz plain *or* wholemeal flour

2 eggs, separated

Small pinch of salt

Makes about 500 g/1 lb 1 oz

Preparation time: 10 minutes, plus 3 hours resting

We use this batter mainly for *amuse-gueules*, like our *Blinis au caviar* (see page 193).

· PREPARATION ·

The leavening: In a bowl, whisk together the lukewarm milk and yeast, then add 25 g/1 oz flour. Cover the bowl with a plate and leave at room temperature (24°C/75°F) for 2 hours.

The batter: Using a spatula, stir in the flour and egg yolks. Cover with a plate and leave at room temperature for 1 hour.

The egg whites: Place in a bowl, beat well, then add a pinch of salt and beat until stiff. Fold them carefully into the batter. The batter is now ready to use.

· NOTES ·

Use the batter as soon as possible, and certainly within an hour, or it will ferment and the flavour will be spoilt.

· EQUIPMENT ·

2 bowls

PATE SUCREE
(Sweet short pastry)

· INGREDIENTS ·

250 g/9 oz flour
100 g/3½ oz butter
100 g/3½ oz icing sugar, sifted
Small pinch of salt
2 × 55-60 g/size 4 eggs, at room temperature

Makes about 520 g/1 lb 2 oz
Preparation time: 15 minutes

This pastry is mainly used for tarts and tartlets, especially those which are baked blind and then filled with fresh fruit (eg, strawberry tart, which has a layer of *crème Chantilly* or *crème Chiboust* between the pastry base and the fruit). It is much easier to work than *pâte sablée*, which, being much finer, is difficult to roll out and shape.

Pâte sucrée is also less fragile when cooked, so it is perfect if you want a tart for a picnic or to transport.

· PREPARATION ·

Put the flour on the work surface and make a well in the centre. Cut the butter into small pieces, place them in the centre, then work with your fingertips until completely softened. Add the sugar and salt, mix well together, then add the eggs and mix. Gradually draw the flour into the mixture.

When everything is thoroughly mixed, work the dough 2 or 3 times with the palm of your hand until it is very smooth.

Roll the dough into a ball, flatten the top slightly, wrap in greaseproof paper or polythene and refrigerate for several hours.

· STORAGE ·

Wrapped in greaseproof paper or polythene, *pâte sucrée* will keep very well in the fridge for several days.

· EQUIPMENT ·

Marble or *wooden pastry board*
Greaseproof paper or polythene

PATE A FONCER
(Lining or flan paste)

· INGREDIENTS ·

250 g/9 oz flour
125 g/4 oz butter, softened
1 × 60 g/size 3 egg
10 g/1½ tsp sugar
5 g/¾ tsp salt
40 ml/2 fl oz water

Makes about 480 g/1 lb
Preparation time: 15 minutes

Traditionally, this dough is used as a base for flans and tartlets.

· PREPARATION ·

Proceed exactly as for *Pâte brisée*, adding the water when the dough is well mixed, but still a little crumbly and not completely homogenous. Knead the dough 2 or 3 times with the palm of your hand, until completely smooth. Wrap in greaseproof paper or polythene and chill in the fridge for several hours before using.

· STORAGE ·

Wrapped in greaseproof paper or polythene, it will keep for several days in the fridge, or can be frozen for several weeks.

· EQUIPMENT ·

Marble or *wooden pastry board*
Greaseproof paper or polythene

BRIOCHES
Large and small, baked in various shapes
(page 32)

CROISSANTS

· INGREDIENTS ·

| 40 g/1½ oz sugar |
| 10 g/1½ tsp salt |
| 300 ml/11 fl oz cold water |
| 17 g/½ oz fresh yeast |
| 25 g/1 oz milk powder |
| 500 g/1 lb 2 oz strong flour |
| 300 g/10 oz butter |
| 1 egg yolk beaten with 1 tbsp milk, to glaze |

Makes 16–18 croissants,
55–60 g/2 oz each

Preparation time: 1½ hours

Rising time: 2½ hours

Cooking time: 15 minutes

· PREPARATION ·

The dough: Prepare the dough 10–12 hours in advance.

Dissolve the sugar and salt in one-third of the cold water. In a separate bowl, beat the yeast into the remaining water with a small wire whisk, then beat in the milk powder.

Place the flour in the bowl of the electric mixer, then at low speed, using the dough hook, beat in first the sugar and salt mixture, then the yeast mixture. Stop beating as soon as the ingredients are well mixed and the dough comes away from the sides of the bowl. This should not take longer than 1½ minutes; do not overwork the dough.

Rising: Cover the dough with a tea towel and leave to rise in a warm place (about 24°C/75°F and not more than 30°C/86°F) for about 30 minutes. The dough should double in size.

Knocking back: Knock back the dough by quickly flipping it over with your fingers to release the carbon gases; do not overwork or the dough will be heavy. Cover with polythene and place in the fridge for 6–8 hours. (If the dough has risen again after an hour, knock it back again as described above.)

Rolling and shaping: Cut a cross in the top of the dough.

On a lightly floured surface, roll out the ball of dough in 4 places, making one-quarter turn each time, so that it looks like 4 large 'ears' around a small head.

Put the butter in the centre; it must be firm but not too hard, and about the same temperature as the dough. Fold the 4 'ears' over the butter, making sure that it is completely enclosed, so that the butter does not ooze out.

Lightly flour the work surface, then carefully roll the dough away from you into a rectangle about 40 × 70 cm/ 16 × 27 in. Brush off the excess flour from the surface of the dough. Fold the dough into 3. Wrap in polythene and refrigerate for at least 20 minutes. Repeat the process, rolling the dough in the opposite direction from before. Wrap and refrigerate as before. Repeat the process once more.

Roll out the dough to a 40 × 76 cm/16 × 30 in rectangle, flouring the work surface very lightly as you roll. Flap up the dough twice to aerate it and prevent shrinkage, taking care not to spoil the shape of the rectangle.

With a large knife, trim the edges, then cut the dough lengthways into 2 equal strips.

Lay one short edge of the triangular template along one long edge of the dough and mark out the outline with the back of the knife. Invert the triangle and mark out the outline as before. Continue in this way until you have marked out 16–18

· EQUIPMENT ·

Electric mixer

Wooden or *marble pastry board*

Isosceles triangular template, 14 × 18 cm/ 6 × 7 in

triangles, then cut them out with a sharp knife (marking out the shapes first will help to prevent mistakes).

Arrange the triangles on a baking sheet. Cover tightly with polythene and refrigerate for a few moments; if the dough becomes too warm, it may soften and crack.

Place the triangles, one at a time, on the work surface, with the long point nearest you. Stretch out the 2 shorter points, then, starting from the short edge, roll up the triangle towards you; use one hand to roll the dough and the other to pull down the long point. Make sure that the central pointed end is in the middle and underneath so that it does not rise up during cooking.

As soon as they are shaped, place the croissants on a baking sheet, turning in the corners in the direction of the pointed end to make a curved crescent shape. Since the sides of the oven are always the hottest, the last row of croissants must face backwards, or the points may dry out or burn.

Lightly brush the croissants with eggwash, working from the inside outwards, so that the layers of dough do not stick together, which would prevent the croissants from rising properly. Leave to rise in a very warm, humid and draught-free place (24°-30°C/75°-85°F) until they have doubled in size; this will take about 2 hours.

· TO COOK ·

Very lightly glaze the croissants again with eggwash. Preheat the oven to 230°C/450°F/gas 9. Bake the croissants in the preheated oven for 15 minutes, then transfer immediately to a wire rack, making sure that they are not touching.

· STORAGE ·

Croissants and *pains au chocolat* freeze very well for up to 2 weeks. Once they are baked and while they are still warm, wrap in plastic bags and freeze immediately. To serve, place, frozen, in an oven at 250°C/500°F/gas 10 for 5 minutes.

To freeze unbaked croissants, place on a baking sheet and freeze before they have risen at all. Leave to rise when you are ready to use. Do not freeze for longer than 8 days.

· FOR PETITS PAINS AU CHOCOLAT ·

While you are making the croissants, any large pieces of dough can be used to make *petits pains au chocolat*. Cut the dough into small rectangles, place one or two squares of plain chocolate on one side, then fold over the dough to make a small, flattish cylinder. Arrange on a baking sheet, glaze with eggwash, then proceed as for croissants, baking for 18 minutes. (Do not re-roll the trimmings; cook them just as they are to enjoy as nibbles.)

Continued overleaf

CROISSANTS

1

Shape the risen dough into a ball and cut a cross in the top.

2

On a lightly floured surface, roll out the dough in 4 places, making a quarter turn each time, leaving a raised platform in the centre, so that it resembles 4 ears surrounding a small head.

3

Place the chilled butter on the 'head'; butter and dough should be at the same temperature.

4

Fold the 4 'ears' over the butter, from front to back, to enclose it completely. Make sure the corners are tucked in so that the butter does not ooze out.

5

On a lightly floured surface, roll the dough into a rectangle about 70 × 40 cm/27 × 16 in. Brush off the excess flour from the surface of the dough.

6

Fold over the ends of the rectangle. Wrap in polythene and chill for at least 20 minutes.

7

Roll and fold the dough in the same way twice more, chilling it each time, until it has been rolled 3 times.

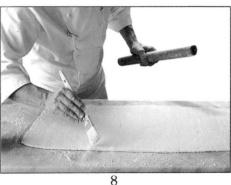

8

Roll out the dough into a 76 × 40 cm/30 × 16 in rectangle, lightly flouring the surface as you roll.

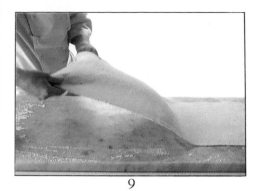

9

Flap up the dough twice to aerate it and to prevent it from shrinking. Take care not to spoil the shape of the rectangle.

9

10

Trim the edges of the dough, then draw the knife across the centre and cut the dough lengthways in half.

10

11

Lay a short edge of the triangular template along the long edge of the dough and cut. Invert the triangle and cut again. To avoid mistakes, mark out the shape with the back of a knife before cutting.

11

12

Lay the dough triangles in overlapping rows on a baking sheet. Cover tightly with clingfilm and leave to rest in the fridge.

12

13

Place a dough triangle on the work surface with the long point nearest to you. Pull the long point downwards with one hand and roll up the triangle towards you with the other.

13

14

Fold the central point underneath the croissant. Place them on a baking sheet, turning the corners inwards to make a crescent.

14

15

Arrange the croissants on the baking sheet in staggered rows. The back and front rows must face backwards, or the points may dry out and burn. Glaze with eggwash and leave to rise until doubled in size.

15

16

Lightly glaze the croissants again. Bake in a preheated oven, then transfer to a wire rack, spacing the croissants well apart.

16

FEUILLETAGE JEAN MILLET
(Jean Millet's puff pastry)

· INGREDIENTS ·

· INGREDIENTS ·

500 g/1 lb 1 oz flour,
plus a little for 'turning'

200 ml/8 fl oz water

12 g/1¾ tsp salt

25 ml/1 fl oz white wine
vinegar

50 g/2 oz butter, melted

400 g/14 oz butter, well
chilled

Makes 1.2 kg/2½ lb
Preparation time: 1 hour 10
minutes, plus about 5 hours
resting time

Many domestic cooks are terrified at the thought of making puff pastry, without just cause. It is certainly a lengthy process, but it is actually quite easy to make.

This recipe was created by our friend Jean Millet, the president of the Confédération de la Pâtisserie, Confiserie, Glacerie de France and MOF in patisserie.

· PREPARATION ·

The dough: Put 500 g/1 lb 1 oz flour on the work surface and make a well in the centre. Pour in the water, salt, vinegar and melted butter and work together with your fingertips. Using your left hand, gradually draw in the flour and mix well.

When all the ingredients are well mixed, work the dough with the palm of your hand until it is completely homogenous, but not too firm. Roll it into a ball and cut a cross in the top to break the elasticity. Wrap in polythene or greaseproof paper and chill in the fridge for 2 or 3 hours.

Incorporating the butter: Lightly flour the work surface. Roll out the ball of dough in four different places, so that it looks like 4 large 'ears' around a small, round head. Hit the chilled butter several times with a rolling pin, so that it is supple but still firm and very cold; place it on the 'head' so that it covers it with no overhang. Fold the 4 'ears' over the butter to cover it completely. Chill in the fridge for 30 minutes to bring the butter and dough to the same temperature.

Turning and folding: Lightly flour the work surface, then progressively roll the dough gently away from you into a rectangle about 70 × 40 cm/27 × 16 in. Fold over the ends to make 3 layers. This is the first turn.

Second turn: On the lightly floured surface, give the rectangle one-quarter turn and again progressively roll it gently away from you into a 70 × 40 cm/27 × 16 in rectangle. Fold the dough into 3. This is the second turn.

Wrap the dough in greaseproof paper or polythene and place in the fridge for 30 minutes to rest and firm up.

Make 2 more turns as above, then, after the fourth turn, wrap the dough and refrigerate again for 30 minutes to 1 hour.

Make 2 more turns, bringing the total to 6. The pastry is now ready to use.

· STORAGE ·

Well wrapped in greaseproof paper or polythene, the pastry will keep for up to 3 days in the fridge, or it can be frozen for several weeks. If you are going to store it, give it only 4 turns

· EQUIPMENT ·

Marble or *wooden pastry board*

Greaseproof paper or *polythene*

For the preparation of Puff pastry dough, refer to the Croissants recipe, steps 1–6 (see page 40).

and complete the 2 final turns on the day you use it. Replace the pastry in the fridge for 30 minutes after these 2 final turns.

· NOTES ·

Once you have cut the puff pastry into your desired shape (*bouchées, vol-au-vent, fleurons, feuilletés, palmiers,* etc) you must let it rest in a cold place for at least 30 minutes before baking, or the pastry will shrink and distort the shape.

Bake puff pastry in a hot oven, at 220°–240°C/425°–475°F/gas 8–10.

FEUILLETAGE MINUTE
(Quick puff pastry)

· INGREDIENTS ·

1 kg/2 lb 2 oz flour, plus a pinch

1 kg/2 lb 2 oz butter, which should be firm but not too hard; (remove from the fridge 2 or 3 hours before using)

20 g/1 tbsp salt

500 ml/18 fl oz iced water (add ice cubes if necessary)

Makes about 2.5 kg/5½ lb
Preparation time: 20 minutes

· PREPARATION ·

Mixing the ingredients: Put the flour on the work surface and make a well in the centre.

Cut the butter into small cubes and put it into the well, together with the salt. Using your fingertips, work the ingredients together, gradually drawing in the flour with your left hand.

When the cubes of butter have become very small and half squashed and the mixture is becoming grainy, pour in the iced water and gradually incorporate it into the pastry. Do not knead it and stop working the pastry as soon as it becomes homogenous, but still contains some little flakes of butter.

Rolling: On a lightly floured surface, roll out the dough away from you into a 40 × 20 cm/16 × 8 in rectangle. Fold and proceed as for ordinary puff pastry (opposite), until you have made 2 turns. Wrap the pastry in greaseproof paper or polythene and chill in the fridge for 20 minutes.

Give the chilled pastry 2 more turns. It is now ready to use. Roll it to your desired shape, then place on a dampened baking sheet, as for classic puff pastry, and chill for 20 minutes before baking.

· STORAGE ·

This pastry is extremely quick and simple to prepare, but does not keep as long as classic puff pastry — only 2 days in the fridge or 3 days in the freezer. Wrap it in greaseproof paper or polythene to store.

· NOTES ·

Quick puff pastry will rise about 30 per cent less than the classic type.

· EQUIPMENT ·

Marble or *wooden pastry board*

Greaseproof paper or *polythene*

LEFT *Wholemeal and white bread rolls and loaves (pages 48–51)*
ABOVE *Pain de mie (page 51)*

PATE A CHOUX
(Choux paste)

· INGREDIENTS ·

125 ml/4½ fl oz water
125 ml/4½ fl oz milk
100 g/3½ oz butter, cut into small pieces
3 g/½ tsp fine salt
5 g/¾ tsp sugar
150 g/5 oz flour
4 × 60 g/size 3 eggs

Makes 22-25 choux buns or éclairs

Preparation time: 20 minutes

Cooking time: 10-20 minutes, depending on the size and shape of the buns

Choux paste is enormously versatile, which makes it a marvellous, indispensable component of all types of cooking and patisserie.

· PREPARATION ·

Preheat the oven to 220°C/425°F/gas 7.

Cooking the paste: Put the water, milk, diced butter, salt and sugar in a saucepan, set over high heat and boil for 1 minute, stirring with a spatula. Take the pan off the heat and, stirring all the time, quickly add the sifted flour.

The next stage — the 'drying out' — is vitally important if you want to make good choux paste. When the mixture is very smooth, replace the pan over the heat and stir with the spatula for 1 minute.

The paste will begin to poach and some of the water will evaporate. Be very careful not to let the paste dry out too much, or it will crack during cooking and your buns or éclairs will not be perfectly smooth. Tip the paste into a bowl.

Adding the eggs: Immediately beat in the eggs, one at a time, using a spatula. Stir well until the paste is very smooth; it is now ready to use. If you do not want to use it immediately, spread one-third of a beaten egg over the surface to prevent a skin or crust from forming, which may easily happen after a few hours.

Piping the paste: Choose an appropriate plain nozzle to pipe out your chosen shape — small or large choux buns, éclairs, swans, *Paris-Brest* or whatever.

Pipe out the paste on baking parchment or a greased baking sheet. If you like, glaze the shapes and mark them lightly with the back of a fork, dipping it into the glaze each time.

· EQUIPMENT ·

1 saucepan
1 fine sieve
1 bowl
1 baking sheet
Baking parchment (optional)
Piping bag with a plain nozzle

Bake in the preheated oven, then open the oven door slightly (about 1–2 cm/¾ in) after 4 or 5 minutes and leave it ajar. Cooking time will vary from 10–20 minutes, depending on the size of the buns.

· STORAGE ·

Stored in an airtight container, choux paste will keep for 3 days in the fridge, or for up to 1 week in the freezer.

PATE SABLEE
(Shortbread dough)

· INGREDIENTS ·

RECIPE 1:

250 g/9 oz flour

200 g/7 oz butter

100 g/3½ oz icing sugar, sifted

Pinch of salt

2 egg yolks

1 drop vanilla *or* lemon essence (optional)

RECIPE 2:

30 g/1 oz ground almonds

250 g/9 oz flour

140 g/5 oz butter

100 g/3½ oz icing sugar, sifted

1 egg

Pinch of salt

1 drop vanilla *or* lemon essence (optional)

Makes about 680 g/1½ lb (recipe 1)
600 g/1¼ lb (recipe 2)
Preparation time: 15 minutes

· PREPARATION RECIPE 1 ·

Sift the flour onto the work surface and make a well in the centre. Dice the butter and place it in the well, then work it with your fingertips until very soft. Sift the icing sugar onto the butter, add the salt and work into the butter. Add the egg yolks and mix well. Gradually draw in the flour and mix until completely amalgamated. Add the vanilla or lemon essence, if you are using it, and rub it into the dough 2 or 3 times with the palm of your hand.

· RECIPE 2 ·

Sift together the ground almonds and flour onto the work surface and make a well in the centre. Proceed as for recipe 1.

Roll the dough into a ball and flatten it out lightly. Wrap in greaseproof paper or polythene and chill in the fridge for several hours.

· STORAGE ·

Wrapped in greaseproof paper or polythene, both doughs will keep very well in the fridge for several days.

· NOTES ·

Flour is always the last ingredient to be added to *pâte sablée*, so that the dough remains crumbly and 'short'. Once you have added the flour, do not overwork the dough, or it will become too elastic. Recipe 1 is very delicate; if you are using the dough to line a flan tin or to make *sablés*, you must work very fast, without overhandling the dough, as it softens extremely quickly. Rolled and cut into different shapes, it is perfect for *petits fours secs*.

Recipe 2 is easier to make, roll out and handle, but because it contains less butter, it is less rich and delicate.

· EQUIPMENT ·

Wooden or *marble pastry board*

1 fine sieve

Greaseproof paper or *polythene*

BREAD

*T*here is one simple reason why French bread has often been imitated but never equalled — nothing goes into it but flour, water, salt and yeast. French flour is different from British flour.

Bread-making is a subject in its own right, which we cannot cover fully here, but we feel we must at least mention the different types of flour used in Britain. The recipes in this chapter are for breads which we bake every day in our restaurants; they are all simple to make at home. We find them extremely satisfying and we know you will too!

We list below a few important definitions:

Extraction ratio is the percentage of flour obtained from a given quantity of wheat.

The ratio of particles or mineral content determines the flour type. The whiter the flour, the fewer impurities it contains, and the lower its bran ratio will be. The main flour types are graded according to their percentage of bran per 100 grammes of dry matter.

The main flour types, characteristics and uses:

Wholemeal or whole wheat flour: Extraction rate 100%, protein 12%, carbohydrate 64.3%, dietary fibre 11.2%. This flour contains the whole wheat grain; nothing is added or taken away during processing.

Uses: Breads, rolls and special bread rolls.

Wheatmeal or brown flours: Extraction rate 85-90%, protein 11.8%, carbohydrate 68.5%, dietary fibre 7.8%.

Uses: Breads, bread rolls and in certain cakes and specialities.

'Strong' white flour – bakers' grade: Extraction rate 70-75%, protein 11.3% minimum (some strong flours have 12-13% protein), carbohydrate 71.5%, dietary fibre 3.15%.

Uses: The most popular type used for all white bread and all other yeast-raised products, puff paste and choux paste.

'Soft' or cake flour, made with an addition of weaker British and other European wheats: Extraction rate 55-75%, protein 8-8.6%, carbohydrate and dietary fibre percentage vary depending on the brands of flour as can the percentage of the extraction rate and protein.

Uses: For all cake making, sponges, biscuits, soft pastes eg. short, sweet etc.

The moisture content is normally 15% for all flours. The 'strength' of the flour refers to the quality as well as the quantity of gluten-forming protein present in the respective flours.

Other flours (rye, rice, soya and cassava): These are often used as improving agents or for flouring around the bread before baking. Rye flour, with a little wheat flour added, is used to make rye bread (*pain de seigle*).

LE PAIN
(Bread rolls)

· PREPARATION ·

The bread can be made either by hand or in an electric mixer.

By hand: Put the flour, sugar and salt into a bowl or basin and make a well in the centre.

In a separate bowl, combine the yeast and water and pour

· INGREDIENTS ·

450 g/1 lb strong flour	
30 g/1 oz sugar	
15 g/2 tsp salt	
15 g/½ oz fresh yeast	
250 ml/9 fl oz water at 16°C/60°F	

Makes 15-20 rolls

Preparation time: 35 minutes

Rising time: 2½ hours

Cooking time: about 12 minutes

into the well. Mix with your hand until the ingredients are thoroughly blended, drawing the flour gradually into the liquid. Do not overwork.

Using an electric mixer: Combine the water and yeast in the bowl and beat lightly with a whisk. Add the flour, salt and sugar and beat, using the dough hook, at the lowest speed until completely homogenous.

Rising: When the dough has reached this stage, leave it in a warm place (about 24°C/75°F), covered with a damp cloth or a baking tray. Leave to rise or 'prove' for about 2 hours; the dough should have doubled in bulk. Knock back the dough by quickly flipping it over with your fingers not more than 2 or 3 times.

Shaping: Place the dough on a marble or wooden surface. Using a sharp knife, divide it into even pieces of the size you require. Shape the dough into rounds or pull into long rolls and place them on a baking sheet.

Make small incisions, 5 mm/¼ in deep in the top of the long rolls, using a razor blade set in a cork, so as not to cut yourself, or use bakers' blades or scissors. Make a cross in the top of the round rolls.

Cover the rolls with clingfilm to prevent them from drying out and forming a crust and to protect them from draughts. Leave in a warm place (about 24°C/75°F) for about 30 minutes to rise again or 'prove'. If you want the rolls to be a deep amber colour, glaze them with beaten egg just before baking.

· TO COOK ·

Preheat the oven to 240°C/475°F/gas 10.

Place a few small tins full of water in the bottom of the oven; these will give off enough steam to bake the bread perfectly. Bake the rolls in the preheated oven for about 12 minutes. If you like a shiny finish, as soon as you take them out of the oven, brush each roll with a very slightly moistened brush.

· STORAGE ·

To freeze the rolls, wrap them in clingfilm and put them in the freezer as soon as they have cooled; they will taste freshly baked if you use them within a few days. It is essential to warm them in a moderate oven (190°C/375°F/gas 6) for about 5 minutes before serving. By keeping a stock of rolls in the freezer, you can enjoy fresh bread every day without having to bake it daily.

· EQUIPMENT ·

1 large mixing bowl or an electric mixer

1 baking sheet

Clingfilm

PICTURE PAGES 44-5

PAIN COMPLET
(Wholemeal rolls)

· EQUIPMENT ·

2 large mixing bowls or an electric mixer
2 baking sheets
Clingfilm

PICTURE PAGES 44-5

· INGREDIENTS ·

THE LEAVENING:

15 g/½ oz fresh yeast

500 ml/18 fl oz water warmed to 16°C/61°F

250 g/9 oz strong flour

250 g/9 oz wholemeal flour

THE DOUGH:

600 g/1¼ lb strong flour

600 g/1¼ lb rye flour

35 g/1 oz salt

500 ml/18 fl oz water warmed to 16°C/61°F

Makes 60 rolls, 40-45 g/ about 1½ oz each

Preparation time: 35 minutes

Rising time: 5½ hours

Cooking time: about 20 minutes

· PREPARATION ·

The leavening: In a large bowl, dissolve the yeast in the water and add the 2 flours. Mix gently without overworking the mixture and set aside in a warm place (about 24°C/75°F) for at least 1 hour, but not more than 2 hours. The leavening should double in volume.

The dough: This can be made either by hand or in an electric mixer.

By hand: Mix the 2 flours in a bowl and make a well in the centre. Mix together the salt and water and pour it into the well, then add the leavening. Mix with your hand until completely homogenous, gradually drawing the flour into the middle. Do not overwork the dough, which should be firm and have some body.

Using an electric mixer: Put the leavening and the salt dissolved in water in the bowl, then add the flours. Beat at the lowest speed until completely homogenous; do not overwork the dough, which should be firm and have some body.

Rising: Cover the bowl with a damp cloth or baking sheet and leave to rise in a warm place (about 24°C/75°F) for about 3 hours. The dough should double in bulk.

Shaping: Knock back the dough by flipping it over quickly with your fingers not more than 2 or 3 times.

Place the dough on a marble or wooden surface and shape it into evenly sized balls, about 40-45 g/1½ oz each.

Place on a baking sheet. Make small crosses, 5 mm/¼ in deep, in the top of the rolls, using a razor blade set in a cork so as not to cut yourself, or use bakers' blades or scissors.

Cover the rolls with clingfilm to prevent them from drying out and forming a crust and to protect them from draughts. Leave in a warm place (about 24°C/75°F) for about 1½ hours to rise again or 'prove'.

· TO COOK ·

Preheat the oven to 240°C/475°F/gas 10. Place a few tins full of water in the bottom of the oven; these will give off enough steam to bake the rolls perfectly.

Bake the rolls in the preheated oven for about 20 minutes.

· STORAGE ·

To freeze the rolls, wrap them in clingfilm and put in the freezer as soon as they have cooled; they will taste freshly baked if you use them within a few days. It is essential to warm them in a moderate oven (190°C/375°F/gas 6) for about 5 minutes before serving.

· NOTES ·

A little flour sprinkled lightly over the rolls before baking will give a nice rustic effect. The same dough can be used to make 1 or 2 'country' loaves which, since they are larger, will take longer to bake. Allow about 45 minutes cooking time for 1 kg/2 lb 2 oz dough.

PAIN DE MIE
(White bread)

· INGREDIENTS ·

750 g/1 lb 10 oz strong flour

30 g/1 oz sugar

20 g/1 tbsp salt

250 ml/9 fl oz lukewarm milk, warmed to about 30°C/86°F

125 ml/5 fl oz water, warmed to 16°C/61°F

3 eggs

60 g/2 oz butter, melted and cooled

30 g/1 oz fresh yeast

50 g/2 oz butter, for greasing

Makes 1 loaf

Preparation time: 20 minutes

Rising time: 2 hours 45 minutes

Cooking time: 40–45 minutes

· PREPARATION ·

The bread can be made either by hand or in an electric mixer. **By hand:** Put the flour, salt and sugar in a bowl and make a well in the centre. In a separate bowl, combine the yeast, warmed milk and water and pour into the well. Mix with your hand until all the ingredients are well blended, drawing the flour gradually into the liquid. Do not overwork.

Add the eggs, one by one, then the cooled melted butter. Work the dough with your hand until it comes away cleanly from the sides of the bowl; it should be smooth, compact and elastic.

Using an electric mixer: Combine the water, milk and yeast in a bowl and beat lightly with a whisk. Add the flour, salt and sugar and, using the dough hook, mix at the lowest speed until almost homogenous. Add the eggs, one at a time, then the cooled melted butter. Continue to beat at low speed until the dough comes away from the sides of the bowl; it will now be smooth, compact and elastic.

Rising: When the dough has reached this stage, leave it in a warm place (about 24°C/75°F), covered with a damp cloth or a baking tray. Leave to rise or 'prove' for about 2 hours, then knock back the dough by flipping it over quickly with your fingers not more than 2 or 3 times.

Shaping: Place the dough on a marble or wooden surface and either plait it or divide it into 4 equal parts and form each into a round ball. Generously butter the loaf tin and put in the plait or the 4 balls, one beside the other.

Cover with clingfilm to prevent the dough from drying out and forming a crust and to protect it from draughts.

Leave in a warm place for about 45 minutes, until the dough has risen to within about 2 cm/1 in from the top of the tin.

Preheat the oven to 220°C/425°F/gas 8.

· EQUIPMENT ·

1 large mixing bowl or an electric mixer

1 black metal rectangular loaf tin, about 41 × 11 cm/ 16 × 4½ in, 10 cm/4 in deep, with a sliding lid

Clingfilm

PICTURE PAGES 44-5

· TO BAKE ·

If you want a loaf with 4 nicely rounded bumps on top and a light, airy texture, do not cover the tin with the lid. If, however, you prefer a rectangular loaf with a closer texture, slide the lid onto the tin. Do not cover the plait, or you will spoil the shape. Bake in the preheated oven for 40–45 minutes.

As soon as you take the bread from the oven, remove the lid if you have used it, taking care not to scald yourself. Unmould the loaf onto a wire rack and leave until completely cold.

· STORAGE ·

To freeze the loaf, wrap it in clingfilm when it is barely cold and freeze at once; it will taste as good as if it were freshly baked when you come to use it. Heat the bread at 190°C/375°F/gas 6 for 10 minutes before serving.

PAIN AUX NOIX
(Walnut bread)

· INGREDIENTS ·

500 g/1 lb 1oz wholemeal flour

5 g/¾ tsp salt

50 g/2 oz brown sugar

25 g/1 oz fresh yeast

4 tbsp water, heated to 16°C/61°F

60 g/2 oz butter

250 ml/9 fl oz milk, warmed to 30°C/86°F

35 g/1 oz shelled walnuts

50 g/2 oz butter, for greasing

Makes 1 loaf

Preparation time: 25 minutes

Rising time: 1 hour 45 minutes

Cooking time: 35 minutes

· PREPARATION ·

The walnut bread can be made by hand or in an electric mixer. **By hand:** Put the flour, salt and brown sugar in a bowl and make a well in the centre. In a separate bowl, mix the yeast and water.

Cook the butter in the saucepan until it is nutty brown, then pass through a conical strainer onto the milk and stir in the yeast mixture.

Pour the mixture into the well, a little at a time, and gently draw the flour into the middle. Mix with your hand until thoroughly blended; do not overwork.

Using an electric mixer: Combine the water, milk, browned butter and yeast in the bowl and stir with a whisk. Add the flour, salt and sugar and, using the dough hook, beat at the lowest speed until thoroughly blended.

Rising: Coarsely chop the walnuts and mix them into the dough. Cover the bowl with a damp cloth or baking tray and leave to rise or 'prove' in a warm place (at about 24°C/75°F) for about 1 hour.

When the dough has proved, knock it back by flipping it over quickly with your fingers not more than 2 or 3 times.

Shaping: Generously grease the loaf tin or terrine, roll the dough into a long sausage shape and place in the mould. Cover with clingfilm to prevent the dough from drying out and a skin from forming, and to protect it from draughts. Leave in a warm place to rise for about 45 minutes.

Preheat the oven to 220°C/425°F/gas 8.

· EQUIPMENT ·

1 large mixing bowl or an electric mixer

1 cast iron terrine mould or a black metal rectangular loaf tin about 32 × 8 cm/ 13 × 3 in, 8cm/3 in deep

1 small saucepan

1 conical strainer

Clingfilm

· TO BAKE ·

Bake the loaf in the preheated oven for 35 minutes, then turn out onto a wire rack.

· STORAGE ·.

This bread is at its best 2 days after baking. To freeze, wrap it in clingfilm when barely cold and freeze at once. Don't reheat it before eating; simply take it out of the freezer 3 or 4 hours in advance. It is delicious with cheese.

SPONGE AND DESSERT BASES

*T*hese bases are made to be filled, masked or decorated but they can be served on their own, although of course they would be less attractive this way. Children enjoy them served plain for tea and they are excellent for those gourmets who prefer their cake without cream. They will keep for several days in a cool, dry place, wrapped in clingfilm. As most can be frozen successfully, you will always have a home-made cake to offer; fill the base with whipped cream and some strawberries or seasonal fresh fruit or simply surround it with a light *crème anglaise*.

BISCUITS
— *(Sponge biscuits for bases, Swiss rolls and fingers)* —

Sponge biscuits are used as a base for numerous desserts, from the simplest to the most elaborate. They can be served simply filled with jam or marmalade, with *crème Chantilly* (see page 66) or chocolate *ganache* (see page 197), but they are also used for almost all charlottes and some decorative *pièces montées*.

· PREPARATION ·

The eggs: Separate them and put the yolks in one bowl and the whites in another.
The yolks: Beat them with two-thirds of the sugar until they form a ribbon.
The whites: Beat in the mixer until well risen, then add the

· INGREDIENTS ·

RECIPE 1:

4 whole eggs
3 egg yolks
85 g/3 oz sugar
35 g/1 oz flour
40 g/1½ oz potato flour

Makes 1 Swiss roll
60 × 40 cm/24 × 16 in

· EQUIPMENT ·

Electric mixer
1 sifter
1 flan ring or sponge tin,
22 cm/8½ in diameter,
4 cm/1½ in deep
1 baking sheet, 60 × 40 cm/
24 × 16 in
Greaseproof paper or baking parchment
Piping bag, with plain nozzles of various sizes

RECIPE 2:

6 eggs

190 g/6½ oz sugar

180 g/6 oz flour

30 g/1 oz icing sugar, for
sponge fingers

*Makes 1 round sponge,
about 22 cm/8½ in diameter,
4 cm/1½ in deep*

*Preparation time: 20
minutes*

*Cooking time: varies
according to the thickness of
the biscuits*

remaining sugar and beat at high speed for 1 minute until firm.

Mixing the yolks and whites: Using a flat slotted spoon, fold about one-third of the whites into the yolks until the mixture is perfectly blended. Tip in the remaining whites all at once and fold them very gently into the mixture. Before it is thoroughly blended, still mixing continuously, scatter in the sifted flour and the potato flour, if you are using Recipe 1. As soon as the mixture is homogenous, stop mixing, or it will become heavy.

Shaping and baking the sponge: The baking time will depend on the shape, thickness and size of the biscuits.

To pipe a rolled biscuit (using Recipe 1): Use a piping bag fitted with a plain nozzle, which can be any size from 5 mm/¼ in to 1.5 cm/½ in, depending on the desired shape. Alternatively, use a ridged nozzle or a palette knife. Pipe or spread the mixture onto a sheet of baking parchment or lightly buttered and floured greaseproof paper.

Slide the paper onto a baking sheet and bake in a hot oven at 220°C/425°F/gas 8 for about 6 minutes, if you are using the 5 mm/¼ in nozzle. Allow longer for a larger nozzle.

The cooked sponge should be about 5 mm/¼ in thick. Invert it onto a tea towel and immediately and carefully peel off the paper. Fill and roll the sponge, as for the *Igloo Douillet* (page 108) or assemble it in layers, alternating the sponge with flavoured cream.

To pipe sponge fingers (using Recipe 2): With a piping bag fitted with a 1.5 cm/½ in nozzle, pipe out 'fingers' about 10 cm/4 in long onto baking parchment or lightly buttered and floured greaseproof paper. Lightly dust them twice with icing sugar, at 5 minute intervals. Bake in a hot oven at 220°C/425°F/gas 8 for 8-10 minutes. Before the sponge fingers have cooled completely, lift them off the paper with a palette knife and place on a wire rack.

To make bases for desserts and centrepieces (using Recipe 2): Pour the mixture into a lightly buttered and floured tin or flan ring and bake in a moderate oven at 190°C/375°F/gas 5 for 15-25 minutes, depending on the diameter of the mould, and therefore on the thickness of the sponge.

As soon as the sponge is cooked, invert it onto a wire rack. Rotate it one-quarter turn every 15 minutes until it has cooled completely to prevent it from sticking to the rack.

· STORAGE ·

Sponge fingers should be eaten on the day they are made; after 2 or 3 days, they dry out and crumble and lose all their delectable moistness.

BISCUIT JOCONDE

(see page 129)

· INGREDIENTS ·

375 g/13 oz *tant pour tant* (equal quantities of icing sugar and ground almonds, sifted together)

5 whole eggs

5 egg whites

25 g/1 oz sugar

40 g/1½ oz butter, melted and cooled

50 g/2 oz flour

30 g/1 oz butter, plus a pinch of flour, for greasing

Makes about 900 g/2 lb (enough for one sponge, 60 × 40 cm/24 × 16 in)

Preparation time: 15 minutes

Cooking time: 2–3 minutes

· EQUIPMENT ·

Electric mixer

1 bowl

1 baking sheet, 60 × 40 cm/ 24 × 16 in

Greaseproof paper or baking parchment

Wire rack

Biscuit joconde is a very fine, delicate sponge which is used to make all kinds of desserts based on mousses and *bavaroises*, and in our *Palmerosa* (see page 129).

· PREPARATION ·

Preheat the oven to 250°C/500°F/gas 10.

The whole eggs: Put the eggs and *tant pour tant* in the bowl of the mixer and beat at high speed for about 10 minutes, until the mixture forms a ribbon. Pour into a bowl and set aside.

The egg whites: Beat until well risen, then add the sugar and beat faster for 1 minute.

The mixture: Using a flat slotted spoon or spatula, fold the cooled butter, then the flour into the whole egg mixture.

Mix in one-third of the egg whites until thoroughly blended, then fold in the rest, taking care not to overmix.

· TO COOK ·

Using a palette knife, spread the sponge mixture over a sheet of baking parchment or lightly buttered and floured greaseproof paper, to a thickness of about 3 or 4 mm/⅒ in Bake immediately in the very hot oven for 2–3 minutes. To test whether the sponge is cooked, touch it with your fingertips. It should not stick to your fingers, but be just firm, yet moist and on no account dry.

Slide the cooked sponge, still on the paper, onto a wire rack. Remove the paper only just before using the sponge.

· STORAGE ·

This sponge freezes well; freeze it, still on the paper, either flat or rolled up like a Swiss roll, which takes up less space.

BISCUIT A L'ORANGE
(Orange sponge biscuit)

· INGREDIENTS ·

4 × 55 g/size 4 eggs

1 × 70 g/size 2 egg

85 g/3 oz finely ground almonds

Zest of ½ orange, finely chopped

25 g/1 oz candied orange peel, very finely chopped

130 g/4½ oz sugar

85 g/3 oz flour, plus a pinch for the mould

1 tsp melted butter

Serves 8

Preparation time: 15 minutes

Cooking time: 25 minutes

This Orange sponge biscuit is used in the recipes for *Rozenn au parfum d'orange mentholé* (see page 112) and *Alméria* (see page 136). It can also be used to make plain biscuits which are delicious served with tea.

· PREPARATION ·

Preheat the oven to 200°C/400°F/gas 7.

The eggs: Separate the eggs and put the yolks in one bowl and the whites in another.

Add the ground almonds, chopped orange zest, candied peel and three-quarters of the sugar to the yolks and beat together until the mixture forms a ribbon.

Beat the whites until soft peaks form, then add the remaining sugar and beat until very stiff.

Mixing the yolks and whites: Using a flat, slotted spoon, fold one-third of the egg whites into the yolk mixture and blend thoroughly. Gently fold in the remaining whites. Just before the whites are completely incorporated, sift in the flour, stirring continuously. Stop stirring as soon as the flour is completely amalgamated.

· TO COOK ·

Brush the inside of the tin or ring with melted butter and coat lightly with flour. Place the ring on a baking sheet lined with baking parchment or buttered and floured greaseproof paper.

Gently pour in the sponge mixture and level the surface with a pastry scraper or palette knife.

Bake the sponge in the preheated oven for 25 minutes. As soon as it is cooked, turn it onto a wire rack and remove the outer ring.

· STORAGE ·

This sponge can be baked 24 hours in advance and keeps very well for up to 48 hours.

· EQUIPMENT ·

Electric mixer

1 loose-bottomed flan or cake tin or Genoise sponge ring 22 cm/9 in diameter, 3.5 cm/1¼ in deep

1 baking sheet

Greaseproof paper or baking parchment

MERINGUE SUISSE
(Swiss meringue)

· INGREDIENTS ·

4 egg whites (125 ml/ 4 fl oz *or* 40 g/4½ oz)

300 g/10 oz sugar

This meringue has a firmer, more solid texture than French meringue and is perfect for making decorations or for dessert bases. It is not, however, as delicate and melting as French meringue.

Preparation time: 20 minutes

Cooking time: 1 hour 45 minutes

· PREPARATION ·

Combine the egg whites and sugar in the mixing bowl. Stand the bottom of the bowl in a bain-marie set over direct heat. Beat the mixture continuously until it reaches a temperature of about 40°C/104°F.

Remove the bowl from the bain-marie and continue to beat until the mixture is completely cold.

· PIPING AND COOKING ·

Preheat the oven to 120°C/250°F/gas 1.

Spoon the mixture onto baking parchment or lightly buttered and floured greaseproof paper, using 2 soup spoons, or use a piping bag fitted with different nozzles to pipe it into various shapes and sizes.

Lower the oven temperature to 100°C/200°F/gas ½ and cook the meringues for 1 hour 45 minutes. They are ready when both the top and bottom are dry.

· EQUIPMENT ·

Electric mixer or *a copper bowl and whisk*

Bain-marie

Greaseproof paper or *baking parchment*

Piping bag and plain or decorative nozzles, depending on the desired effect

MERINGUE FRANCAISE
(French meringue)

· INGREDIENTS ·

4 egg whites (125 ml/ 4 fl oz or 140 g/4½ oz)

125 g/4 oz sugar

125 g/4 oz icing sugar, sifted

Preparation time: 15 minutes

Cooking time: 1 hour 45 minutes

· PREPARATION ·

Whisk the egg whites until soft peaks form. Beat in the sugar, a little at a time, and continue to beat for 10 minutes. The mixture should be firm and very smooth and shiny.

Gradually sift in the icing sugar, folding it gently into the mixture with a slotted spoon. Do not overwork the mixture. Use the meringue immediately.

· PIPING AND COOKING ·

Preheat the oven to 120°C/250°F/gas 1.

Pipe or spoon the mixture onto baking parchment or lightly buttered and floured greaseproof paper, using 2 soup spoons or a piping bag fitted with the appropriate nozzle.

Lower the oven temperature to 100°C/200°F/gas ½ and cook the meringues for 1 hour 45 minutes. They are ready when both the top and bottom are dry.

· STORAGE ·

Meringues will keep very well for up to 2 weeks in an airtight tin or tightly sealed container. Keep in a dry place.

· NOTES ·

You should always keep a few prepared meringue shells or cases ready for impromptu meals. You can then rustle up a marvellous dessert by combining the meringue with some

· EQUIPMENT ·

Electric mixer or *a copper bowl and whisk*

Greaseproof paper or *baking parchment*

Piping bag and plain or patterned nozzles, depending on the desired effect

whole fruits or a fruit mousse, some whipped cream, ice cream or a sorbet.

If you prefer a pale golden meringue, cook it at 150°C/300°F/gas 3, but reduce the cooking time by about 30 minutes.

M E R I N G U E   I T A L I E N N E
(Italian meringue)

· INGREDIENTS ·

80 ml/3 fl oz water

360 g/12 oz sugar

30 g/1 oz glucose (optional)

6 egg whites

Preparation time: 7 minutes

Cooking time: 15–20 minutes

· PREPARATION ·

Cooking the sugar: Put the water in the copper pan, then add the sugar and glucose, if using. Place over moderate heat and stir the mixture with a skimmer until it boils. Skim the surface and wash down the sugar crystals which form inside the pan with a brush dipped in cold water. Now increase the heat so that the syrup cooks rapidly. Insert the sugar thermometer to check the temperature.

The egg whites: When the sugar reaches 110°C/230°F, beat the egg whites in an electric mixer until stiff. Keep an eye on the sugar and take the pan off the heat when it reaches 121°C/248°F.

Mixing the sugar with the egg whites: When the egg whites are well risen and firm, set the mixer to the lowest speed and gently pour on the cooked sugar in a thin stream, taking care not to let it run onto the whisks. Continue to beat at low speed until the mixture is almost completely cold; this will take about 15 minutes. The meringue is now ready to use.

· STORAGE ·

Meringue italienne can be kept in the fridge for several days, stored in an airtight container.

· NOTES ·

The glucose prevents crystals from forming in the egg whites or at the edge of the bowl when the sugar is added.

The quantity of sugar used in this recipe may vary, depending on how the meringue will be used. If you want a light meringue, 50 g/2 oz sugar per egg white will be enough; if, however, you need a very firm, stiff mixture, you will need 70 g/2½ oz sugar for each white.

The quantities given here are the smallest possible needed to achieve a really good result.

You can make an excellent buttercream using *Meringue italienne* (see page 66).

· EQUIPMENT ·

1 copper sugar pan

Sugar thermometer

Electric mixer

FOND DE PROGRES AUX AMANDES OU NOISETTES
(Almond or hazelnut meringues 'Japonais')

The almonds and hazelnuts make this a more sophisticated mixture than plain meringue.

· PREPARATION ·

Preheat the oven to 150°C/300°F/gas 3.

The egg whites: Beat until soft peaks form, then add the sugar and beat until firm.

Scatter in the *tant pour tant* and 15 g/½ oz flour and fold into the whites with a flat slotted spoon, stopping as soon as they are well mixed. Do not overwork.

Piping the mixture: Line the baking sheet with baking parchment or buttered and floured greaseproof paper. Draw your desired shape on the paper, or press the cutters into the flour to mark out the shape. Leave plenty of space between the circles.

Starting from the centre of the circles, pipe out the mixture in a spiral, using the 1 cm/½ in nozzle for the larger circles and the 5 mm/¼ in nozzle for the individual bases. Sprinkle with flaked almonds or hazelnuts and bake at once in the preheated oven.

· TO COOK ·

Cook the large bases for 1 hour and the small ones for 40 minutes, or until they are completely dry, like meringues, and a pale, creamy colour.

· TO SERVE ·

Cover one of the bases with *crème mousseline* (see page 63), chocolate or coffee *Chantilly* (see page 66), or *crème pralinée* (see page 63) and top with another circle, then make a third layer in the same way. Serve this simple, luscious dessert as soon as possible. To make it even more special, garnish with fruits in season and a *coulis* made from the same fruits and poured around the edge in a ribbon.

· STORAGE ·

These bases will keep very well for 8–10 days, stored in an airtight container in a dry place. Keep some handy in case of unexpected guests.

GENOISE NATURE
(Plain Genoise sponge)

A plain Genoise served with a fresh fruit *coulis* makes a delicious, healthy tea-time treat for children.

· PREPARATION ·

Preheat the oven to 190°C/375°F/gas 6.

Preparing the mixture: Put the sugar and eggs in the bowl of the mixer and whisk immediately. Set the bowl in a bain-marie and, still whisking, heat until the mixture reaches about 30°C/86°F.

Remove the bowl from the bain-marie and beat the mixture at medium speed for 10 minutes, until well risen, then reduce the speed and beat for a further 10 minutes until the mixture cools and has a ribbon consistency.

Moulding the sponge: Sift in the flour and fold it gently into the mixture with a flat slotted spoon, taking care not to overwork it.

If you are using the clarified butter, add it at this stage. Divide the mixture between the lightly buttered and floured tins or moulds and bake immediately in the preheated oven.

· TO COOK ·

Cooking time will vary according to the size of the mould you use; a 22 cm/8½ in sponge will take 30 minutes, while the very large sponge used in *Le Fraisier* (see page 114) will need 1 hour.

As soon as the sponge is cooked, invert it onto a wire rack and unmould. Give the cake one-quarter turn every 15 minutes until it is completely cold; this will prevent it from sticking to the rack and spoiling.

· STORAGE ·

Wrapped in clingfilm, Genoise sponges freeze very well for up to 2 weeks, and they will also keep in the fridge for 3 days.

· NOTES ·

Genoise sponges are generally baked the day before they are eaten. They will then hold their shape better when sliced for filling.

If you plan to serve a Genoise plain, the addition of the clarified butter will improve it greatly. Add the butter immediately after the flour.

· EQUIPMENT ·

Electric mixer
Bain-marie
*1 or more tins or moulds
(eg 2 × 22 cm/8½ in
diameter tins)*
Wire rack

CREAMS, SAUCES, FRUIT COULIS AND JELLY

*L*ike sauces, fruit *coulis* should be served either directly on the plate with the dessert arranged on top, or trickled around the edge in a ribbon, but never poured over the dessert, as this would spoil its appearance.

With their varied colours and textures, creams are velvety and delicately flavoured, while fruit *coulis* also add a refreshing tang. Whether they are used to coat the base of a pudding or served as an accompanying sauce to fresh fruits, they are always delicious; gourmands will not hesitate to sup them up with a spoon.

By the judicious mixing of different creams, you can obtain some surprising and delectable results, with unusual colours and flavours. Be careful, though; practice at home first and never experiment if you are expecting guests!

Creams do not keep well — two or three days in the fridge at most — and very few can be frozen. To store in the fridge, put the creams in an airtight container or a bowl covered with clingfilm and remove from the fridge 30 minutes before using.

CREME PATISSIERE
(Confectioners' custard: vanilla, coffee and chocolate)

· INGREDIENTS ·

6 egg yolks
125 g/4½ oz sugar
40 g/1½ oz flour
500 ml/18 fl oz milk
1 vanilla pod, split

Makes about 750 g/1 lb 9 oz
Preparation time: 15 minutes

Crème pâtissière is to patisserie what veal stock is to cooking — it forms the basis for innumerable recipes. It is as simple to make as it is delicious.

· PREPARATION ·
Place the egg yolks and about one-third of the sugar in a bowl and whisk until they are pale and form a light ribbon. Sift in the flour and mix well.

· TO COOK ·
Combine the milk, the remaining sugar and the split vanilla pod in a saucepan and bring to the boil. As soon as the mixture

· EQUIPMENT ·

1 bowl
1 saucepan

PICTURE PAGES 68-9

bubbles, pour about one-third onto the egg mixture, stirring all the time. Pour the mixture back into the pan and cook over gentle heat, stirring continuously. Boil for 2 minutes, then tip the custard into a bowl. Flake a little butter over the surface or dust lightly with icing sugar to prevent a skin from forming as the custard cools.

· NOTES ·

Add a little cocoa or coffee powder to the custard instead of the vanilla to give you a chocolate or coffee-flavoured cream. If you use cocoa, use a little less flour and add a touch more sugar.

CRÈME CHIBOUST

· INGREDIENTS ·

FOR THE *CRÈME PÂTISSIÈRE:*

6 egg yolks

80 g/3 oz sugar

30 g/1 oz custard powder

350 ml/12 fl oz milk

½ vanilla pod

1 quantity *Meringue italienne* (see page 58)

50 ml/2 fl oz Curaçao, Grand Marnier *or* rum (optional)

Makes 1.3 kg/2 lb 14 oz

Preparation time: 25 minutes

· PREPARATION ·

The crème pâtissière: Follow the recipe on page 61. Take the pan off the heat and stir in the alcohol, if you are using it, or simply leave it flavoured with vanilla. Dot the surface with butter to prevent a skin from forming and set aside in a warm place.

The crème Chiboust: Leave the *crème pâtissière* until it is just tepid. Remove the vanilla pod. Using a whisk, stir in one-third of the *meringue italienne*, then, with a spatula, gently fold in the rest until the mixture is completely homogenous. Do not overwork, or the cream will collapse and lose its lightness.

· STORAGE ·

The cream will freeze very well for up to a week, but only if you freeze the entire dessert, already assembled.

· NOTES ·

You must use this cream as soon as you have mixed in the *meringue italienne*, so it is essential to have your bases (for *St Honoré, puits d'amour* or *tarte princesse* with redcurrant pearls etc.) completely ready before finishing the *crème Chiboust*.

We prefer not to use gelatine for this cream so that it stays very light, delicate and ultra-smooth, but it is fragile. If you need to transport a dessert made with *crème Chiboust*, we suggest that you add 1½ gelatine leaves to the *crème pâtissière* as soon as it is taken off the heat and before adding the alcohol.

· EQUIPMENT ·

1 saucepan

PICTURE PAGES 68-9

CRÈME MOUSSELINE

· INGREDIENTS ·

| 4 whole eggs |
| 2 egg yolks |
| 220 g/7½ oz sugar |
| 50 g/2 oz flour |
| 500 ml/18 fl oz milk |
| 250 g/9 oz butter, at room temperature |
| Flavouring of your choice – eg, caramel, chocolate, coffee, praline, Grand Marnier (optional) |

Makes about 1.3 kg/ 2 lb 14 oz

Preparation time: 30 minutes plus cooling

Crème mousseline makes a perfect filling for biscuits, sponges and other dessert bases. It is not as rich as buttercream, and is very light and palatable.

· PREPARATION ·

The crème pâtissière: Make a *crème pâtissière* using all the ingredients except the butter and flavouring, following the method on page 61.

Adding the butter to the cream: As soon as the *crème pâtissière* is cooked, take the pan off the heat and beat in one third of the butter, cut into small pieces. Pour into a bowl and keep in a cool place, stirring from time to time to prevent a skin from forming and to help the mixture to cool faster.

Place the remaining butter in the bowl of the mixer and beat at low speed for about 3 minutes, until rather pale. Increase the speed to medium and add the cooled *crème pâtissière*, a little at a time. Beat for 5 minutes, until the cream is perfectly light and creamy. Add the flavouring of your choice, or leave the cream plain. It is now ready to use.

· STORAGE ·

The cream will keep well in the fridge for up to 4 days. Store in an airtight container or bowl covered with clingfilm.

· EQUIPMENT ·

| 1 bowl |
| 1 saucepan |
| Electric mixer |

PICTURE PAGES 68-9

CRÈME PRALINÉE
(Praline cream)

· INGREDIENTS ·

| 500 g/1 lb 2 oz *Crème pâtissière* (see page 61) |
| 500 g/1 lb 2 oz *Crème Chantilly* (see page 66) |
| 150 g/5 oz praline *or* nougat paste |
| 100 g/3½ oz hazelnuts, shelled (optional) |
| Pinch of icing sugar |

Makes about 1.25 kg/ 2 lb 12 oz

Preparation time: 20 minutes

This is one of those creams which seem particularly delicious in winter. Its delicate, nutty flavour makes it perfect for filling all kinds of biscuit- and sponge-based desserts.

· PREPARATION ·

The crème pralinée: In a bowl, combine one-third of the *crème pâtissière* with the paste and whisk together until thoroughly mixed. Add the rest of the *crème pâtissière* and mix well again with the whisk.

Using a spatula, gently fold in the *crème Chantilly*. The *crème pralinée* is now ready to use.

The hazelnuts: If you want to add hazelnuts to the mixture, first place them under a very hot grill to detach the papery skin, then rub them in a cloth to remove the skin completely.

Arrange the nuts in a grill pan, sprinkle with icing sugar

· EQUIPMENT ·

| 1 bowl |
| 1 grill pan (optional) |

PICTURE PAGES 68-9

and replace under the grill until lightly caramelized. Leave to cool completely.

When the nuts have cooled, chop them with a knife, or crush coarsely with a rolling pin.

Fold them into the *crème pralinée* at the very last moment so that they remain crunchy.

· STORAGE ·

You can keep it in the fridge for up to 2 days in an airtight container, but it will have lost some of its exquisite lightness when you come to use it. Remove the cream from the fridge an hour before using, then beat lightly to restore its smoothness, but not, alas, its original volume.

SAUCE CARAMEL
(Caramel sauce)

· INGREDIENTS ·
80 ml/3 fl oz water

100 g/3½ oz sugar

500 ml/18 fl oz double cream

2 egg yolks, lightly beaten (optional)

Makes about 700 ml/1¼ pints

Preparation time: 5 minutes, plus chilling

· EQUIPMENT ·
1 large saucepan

1 bowl

Conical strainer

PICTURE PAGES 68-9

Caramel sauce makes a quite delicious accompaniment to numerous desserts. It should be served very cold. It can also be churned in an ice cream maker to make a caramel ice cream.

· PREPARATION ·

Cooking the sugar: Pour the water into a large saucepan and add the sugar. Set over low heat until the sugar has completely melted and is beginning to boil. Wash down the inside of the pan with a pastry brush dipped in cold water to prevent any crystals from forming. Cook the sugar until it turns a lovely deep amber and the surface begins to smoke slightly. Take the pan off the heat immediately and beat in the cream, stirring constantly with a whisk.

Cooking the sauce: Set the pan back over a high heat and stir with the whisk. Let the mixture bubble for 2 or 3 minutes, then remove from the heat.

Still stirring, pour a little of the sauce onto the egg yolks, then return this mixture to the pan but do not cook it. Pass the sauce through a conical strainer into a bowl and keep in a cool place. Stir the sauce from time to time to prevent a skin from forming.

· STORAGE ·

The sauce will keep in the fridge for up to 48 hours stored in an airtight container.

· NOTES ·

The egg yolks are not essential, but they do make the sauce smoother, less liquid and more refined.

CREME D'AMANDE
(Almond cream)

· INGREDIENTS ·
250 g/9 oz butter

500 g/1 lb 2 oz *tant pour tant* (equal quantities of icing sugar and ground almonds sifted together)

50 g/2 oz flour

5 eggs

50 ml/2 fl oz rum (optional)

Makes 1 kg 150 g/2½ lb

Preparation time: 20 minutes

This cream forms the basis of several desserts, particularly *Pithiviers* and various tarts. It can be made moister and more velvety by stirring in 20-30 per cent of *crème pâtissière* just before using.

· PREPARATION ·
Work the butter with the beater or spatula until very soft. Still beating, work in the *tant pour tant* and the flour, then the eggs one by one, beating between each addition. The mixture should be light and homogenous. Stir in the rum.

· STORAGE ·
The cream will keep very well for 4 or 5 days; keep it in the fridge in an airtight container or a bowl covered with clingfilm. Take it out of the fridge 30 minutes before using.

· EQUIPMENT ·
Electric mixer or food processor with a paddle beater or flat whisk or mixing bowl and spatula

PICTURE PAGES 68-9

CREME AU CHOCOLAT
(Chocolate cream)

· INGREDIENTS ·
200 ml/7 fl oz double cream

150 g/5 oz sugar

120 g/4 oz cocoa powder, sifted *or* unsweetened bitter chocolate, chopped

300 g/10 oz butter, at room temperature

Makes about 750 g/1 lb 10 oz

Preparation time: 15 minutes, plus cooling

This chocolate cream is very rich and velvety, without being sickly. It is used mostly in biscuit- and sponge-based desserts and all sorts of chocolate confections, from the simplest to the most elaborate.

· PREPARATION ·
Cooking the cream: Put the cream and sugar in a saucepan, place over high heat and bring to the boil, stirring continuously. Boil for 3 minutes, then take the pan off the heat and whisk in the cocoa or chopped chocolate and half the butter, a little at a time. Pour the mixture into a bowl and leave in a cool place until completely cold. Whisk from time to time to prevent a skin from forming.

Combining the butter with the cream: In the electric mixer, or a bowl, beat the remaining butter for 3 minutes, until very light. Still beating, incorporate the cold chocolate cream, 1 spoonful at a time and beat for about 5 minutes, until the mixture is homogenous and very light in texture, almost like a mousse. The cream is now ready to use.

· STORAGE ·
The cream keeps very well for up to 3 days in the fridge, stored in an airtight container.

· EQUIPMENT ·
1 saucepan

Electric mixer or a bowl and whisk

PICTURE PAGES 68-9

CRÈME AU BEURRE
(Buttercream)

· INGREDIENTS ·

250 ml/9 fl oz water

700 g/1 lb 8 oz sugar

50 g/2 oz glucose
(optional)

9 egg whites

1 kg/2 lb 2 oz butter, at
room temperature

Makes about 2.3 kg/5 lb

*Preparation time: 20
minutes, plus cooling·*

*Cooking time: 15-20
minutes*

· EQUIPMENT ·

1 copper sugar pan

Sugar thermometer

Electric mixer

PICTURE PAGES 68-9

Buttercream made with *meringue italienne* is a simple, easy-to-make cream, which can be used in many recipes, including all sorts of biscuit- and sponge-based desserts. Its great advantage is that it is neither too rich nor too sickly and so is easily digestible.

· PREPARATION ·

The meringue italienne: Make the meringue with all the ingredients except the butter, following the recipe given on page 58.

Adding the butter: When the meringue is almost cold, set the mixer on low speed and beat in the butter, a little at a time. Beat for about 5 minutes, until the mixture is very smooth and homogenous. The buttercream is now ready to use.

· STORAGE ·

It will keep well in the fridge for up to a week stored in an airtight container. Before using the buttercream, leave at room temperature for 1 hour, then mix well until smooth.

CRÈME CHANTILLY
(Plain, chocolate and coffee)

· INGREDIENTS ·

FOR ALL THE CREAMS:

500 ml/18 fl oz whipping
cream, well chilled

50 g/2 oz icing sugar
or 50 ml/2 fl oz Sorbet
syrup (see page 168)

Vanilla powder *or*
extract, to taste
(optional)

FOR THE
CHOCOLATE CREAM:

150 g/5 oz plain
chocolate *or* 2 tbsp
cocoa powder, sifted

FOR THE COFFEE CREAM:

1 tbsp hot milk

2 tbsp instant coffee *or*
1 tbsp coffee extract

· EQUIPMENT ·

*Electric mixer or a bowl and
whisk, chilled*

PICTURE PAGES 68-9

Crème Chantilly is used to lighten and enrich numerous creams — the *crème pâtissière* in an *Alméria* (see page 136) for example. It can also be served just as it is and will complement many desserts, fruits and ice creams.

· PREPARATION ·

Plain crème Chantilly: Combine the well-chilled cream with the sugar or sorbet syrup and vanilla in a chilled mixer bowl and beat at medium speed for 1 or 2 minutes. Increase the speed and beat for 3 or 4 minutes, until the cream begins to thicken. Do not overbeat, or the cream may turn into butter. It should be a little firmer than the ribbon stage.

Chocolate Chantilly: Melt the plain chocolate in a double boiler; the temperature should not exceed 35°C/95°F. Remove from the heat and whisk in one-third of the plain *crème Chantilly*. Fold gently and delicately into the remaining *crème Chantilly;* do not overwork the mixture.

If you are using cocoa instead of the plain chocolate, add it when you beat the cream.

Makes about 600 g/1 lb 4 oz
Preparation time: 8 minutes

Coffee Chantilly: Dissolve the coffee in the hot milk and leave to cool. Add it when you beat the cream. Alternatively, add a tablespoon of coffee extract when you whip the cream.

· STORAGE ·

It is best to use the *Chantilly* as soon as you have made it, but it can be kept in the fridge in an airtight container for up to 24 hours.

· NOTES ·

If you haven't any whipping cream, but only double cream, add some very cold milk to the cream before whipping. You will need 15 per cent of the volume of the cream (which will be about 75 ml/3 fl oz). Proceed as for whipping cream.

SAUCE CHOCOLAT
(Chocolate sauce)

· INGREDIENTS ·

200 g/7 oz bitter chocolate *or* plain *couverture*
150 ml/5 fl oz milk
2 tbsp double cream
30 g/1 oz sugar
30 g/1 oz butter

Makes about 460 g/1 lb
Preparation time: 10 minutes

· EQUIPMENT ·

Double saucepan or *bain-marie*
1 *saucepan*
Conical strainer

PICTURE PAGES 68-9

Chocolate sauce is used as the base for innumerable desserts, ice creams etc. Served hot, it is delicious with profiteroles, vanilla ice cream and *Soufflé tiède aux poires* (see page 151). Served cold, it adds the finishing touch to a *vacherin* or a slice of toasted *brioche*.

· PREPARATION ·

The chocolate: Melt it in the double saucepan or a bain-marie.
To cook the sauce: Put the milk, cream and sugar in a saucepan and set over high heat. Stir gently with a whisk until the mixture boils. Pour it onto the melted chocolate, stirring constantly. Tip the whole mixture into the saucepan and let it bubble for 15 seconds.

Take the pan off the heat and beat in the butter, a little at a time, until the sauce is completely homogenous. Pass through a conical strainer.

· STORAGE ·

The sauce keeps very well in the fridge for up to 3 days; store it in a bowl covered with clingfilm, or in an airtight container.

2

6

3

4

5

1

1 *Coulis de fruits rouges (page 71);* **2** *Crème d'amande (page 65);* **3** *Crème pralinée (page 63);* **4** *Crème ganache (page 197);* **5** *Sauce caramel (page 64);* **6** *Gelée de pommes (page 70);* **7** *Crème au chocolat (page 65);* **8** *Crème Chiboust (page 62);* **9** *Crème pâtissière (page 61);* **10** *Crème au beurre (page 66);* **11** *Crème mousseline (page 63);* **12** *Sauce chocolat (page 67);* **14** *Crème anglaise (page 70);* **15** *Crème Chantilly (page 66).*

CRÈME ANGLAISE
(Custard cream)

· INGREDIENTS ·

12 egg yolks	
250 g/9 oz sugar	
1 lt/1¾ pt milk	
1 vanilla pod, split	

Makes about 1.55 lt/2½ pints
Preparation time: 15 minutes
Cooking time: 8 minutes
approximately

Crème anglaise is used as a base for numerous desserts, sweets and ice creams. It is delicious served like a *coulis* or sauce with cakes or red fruits; serve it well chilled.

· PREPARATION ·

Put the egg yolks in a bowl with one-third of the sugar (about 85 g/3 oz). Beat with a whisk until the mixture forms a ribbon.

· TO COOK ·

Combine the milk, split vanilla pod and the remaining sugar in a saucepan and bring to the boil. Pour the boiling milk onto the egg mixture, whisking continuously.

Pour the mixture back into the pan, set over low heat and cook, stirring continuously with a spatula, until the custard is thick enough to coat it. On no account let the custard boil.

Pass the custard through a conical strainer and keep in a cool place until completely cold. Stir from time to time to prevent a skin from forming.

· STORAGE ·

The custard keeps very well in the fridge for 2 or 3 days. Pass it through a conical strainer again before serving.

· NOTES ·

If you prefer a much less rich and creamy sauce, you can reduce the number of egg yolks, but do not use fewer than 8 yolks for each litre (1¾ pints) of milk.

The vanilla pod can be replaced by 3 tablespoons of instant coffee or 100 g/3½ oz melted plain chocolate.

· EQUIPMENT ·

1 bowl	
1 saucepan	
1 conical strainer	

PICTURE PAGES 68-9

GELÉE DE POMMES
(Apple jelly)

· INGREDIENTS ·

500 ml/18 fl oz water	
250 g/9 oz sugar	
500 g/1 lb 2 oz eating apples (preferably Cox's)	
6 leaves of gelatine	

This delicately flavoured apple jelly is translucent, which makes it ideal for 'neutral' glazes where no colour is required. It is perfect for all kinds of mousse-based desserts, like our *Délice aux fruits de la passion* (see page 132) and adds a beautiful sheen. It can also be used to coat peeled fruits to prevent them from discolouring or drying out, and it makes a good glaze for fruit tarts.

· EQUIPMENT ·

1 saucepan with a lid	
Conical strainer or a jelly bag	
1 bowl	

PICTURE PAGES 68-9

Makes 500 ml/18 fl oz

Preparation time: 20 minutes

Cooking time: about 15 minutes

· PREPARATION ·

The syrup: Pour the water into the pan and add the sugar. Heat until the sugar has dissolved completely and is beginning to boil, stirring with a whisk from time to time. Skim the surface if necessary.

The gelatine: Soak the leaves in cold water for 20 minutes, then drain.

The apples: Wash or wipe them, but do not peel. Coarsely chop the whole apples, including the core, and drop them into the boiling sugar syrup. Cover the saucepan and simmer for about 7 minutes. Take the pan off the heat and push the apples to one side so that you can drop in the drained gelatine and dissolve it. When it has dissolved, pass the mixture carefully through a conical strainer or jelly bag set over a bowl.

Use the jelly as a glaze for various desserts when it is cold, but before it begins to set.

· STORAGE ·

The jelly will keep in an airtight container for up to 4 days. Reheat it, then leave to cool again before using.

C O U L I S   D E   F R U I T S
(Fruit coulis)

· INGREDIENTS ·

800 g/1 lb 12 oz fresh fruit (eg, strawberries, raspberries, wild strawberries, redcurrants, pineapple, apricots, peaches, kiwi fruit)

Juice of 1 lemon

250 ml/9 fl oz Sorbet syrup (see page 168)

Makes about 800 g–1 kg/ 1lb 12 oz–2 lb 2 oz, depending on the density of the fruit

Preparation time: 15 minutes

· EQUIPMENT ·

Blender or food processor

1 conical strainer

PICTURE PAGES 68-9

Fruit *coulis* go wonderfully well with all kinds of desserts, from mousses to tarts, gâteaux and ice creams. Almost any fruit is suitable for this *coulis*, depending on the desired flavour, but do not mix different fruits.

· PREPARATION ·

Wash, drain, hull, peel or core the fruit as appropriate. Place in the blender or food processor with the lemon juice and syrup and process until smooth. Pass through the strainer and keep in the fridge until you are ready to use the *coulis*.

· STORAGE ·

Fruit *coulis* freeze very well; beat well as soon as they have thawed. You can perfectly well use bottled or tinned fruits in syrup instead of fresh fruit. Use only 125 ml/4 fl oz sorbet syrup and top it up with the same amount of water.

· NOTES ·

Allow at least 100 ml/4 fl oz of *coulis* per person.

Two tablespoons of fruit *coulis* in a glass of champagne makes the most delectable cocktail.

A SELECTION OF FRUIT TARTLETS
AND BARQUETTES

*Included are: Red fruits in a pâte sablée case
lined with crème Chantilly (strawberry, raspberry
dusted with icing sugar, wild strawberry and
redcurrant); baked and glazed with redcurrant
jelly (cherry, apricot and mirabelle) in puff pastry cases.
The fruits include white and black grapes, fig,
nectarine with mint, damson, gooseberry and
mirabelle.*

CHAPTER
· 3 ·

DESSERTS

*R*ichly-hued, light and delicate, a dessert should add the final flourish, like the royal seal on a regal missive. The preparation, therefore, demands a great deal of attention and a modicum of patience.

In France, the country of gastronomy, desserts have always played a very important part in family gatherings and social occasions as well as in religious festivals: yule logs at Christmas, *galettes des rois* at Epiphany, chocolate eggs and animals at Easter. Baptisms, first communions and weddings are occasions for towering *croquembouches* or *pièces Bretonnes*, while Mother's Day inspires cakes decorated with love and affection.

We French associate a large, fine cake with joyful occasions and shared friendship.

Nowadays, it is quite usual for guests to present their hostess with a beautiful pastry instead of a bunch of flowers. Even though fellow guests may not be hungry by this stage of the meal, if the dessert is simple, original and unusual, no one will resist a taste.

· USING FRUIT IN DESSERTS ·

Fruit is the best-loved and most sought after of all natural ingredients. Whether frozen, bottled or canned, but best of all fresh, it is the pre-eminent natural product — fruit is the king!

Its sugar, juice and pure flavour makes it the most delicate of all ingredients in any dessert; there is nothing to beat it. There is no limit to its uses — virtually all fruits will grace any cake or gateau — hence the ever-growing demand from the customer for every type of fruit.

Even out of season, thanks to refrigerated air and road transport, we can always obtain fresh red fruits from Europe, particularly Italy, Spain and France. Thus from late May right through until October, city dwellers always find raspberries and strawberries, with their sweet flavour and delicate scent.

Depending on the fruits you use and the effect you want to create, you can produce all manner of desserts — light, refreshing, sweet or sharp-tasting; no one will be able to resist the shimmering, appetizing colours of a fruit dessert.

· WHAT TO DRINK WITH DESSERTS ·

If you want to devote your tastebuds entirely to the delights of the dessert, you should drink only iced water; however, if you are feeling festive and want to marry a wine with your pudding, remember that the wine you choose should vary according to the type of pudding and the season of the year; depending on whether the dessert is very sweet or not and on the basic ingredients — fruits, chocolate, sponge biscuit or mousse. The appropriate wine could be Sauternes and Barsac, Beaumes de Venise, Monbazillac, Banyuls or medium dry white or pink champagne. A medium sweet cider can make a delicious accompaniment.

TARTS

*W*arm or cold (but never chilled), tarts can be served on almost any occasion; after lunch, for tea, at a buffet or even after dinner. We have never been able to resist that most seductive lure of a little tartlet, filled with wild strawberries, accompanied of course by those scintillating little bubbles which one finds in a glass of pink champagne!

Make different pastry cases to suit the occasion; the type will vary according to the kind of fruit you use, the preferences of your guests and the time of day when you are going to serve the tart. After dinner, for example, it is best to use a fine, light, delicate pastry, such as puff pastry or trimmings, *pâte sucrée* or *sablée;* for tea, a *brioche* dough, shortcrust or flan pastry would be more suitable.

Adorned with exotic fruits like mangoes and lychees, their iridescent colours and fragrances make them truly alluring. Even decorated with such humble fruits as apples and pears, they are still delicious, though more simple and rustic.

As children, we adored helping our mother to roll out the pastry and to decorate the

Continued on page 78

TOP LEFT *Tarte chaude aux deux fruits (page 88)*
BOTTOM LEFT *Tarte aux mirabelles (page 79)*
ABOVE *Tarte al'coloche (page 93)*

tarts, arranging the fruit with our nimble fingers! For these are simple desserts, so easy to prepare that they are often the first task of the youngest apprentices in a patisserie.

FRUIT TARTLETS AND BARQUETTES

*F*or tartlets and *barquettes* filled and baked with a little *crème pâtissière* in the bottom and topped with fruit, such as apricots, apples, plums etc., use *pâte brisée, pâte à foncer* or puff pastry trimmings.

For more delicate fruits like red fruit, grapes, peaches etc., use *pâte sucrée* or *sablée*, baked blind. For a delicious flavour, spread a little *crème Chantilly* or *Chiboust* over the pastry just before filling the *barquettes* or tartlets with soft fruit.

The tartlets can be served just as they are, or sprinkled with sugar, or lightly brushed with apricot glaze or redcurrant jelly; where appropriate, arrange a few small sprigs of mint amongst the fruit.

TARTE AUX NOISETTES
(Hazelnut tart)

· INGREDIENTS ·

300 g/10 oz *Pâte sablée* (see recipe 2, page 47)
Pinch of flour
Butter, for greasing
4 eggs
250 ml/8 fl oz double cream
100 g/3½ oz clear honey
2 tbsp demerara sugar
150 g/5 oz fresh hazelnuts *or* cob nuts shelled and skinned if the skins are hard

Serves 6
Preparation time: 35 minutes
Cooking time: 40 minutes

· PREPARATION ·

Preheat the oven to 220°C/425°F/gas 8.

The pastry case: On a lightly floured surface, roll out the pastry to a thickness of about 3 mm/⅛ in.

Grease the flan ring, then line it with the pastry. Place on a baking sheet. Line the bottom of the pastry case with greaseproof paper and fill it with baking beans. Bake blind in the preheated oven for 20 minutes.

Use a spoon to remove the baking beans, then remove the greaseproof paper. Set aside at room temperature.

The filling: In a bowl, using a wire whisk, lightly beat together the eggs, cream, honey and sugar. Do not overwork the mixture.

· TO COOK ·

Pour the filling into the part-baked pastry case and bake at 220°C/425°F/gas 8 for about 15 minutes. Cut the hazelnuts in half and after 15 minutes lay the nuts, flat side down, on top of the half-cooked filling. Return to the oven and bake for a further 5 minutes, until the nuts are a pale golden brown.

Remove the flan ring before the tart is completely cold.

· EQUIPMENT ·

Wooden or marble pastry board
Flan ring, 22 cm/8½ in diameter, 3 cm/1¼ in deep
Baking sheet
Greaseproof paper
Baking beans

PICTURE PAGES 82-3

· TO SERVE ·

Slide this delicate tart onto a round plate and slice it at the table. Serve it cold but not chilled, dusted with icing sugar; it needs no accompaniment.

· NOTES ·

If you cannot find fresh hazelnuts, use dried instead, although they will not be quite as delicious. To remove the skins, grill them or place in a hot oven for a few minutes, until the skins split, then rub in a tea towel. Soak them in cold milk for 3 or 4 hours; this will give them the creamy texture of fresh nuts. Drain and dry them with a cloth before halving them.

TARTE AUX MIRABELLES
(Mirabelle tart)

· INGREDIENTS ·

300 g/10 oz *Pâte brisée* (see page 31)

Pinch of flour

Butter, for greasing

150 g/5 oz (about 5 tbsp) *Crème pâtissière* (see page 61)

800 g/1 lb 12 oz fresh mirabelles poached in syrup, *or* canned mirabelles, drained

50 g/2 oz apricot jam, sieved

Serves 8

Preparation time: 25 minutes

Cooking time: 40 minutes

This is a lovely tart which all your friends will enjoy. It is a feast for the eye and palate, with its delicate, sugary flavour. The unusual fruits give it an autumnal air, with their warm glowing tones of yellow and amber.

· PREPARATION ·

Preheat the oven to 220°C/425°F/gas 8.

Preparing the base: On a lightly floured surface, roll out the pastry into a circle about 3 mm/⅛ in thick. Lightly grease the flan ring, place on the greased baking sheet, then line it with the pastry. You will have about 30 g/1 oz trimmings left over.

With your fingertips, lightly pinch up the edges of the pastry to form a little crest. Crimp diagonally all round the edge with a pastry crimper or use your thumb and forefinger to achieve an attractive effect. Chill for 20 minutes.

Filling: Spread the *crème pâtissière* evenly over the pastry base. Arrange the whole, pitted mirabelles on top, taking care not to leave any gaps between them.

· TO COOK ·

Bake in the preheated oven for 40 minutes.

When you remove the tart from the oven, leave it in the flan ring and on the baking sheet for about 10 minutes. Once it has cooled, remove the ring and transfer to a wire rack.

Heat the apricot jam until boiling, then brush it lightly and evenly over the mirabelles.

· TO SERVE ·

Serve the tart as soon as it has cooled; on no account refrigerate it. Present it whole for your guests to help themselves.

· EQUIPMENT ·

Wooden or *marble pastry board*

1 flan ring, 22 cm/8 ½ in diameter, 2 cm/¾ in deep or a loose-bottomed flan tin

1 baking sheet

Pastry crimper

Wire rack

Small saucepan

PICTURE PAGE 76

1

Spread all the butter thickly and evenly over the base of the pan or heatproof dish.

2

Pour over the sugar.

3

Arrange the peeled, cored and halved apples, rounded side down.

4

Loosely roll the pastry on to the rolling pin, then unroll it over the apples.

5

Tuck in the pastry at the edge of the pan and trim off the excess with a knife.

6

When the tart is cooked, carefully invert it on to a round dish, using a cloth to protect your arms and hands, as it will be very hot.

TARTE DES DEMOISELLES TATIN
(Tart Tatin)

PICTURE PAGES 82–3

This easy-to-make winter pudding makes a pleasant change from a classic apple tart. Don't eat it too greedily, or you may burn your tongue on the delicious golden caramel coating the apples!

· PREPARATION ·

Preheat the oven to 220°C/425°F/gas 8.

The apples: Peel, core and halve them. Sprinkle with lemon juice and place in the fridge.

Assembling the tart: Evenly grease the base of the frying pan or dish with butter. Cover the bottom of the pan with the sugar, then arrange the apples, rounded side down, on the bottom of the pan.

On a lightly floured surface, roll out the puff pastry into a circle about 3 mm/⅛ in thick. Lay the pastry over the apples, allowing an overlap of about 2 cm/¾ in all round. Trim off the excess with a sharp knife.

Leave to rest in a cool place for at least 20 minutes.

· TO COOK ·

Set the pan or dish over fierce direct heat for 15–20 minutes, until the butter and sugar are bubbling and have become a deep amber colour. With a small palette knife, lift a little of the pastry away from the edges to ensure even cooking.

Cook in the preheated oven for 20 minutes, until the pastry is risen and golden.

· TO SERVE ·

As soon as the tart is cooked, invert it quickly onto a round serving dish, taking care not to burn yourself. The pastry will now be on the bottom of the plate, with the apples on top. If any have slipped, push them back into place with a small knife. Serve the tart piping hot.

· NOTES ·

For an original variation on a classical idea, make small individual tarts Tatin using mangoes instead of apples and halving the quantity of butter. Serve with a *coulis* made from equal quantities of mango and passion fruit.

· INGREDIENTS ·

6 medium dessert apples, preferably Cox's

Juice of ½ lemon

120 g/4 oz butter

200 g/7 oz sugar

250 g/9 oz Puff pastry *or* trimmings
(see pages 42-3)

Pinch of flour

Serves 4

Preparation time: 20 minutes plus 20 minutes resting time

Cooking time: 40 minutes

· EQUIPMENT ·

Deep frying pan or round heatproof dish, 26 cm/10 in diameter, 7 cm/2¾ in deep

Wooden or marble pastry board

1 and 4 *Tarte princesse aux pruneaux*
(page 84); 2 and 3 *Tarte des Demoiselles Tatin*
(page 81); 5 and 6 *Tarte marguerite (page 85);*
7 and 11 *Tarte aux perles de groseilles (page 92);*
9 and 10 *Tarte aux fruits de saison: Reine*
Claude and quetsches (page 91); 8 and 12 *Tarte*
aux noisettes (page 78)

TARTE PRINCESSE AUX PRUNEAUX
(Prune tart 'Princess')

PICTURE PAGES 82-3

· INGREDIENTS ·

520 g/1 lb 2 oz *Pâte à foncer* (see page 35) or puff pastry trimmings

2 pinches of flour

30 g/1 oz butter, for greasing

Eggwash, made with 1 egg yolk and 1 tbsp milk

900 ml/1½ pt double cream

7 eggs

250 g/9 oz sugar

Finely grated zest of 1 orange

50 soft prunes, stoned and steeped in 150 ml/5 fl oz Armagnac for about 15 minutes

1 quantity *Crème Chiboust* (see page 62), with 1 leaf of gelatine added

50 g/2 oz sugar, to glaze

Makes 2 tarts, each serving 8

Preparation time: 30 minutes, plus 20 minutes chilling

Cooking time: 45 minutes

· PREPARATION ·

Preheat the oven to 220°C/425°F/gas 8.

The pastry cases: On a lightly floured surface, roll out half the pastry into a circle about 2 mm/¹⁄₁₆ in thick.

Grease a flan ring, place on a baking sheet and line the ring with the pastry. Pinch up the edges so they come about 4 mm/¼ in above the ring. You will have about 30 g/1 oz pastry left over. Repeat the operation for the second pastry case.

Leave to rest in the fridge for at least 20 minutes.

Baking blind: Prick the pastry bases with a fork or the point of a knife. Line them with greaseproof paper or foil and fill with baking beans. Bake in the preheated oven for 15 minutes.

Remove the paper and beans, then brush the insides of the cases with eggwash and bake for a further 5 minutes, or until the glaze is lightly coloured. Set aside, in the rings, at room temperature. Reduce the oven to 200°C/400°F/gas 7.

The cream filling: Combine the double cream, eggs, sugar and grated orange zest in a bowl and mix lightly together.

Baking the tarts: Spread the prunes over the bottom of the pastry cases and pour over the cream mixture. Bake at 200°C/400°F/gas 7 for 25 minutes, until the cream has set.

Take the tarts out of the oven and, with a small knife, trim the crimped edges so that they are almost level with the cream filling. Slide a knife blade between the flan ring and the tart and lift off the ring, rotating it a quarter turn as you do so. Place on a wire rack and leave at room temperature.

Decorating and glazing: Heat the glazing iron over a gas flame, or switch it on if it is electric; alternatively, preheat the grill. Pipe the *crème Chiboust* onto the tarts in stars or rosettes so that the surface of the tarts is raised by about 2 cm/¾ in.

Sprinkle the surface with sugar and touch the top of each star or rosette for barely 1 second with the hot iron, to make a thin layer of caramel. Alternatively, place the tarts under the hot grill until the sugar caramelizes.

· TO SERVE ·

Serve the tarts whole not more than 2 or 3 hours after filling them, and let your guests help themselves.

· NOTES ·

Since it is difficult to reduce the quantities for the *Tarte princesse* without spoiling the proportions, it is better to make

· EQUIPMENT ·

Wooden or *marble pastry board*

2 *flan rings, 22 cm/8½ in diameter, 3 cm/1¼ in deep*

1 *baking sheet*

Greaseproof paper or *foil*

Baking beans

Glazing iron or *grill*

1 *bowl*

Piping bag fitted with a 1 cm/½ in plain or patterned nozzle

2 at one time. The second tart can be frozen, unglazed, for up to 3 days. To serve, place in the fridge to thaw gradually for 3 or 4 hours, then leave it at room temperature for another 2 or 3 hours, and finally glaze it just before serving.

Dried apricots make a delicious substitute for the prunes.

Gelatine is added to the *crème Chiboust* to help it hold its shape when it is caramelized.

TARTE MARGUERITE TUTTI FRUTTI
(Marguerite tart)

· INGREDIENTS ·

150 g/5 oz Puff pastry (see pages 42-3) *or* trimmings, *or Pâte brisée* (see page 31)

Pinch of flour

Eggwash, made with 1 egg yolk and 1 tbsp milk

250 ml/9 fl oz *Pâte à choux* (see page 46; ½ recipe quantity)

350 g/12 oz *Crème Chantilly* (see page 66)

150 g/5 oz each of various fruits: eg: gooseberries, blackberries, wild strawberries, cherries, golden raspberries, bilberries, loganberries, washed and hulled as necessary

Sprig of fresh mint, to garnish

Serves 7

Preparation time: 30 minutes

Cooking time: 35 minutes

This unusual tart with its rainbow colours presents an interesting contrast between the soft choux pastry and the crisp puff pastry. You can substitute other seasonal fruits.

· PREPARATION ·

Preheat the oven to 200°C/400°F/gas 7.

The pastry base: On a lightly floured surface, roll out the pastry as thinly as possible (about 1 mm/¹⁄₁₆ in) into a circle. Roll the circle on to a rolling pin, then unroll it on to a dampened baking sheet. Place the flan ring or template on the pastry and, with a sharp knife, cut around the outside edges following the contours of the mould. You will have about 50 g/2 oz pastry left over.

Lift off the flan ring and prick the pastry with a fork. Glaze the outside edges with eggwash, then brush lines of eggwash from the points where the rounded edges meet towards the centre to mark out 7 sections (see diagram).

The choux paste: Pipe out the choux paste following the lines of eggwash, then glaze the choux paste with eggwash. Leave to rest at room temperature for 5 minutes.

· TO COOK ·

Bake the prepared base in the preheated oven for about 35 minutes. Using a palette knife, slide the base on to a wire rack and keep at room temperature.

· TO SERVE ·

The base can be baked several hours in advance, but should only be filled at the last moment. Spread 50 g/2 oz *crème Chantilly* inside each choux pastry triangle and fill each with a different kind of fruit. Garnish the centre of the tart with a sprig of mint and serve at once.

· EQUIPMENT ·

Wooden or marble pastry board

1 baking sheet

1 daisy-shaped flan ring, or a template with 7 rounded edges, 26 cm/10 in diameter (see diagram)

Piping bag with a plain 1 cm/½ in nozzle

PICTURE PAGES 82-3

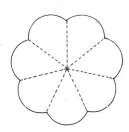

ABOVE *Tarte à l'orange (page 89)*
RIGHT *Tarte au citron (page 90)*

TARTE CHAUDE AUX DEUX FRUITS
(Hot two-fruit tart with sabayon sauce)

· INGREDIENTS ·

200 g/7 oz Puff pastry
trimmings (see
pages 42-3) or Pâte brisée
(see page 31)

Pinch of flour

5 crisp dessert apples,
(about 500 g/1 lb 1 oz)
preferably Cox's

75 g/2½ oz butter

60 g/2 oz sugar

75 ml/3 fl oz Calvados

80 g/3 oz bilberries in
syrup, drained or
50 fresh bilberries
poached in syrup

4 egg yolks

Serves 4

Preparation time: 35
minutes

Cooking time: 15 minutes

This delicate tart is very quick and easy to make.

· PREPARATION ·

Preheat the oven to 240°C/475°F/gas 10.

The pastry: On a lightly floured surface, roll out the pastry into a circle about 24 cm/9 in diameter and 2 mm/¹⁄₁₆ in thick. Place on a baking sheet brushed with cold water and prick the surface with a fork or a sharp knife. Leave to rest in the fridge.

The apples: Peel, halve and core them, then cut each half into ten even slices. Place in the sauté pan with the butter and sauté over high heat for 1 minute. Add the sugar, then flambé with 15 ml/1 tbsp of the Calvados. Drain the apples and keep the cooking juices and the apples separately in a cool place.

Assembling the tart: Arrange the cold apples in an attractive rosette pattern on the pastry base.

Cooking: Bake the tart in the preheated oven for 12 minutes.

Drain the bilberries thoroughly and arrange them in little heaps on top of the apples. Sprinkle 30 g/1 oz of the sugar over the top and return the tart to the oven for a further 3 minutes.

The sabayon sauce: In a shallow pan, combine the egg yolks, the remaining Calvados, 1 tablespoon water and the cooking juice from the apples. Set the pan over gentle, indirect heat or in a bain-marie and beat the mixture continuously with a whisk until you have a very smooth lukewarm froth (about 50°C/120°F).

· TO SERVE ·

Serve the tart on a round china plate, or, better still, on the baking sheet. Serve the sauce separately in a sauceboat, or poured around the tart in a ribbon, if you are using individual plates.

· NOTES ·

Never make the *sabayon* sauce more than 10 minutes before serving, or it will lose its frothiness. If you prefer, you can make individual tartlets instead of 1 large tart. Try adding a thin layer of 2 tablespoons *crème pâtissière* between the pastry base and the apples for a real treat.

· EQUIPMENT ·

Wooden or marble pastry
board

Baking sheet

1 sauté pan

1 shallow pan

1 strainer

PICTURE PAGE 76

TARTE A L'ORANGE
(Orange tart)

· INGREDIENTS ·

380 g/13 oz *Pâte sucrée* (see page 35)
Pinch of flour
Butter, for greasing
250 g/9 oz *Crème d'amande* (see page 65)
150 g/5 oz (about 5 tbsp) *Crème pâtissière* (see page 61)
2 large oranges, total weight about 600 g/ 1 lb 6 oz
500 ml/18 fl oz Sorbet syrup (see page 168)
1 tbsp apricot jam, sieved

Serves 8
Preparation time: 35 minutes
Cooking time: 30 minutes

· PREPARATION ·

Preheat the oven to 200°C/400°F/gas 7.

Preparing the base: On a lightly floured surface, roll out the pastry into a circle about 3 mm/⅛ in thick. Lightly grease the flan ring, place on the baking sheet, then line it with the pastry. You will be left with about 60 g/2 oz trimmings.

With your fingertips, lightly pinch up the edges of the pastry to form a little crest. Crimp diagonally all round the edge with a pastry crimper, or simply use your thumb and forefinger to shape the pastry. Chill for 20 minutes.

Filling: Mix together the two creams and spread them evenly over the chilled pastry base.

Cooking the base: Bake in the preheated oven for 30 minutes. When you remove the tart from the oven, leave it in the flan ring and on the baking sheet for about 10 minutes. Once it has cooled, remove the ring and transfer to a wire rack.

Preparing the oranges: Using a cannelizing knife, peel off about 12 long strips of zest at regular intervals from top to bottom of the oranges, then cut the oranges in half vertically.

Place the fruit on a board, cut side down and, with a fine serrated knife, cut into very fine, neat slices, about 2 mm/¹⁄₁₂ in thick. Spread them in a single layer in a deep dish. Bring the sorbet syrup to the boil and pour it over the orange slices. Cover with non-absorbent greaseproof paper, so that the fruit is thoroughly steeped in syrup.

Leave for about 30 minutes, until the syrup is completely cold, then carefully drain the orange slices and reserve the syrup.

Garnishing the tart: Arrange the orange slices in a spiral shape, starting from the outside of the tart (see the picture on page 86).

If you like, you can stand a few orange segments upright in the centre of the tart; cut the bases so that they stand firmly to give a very attractive effect.

Glazing: Mix 6 tablespoons of the reserved syrup with the apricot jam. Reduce by two-thirds over high heat, then carefully and evenly brush the glaze over the orange slices, taking care not to displace them.

· TO SERVE ·

Present the tart whole to your guests, then take it back to the kitchen and slice it with a serrated knife or a ham knife, taking care not to disarrange the oranges. The tart should be served at room temperature; on no account chill it before serving.

· EQUIPMENT ·

Wooden or marble pastry board
1 flan ring, 22 cm/8½ in diameter, 2 cm/¾ in deep, or a loose-bottomed flan tin
1 baking sheet
Pastry crimper
Cannelizing knife
1 small saucepan
1 large, deep dish
Wire rack

PICTURE PAGE 86

TARTE AU CITRON
(Lemon tart)

PICTURE PAGE 87

· INGREDIENTS ·

20 g/1 tbsp butter, for greasing

650 g/1 lb 6 oz *Pâte sablée* (see page 47)

Pinch of flour

4 lemons

9 eggs

375 g/13 oz sugar

300 ml/11 fl oz double cream

Eggwash, made with 1 egg yolk and ½ tsp milk

50 g/2 oz icing sugar, to serve

Serves 8

Preparation time: 40 minutes

Cooking time: about 1 hour 35 minutes

· EQUIPMENT ·

Wooden or marble pastry board

2 bowls

1 flan ring, 22 cm/ 8½ in diameter, 3.5 cm/1½ in deep

1 baking sheet

1 conical strainer

Foil or greaseproof paper

Baking beans

This lemon tart is one of our most popular recipes. It tastes much better if it is made in advance, which gives you a welcome opportunity to do some pre-preparation.

· PREPARATION ·

Preheat the oven to 200°C/400°F/gas 7.

The pastry case: Butter the flan ring and place in the freezer for about 10 minutes.

On a lightly floured surface, roll out the pastry to a thickness of about 4 mm/¼ in. Place the prepared flan ring on a baking sheet and line with the pastry. Use a sharp knife to trim the pastry, then pinch up the edges to make a little frill about 1 cm/½ in above the rim of the flan ring. Leave to rest in the fridge for 15 minutes.

The lemons: Wash them and grate the zests. Squeeze the lemons, strain the juice and reserve it with the zests.

The eggs: Break them into a bowl, add the sugar and beat lightly with a whisk until smooth and well blended.

The cream: Put it in a bowl and whisk very lightly for 10 seconds, until slightly thickened.

The filling: Stir the lemon zests and juice into the beaten eggs, then whisk in the cream. Place in the fridge.

Baking blind: Line the whole interior of the pastry case with foil or greaseproof paper and fill with baking beans. Bake in the preheated oven for 15 minutes, then remove from the oven, take out the beans and paper or foil and keep warm. Do not remove the flan ring. Brush the inside with eggwash and return to the oven for about 5 minutes, until the glaze is lightly coloured. Lower the oven temperature to 150°C/300°F/gas 3.

Filling the tart: Lightly stir the filling and pour into the case; bake at once at 150°C/300°F/gas 3 for about 1¼ hours.

When it is cooked, trim the edges of the pastry with a small knife, so that the rim of the tart stands about 3-5 mm/¼ in above the filling. Do this carefully, as *pâte sablée* is extremely fragile. Slide a knife between the flan ring and the tart and as you gently lift off the ring, rotate it a quarter turn.

· TO SERVE ·

Leave the tart to cool for at least 4 hours, sprinkling the top with icing sugar before serving. Serve it whole or in slices.

· NOTES ·

On no account put the tart in the fridge; keep it at room temperature otherwise the *pâte sablée* will soften.

TARTE AUX FRUITS DE SAISON: REINE CLAUDE ET QUETSCHE
(Greengage and damson tart)

PICTURE PAGES 82-3

· INGREDIENTS ·

300 g/10 oz *Pâte à foncer* (see page 35) *or* puff pastry trimmings
Pinch of flour
400 g/14 oz Reine Claude plums *or* greengages
400 g/ 14 oz Quetsche plums *or* damsons
30 g/1 oz butter, for greasing
60 g/2 oz sugar
150 g/5 oz (about 5 tbsp) *Crème pâtissière* (see page 61)
50 g/2 oz apricot jam, sieved

Serves 6

Preparation time: 30 minutes

Cooking time: 40 minutes, plus 5 minutes for the plums

This tart, which is easy to make, is a delight to both eye and palate, with its warm, glowing colours. The slightly acid Quetsche plums marry sublimely with the sweet, sugary Reine Claudes. If these plums are not available, you could use Victorias instead.

· PREPARATION ·

Preheat the oven to 220°C/425°F/gas 8.

The pastry case: On a lightly floured surface, roll out the pastry into a circle about 3-4 mm/⅛ in thick.

Grease the flan ring, slide it onto the baking sheet and line it with the pastry. You will have about 30 g/1 oz left over.

Carefully flute the edges with your fingertips, then crimp them diagonally with your fingertips or a pastry crimper to give an attractive effect. Leave to rest in the fridge for 20 minutes.

The plums: Wash them, cut in half and remove the stones. Place the plums on a baking sheet, skin side down and sprinkle over the sugar. Place in the preheated oven for 5 minutes to precook them and, most importantly, to let some of the juices run. Carefully transfer to a colander set over a bowl to catch the juice.

Assembling the tart: Spread the *crème pâtissière* evenly over the pastry base and arrange the plums on top, skin side up, placing them very close together, alternating the 2 sorts of plums.

Bake in the preheated oven for 40 minutes.

When the tart is cooked, leave it on the baking sheet for 10 minutes, then lift off the flan ring and slide the tart on to a wire rack.

To glaze: Heat the apricot jam in the saucepan until it begins to boil. Add the reserved plum juice and carefully brush the glaze evenly over the plums.

· TO SERVE ·

Serve the tart whole; it should be at room temperature, never chilled.

· EQUIPMENT ·

Wooden or *marble pastry board*
1 *flan ring, about 22 cm/ 8½ in diameter, 2 cm/¾ in deep*
1 *baking sheet*
1 *roasting pan*
1 *colander*
1 *small saucepan*

TARTE AUX PERLES DE GROSEILLES
(Tart with redcurrant pearls)

· INGREDIENTS ·

360 g/12 oz *Pâte sablée* (see page 47)

Pinch of flour

Butter, for greasing

CREAM FILLING:

4 eggs

440 ml/16 fl oz double cream

135 g/4½ oz sugar

½ vanilla pod, split *or* a few drops of pure vanilla essence

700 g/1 lb 8 oz redcurrants

60 g/2 oz white currants, to garnish (optional)

180 g/6 oz (about 6 tbsp) redcurrant jelly

Serves 8

Preparation time: 30 minutes

Cooking time: 50 minutes

· EQUIPMENT ·

Wooden or *marble pastry board*

1 flan ring, 22 cm/8½ in diameter, 4 cm/1½ in deep, or a loose-bottomed flan tin

Greaseproof paper

Baking beans

1 baking sheet

1 small saucepan

PICTURE PAGES 82–3

The colours of this unusual tart are stunning.

· PREPARATION ·

Preheat the oven to 220°C/425°F/gas 8.

Preparing the base: On a lightly floured surface, roll out the pastry to a thickness of about 3 mm/⅛ in. Grease the flan ring, place it on the baking sheet and line with the pastry. You will have about 60 g/2 oz trimmings left over.

Place a circle of greaseproof paper inside the pastry and fill with baking beans. Bake blind in the preheated oven for 20 minutes. Remove the baking beans with a spoon and lift out the paper. Set aside at room temperature. Lower the oven temperature to 180°C/350°F/gas 5.

The filling: In a bowl, whisk together the eggs, cream and sugar. Add the seeds from the split vanilla pod or the vanilla essence.

Baking the filled tart: Pour the filling into the part-baked tart case. Bake at 180°C/350°F/gas 5 for about 30 minutes, until the filling is set. Remove the flan ring before the tart has cooled completely.

The redcurrants: Remove the redcurrants from their stalks by sliding the prongs of a fork right down the stalk. Discard any damaged berries and place the rest in a bowl. Leave the white currants on their stalks.

Scatter the prepared redcurrants over the surface of the flan, so that they cover the entire surface and come right up to the top of the crust.

Glazing: Gently melt the redcurrant jelly and leave to cool. When it is almost cold, use a spoon to apply an even coating of glaze to the redcurrants. Decorate the tart with the white currants. You could, for example, use them to mark out each portion (see photo, pages 82–3).

· TO SERVE ·

Slide the tart on to a round serving plate and serve it whole, leaving your guests to help themselves. If you like, offer each guest a glass dish of vanilla ice cream. Its subtle, luscious richness and tiny speckles of black vanilla will complement the tart beautifully and offset its sharp flavour.

TARTE AL' COLOCHE

· INGREDIENTS ·

350 g/12 oz *Pâte Brisée*
(see page 31)

Pinch of flour

20 g/1 tbsp butter, for
greasing

12 medium dessert
apples, preferably Cox's

½ cinnamon stick *or* a
pinch of ground
cinnamon

4 turns of the pepper
mill (about 5 g/¾ tsp)

100 g/3½ oz butter

150 g/5 oz sugar

500 ml/18 fl oz double
cream

2 eggs

Serves 8

*Preparation time: 40
minutes*

Cooking time: 45 minutes

This tart takes its name from the bubbling caramel, which puffs up and *coloche* (bubbles). It makes a divine winter pudding — creamy and delicate, with the apples all coated in caramel. Christian Germain, the *chef patron* of the Chateau de Montreuil in France, makes the best *tarte al' coloche* in the world!

· PREPARATION ·

Preheat the oven to 220°C/425°F/gas 8.

The pastry base: On a lightly floured surface, roll out the pastry to a thickness of about 3 mm/⅛ in.

Grease the flan ring and place it on a baking sheet. Line the whole ring with pastry, cutting off any excess with a sharp knife. Lightly crimp up the edges of the pastry to form a sort of frill above the edge of the ring.

Leave to rest in the fridge for 20 minutes before baking.

The apples: Peel, quarter and core them.

Place 4 quartered apples in a saucepan with 2 tablespoons water and the cinnamon. Cover the pan and cook gently until soft. Remove the cinnamon stick and add the pepper. Beat vigorously until they have the consistency of a compote. Set aside at room temperature.

Baking blind: Line the base and sides of the pastry with greaseproof paper. Fill with baking beans and bake in the preheated oven for 20 minutes.

As soon as the pastry is half-cooked, remove the beans and paper and leave the base in a warm place.

Reduce the oven temperature to 200°C/400°F/gas 7.

In a large, thick-bottomed pan, melt the butter, then immediately add the sugar. Cook gently until it becomes a very pale caramel. Add the remaining apple quarters and roll them in the caramel for 4 minutes. They should be cooked but still firm. Set aside in a cool place.

· ASSEMBLING THE TART ·

Spread the apple compote over the base of the tart, then arrange the quarters on top. Pour the remaining caramel into a bowl and stir in the cream and eggs. Beat together lightly, then pour the mixture over the apples.

Bake the tart at 200°C/400°F/gas 7 for 25 minutes.

· TO SERVE ·

Serve the tart warm and cut it at the table. Sprinkle lightly with icing sugar if you like.

· EQUIPMENT ·

Marble or *wooden pastry
board*

*1 flan ring, 24 cm/9½ in
diameter, 3.5 cm/1½ in deep*

Baking sheet

1 saucepan

Thick-bottomed pan

Greaseproof paper

Baking beans

PICTURE PAGE 77

CLAFOUTIS AUX CERISES
(Cherry clafoutis)

· INGREDIENTS ·

220 g/8 oz *Pâte brisée*
(see page 31)

2 pinches of flour

30 g/1 oz butter, for
greasing

500 g/1 lb 1 oz very ripe
black cherries

120 ml/4 fl oz milk

120 ml/4 fl oz double
cream

½ vanilla pod, split

4 eggs

170 g/6 oz sugar

2 drops orange blossom
water or a little Kirsch
(optional)

30 g/1 oz granulated
sugar

Serves 8

Preparation time: 30
minutes

Cooking time: 45 minutes

· EQUIPMENT ·

Wooden or marble pastry
board

1 loose-bottomed flan tin or
flan ring,
24 cm/9 in diameter,
2 cm/¾ in deep

Greaseproof paper

Baking beans

1 baking sheet

1 saucepan

1 bowl

When we were children, our mother used to make this very easy dessert for us as a treat (and she still does!). In winter, pears or apples can be used instead of the cherries.

· PREPARATION ·

Preheat the oven to 220°C/425°F/gas 8.

The pastry case: On a lightly floured surface, roll out the pastry into a circle about 2-3 mm/⅛ in thick.

Lightly grease the flan tin, place on a baking sheet, then line it with the pastry. Roll the rolling pin over the top edge of the tin to cut off the excess pastry. You will have about 40 g/1½ oz trimmings. Leave to rest in the fridge for about 20 minutes.

Line the whole surface of the pastry with greaseproof paper and fill with baking beans.

Baking blind: Bake in the preheated oven for 20 minutes. Use a spoon to lift out the baking beans and remove the greaseproof paper. Keep at room temperature.

Reduce the oven temperature to 200°C/400°F/gas 7.

The cherries: Remove the stalks and stone the cherries, using a small piece of wire bent back at one end to make a loop; you should be able to remove the stones without cutting open the fruit.

The mixture: Combine the milk, cream and vanilla pod in a saucepan and boil for 1 minute.

In a bowl, whisk the eggs and sugar until light and frothy. Add a pinch of flour.

Discard the vanilla pod and pour the milk mixture on to the eggs, whisking lightly. Stir in the orange blossom water or Kirsch, if you are using it. Leave the mixture in a cool place, stirring from time to time.

Filling and cooking the pastry case: Arrange the cherries in the pastry case and pour over the mixture, which should still be slightly warm. Bake immediately at 200°C/400°F/gas 7 for 25 minutes.

As soon as the dessert is cooked, remove the side of the flan tin, leaving the *clafoutis* on the bottom.

· TO SERVE ·

Sprinkle the top of the *clafoutis* with granulated sugar just before serving. Serve the dessert while it is still warm so that the full flavour of the cherries comes through.

COLD DESSERTS AND SWEETS

Any number of cold sweets and desserts can be prepared in advance to make life easier for the cook — but make sure they are served chilled and not tepid.

Some desserts like *sablés* or *feuilletés* cannot be finally assembled until the last moment.

Almost all the recipes in this chapter are prepared with fruit, which lends a delicate texture and flavour to our desserts.

Most of these recipes can be frozen without harming their flavour or appearance, so why not prepare two or three desserts at the same time? Then, if you issue a last-minute invitation, you will have a delicious home-made dessert to offer your guests. We have indicated in each recipe whether or not it is suitable for freezing.

FEUILLETES AUX FRAMBOISES OU AUX FRAISES
(Raspberry or strawberry feuilletés)

· INGREDIENTS ·

400 g/14 oz raspberries
or strawberries

600 ml/1 pt red Fruit
coulis (see page 71)

500 ml/18 fl oz double
cream

50-100 ml/2-3 fl oz
Sorbet syrup (see
page 168), depending on
the tartness of the fruit,
well chilled

60 g/2 oz icing sugar

350 g/12 oz Puff pastry
(see pages 42-3)

· PREPARATION ·

The raspberries or strawberries: Wash the fruit, hull if necessary and, if you are using strawberries, halve or quarter them, depending on their size. Mix them in a bowl with about 300 ml/11 fl oz red fruit *coulis* and keep in the fridge.

The double cream: In a well-chilled bowl, whip the cream until it forms a ribbon. Add the chilled syrup and whip until almost stiff. Chill in the fridge, together with the piping bag and nozzle.

The puff pastry: Preheat the oven to 220°C/425°F/gas 8.

Dust the pastry board with icing sugar, not with flour, and roll out the pastry to a thickness of about 4 mm/⅛ in. Cut out 8 circles with the pastry cutter and place them on a baking sheet brushed with cold water. Leave to rest in a cold place for 20 minutes before baking.

· TO BAKE ·

Bake the circles in the preheated oven for about 10 minutes.

· EQUIPMENT ·

1 well-chilled bowl

Wooden or marble pastry
board

1 plain round pastry cutter,
9 cm/3½ in diameter

1 baking sheet

Piping bag, with a medium
plain or ridged nozzle

Wire rack

PICTURE PAGE 99

Serves 4

Preparation time: 25 minutes

Cooking time: 10 minutes

The icing sugar from the pastry board will have given the tops an attractive glaze. Use a palette knife to transfer the circles to a wire rack.

· TO SERVE ·

Using a small, sharp knife, make a small cavity in the centre of 4 of the pastry circles. Spread a little of the whipped cream over the bottom of each cavity, then fill generously with raspberries or strawberries. Pipe a pretty border of whipped cream around the rim of each filled circle, then top with the second pastry circle. Place on individual plates, pour a ribbon of fruit *coulis* around each *feuilleté* and pipe a little rosette of whipped cream on top of each one. Decorate with a raspberry or strawberry.

· NOTES ·

Never bake the pastry for these light, delicate, crisp *feuilletés* more than an hour or two before serving, and fill them at the very last moment. They are also delicious filled with wild strawberries. The sorbet syrup can be replaced by 50-100 g/2-4 oz icing sugar, depending on the tartness of the fruit.

ROULE MARQUIS
(Chocolate roulade with raspberries)

· INGREDIENTS ·

3 egg yolks

175 g/6 oz icing sugar

4 egg whites

50 g/2 oz cocoa powder

15 g/2 tsp potato flour *or* cornflour

1 tsp butter

Pinch of flour

250 ml/9 fl oz single cream

250 ml/9 fl oz red Fruit *coulis* (see page 71)

2 tbsp *framboise* liqueur (optional)

150 g/5 oz fresh raspberries

60 g/2 oz coffee liqueur beans (optional)

· PREPARATION ·

Preheat the oven to 200°C/400°F/gas 7.

The chocolate sponge: Beat together the egg yolks and 80 g/3 oz icing sugar until they form a ribbon.

Beat the egg whites until half-risen. Add 45 g/1½ oz icing sugar and beat at high speed for 1 minute until very stiff.

Using a flat slotted spoon, mix one-third of the egg whites into the yolks and stir until completely blended. Very carefully tip in the remaining egg whites all at once and mix gently.

Before the mixture becomes completely homogenous, sift in the cocoa and potato flour or cornflour, folding all the time. As soon as the mixture is well blended, stop folding, or it will become heavy.

Line a baking sheet with baking parchment or lightly buttered and floured greaseproof paper. Using a palette knife, spread the roulé mixture evenly over the paper to make a rectangle about 26 × 30 cm/10 × 12 in and 1.5 cm/½ in thick.

Bake in the preheated oven for 8-10 minutes. The top of the sponge should feel springy when pressed with the fingertips.

· EQUIPMENT ·

Electric mixer

Baking sheet

Baking parchment *or* greaseproof paper

Wire rack

1
Remove the cooked sponge from the oven and cover with a tea towel.

2
Immediately invert it on to a wire rack, so that the tea towel covers the rack. Carefully peel off the greaseproof paper.

1

2

3
Brush the sponge with a mixture of framboise liqueur and fruit coulis.

4
Scatter over the raspberries and then the coffee liqueur beans.

3

4

5
Using the tea towel to help you, roll up the filled sponge like a Swiss roll. Chill for 2-3 hours before serving.

6
After chilling, serve the roulé cut into diagonal slices. Dredge each slice with icing sugar and serve on chilled plates. Serve the reserved coulis separately.

5

6

Serves 6
Preparation time: 20 minutes
Cooking time: 8-10 minutes

If it is not sufficiently cooked, it will stick to the cloth after baking.

Remove from the oven and immediately invert the sponge onto a wire rack covered with a tea towel. Carefully peel off the paper, then leave in a cool place for 5-10 minutes.

The filling: Whip the cream with the remaining icing sugar until it forms a ribbon. Mix together the *framboise* liqueur and the fruit *coulis*. Brush the sponge with a quarter of the *coulis*. Reserve the rest to serve separately.

Trim the edges of the sponge with a knife, cutting off any slightly overcooked or dry parts.

Continued on page 100

Using a palette knife, spread the whipped cream to within 1.5 cm/½ in of the edges of the sponge. Scatter over the raspberries and coffee liqueur beans.

Using the tea towel to help you, roll up the sponge like a Swiss roll. Chill in the fridge for 2-3 hours before serving.

· TO SERVE ·

Cut into diagonal slices. Dredge with icing sugar and serve on very cold plates. Serve the remaining fruit *coulis* separately in a sauceboat.

· NOTES ·

This luscious, light dessert can be made in advance and refrigerated for up to 24 hours. Use strawberries when raspberries are not available. The raspberry liqueur is not essential, but it does bring out the flavour of the fruit beautifully.

Coffee liqueur granules are available from specialist foodshops and add a delicious crunch to the filling.

ST. HONORE,
CREME CHIBOUST
(St. Honoré with crème Chiboust)

· INGREDIENTS ·

220 g/8 oz puff pastry trimmings *or* *Feuilletage minute* (see page 43)

Pinch of flour

1 quantity *Pâte à choux*, about 250 ml/9 fl oz (see page 46)

Eggwash made with 1 egg yolk and 1 tbsp milk

30 g/1 oz butter

200 g/7 oz sugar

1 quantity *Crème Chiboust* (see page 62)

· PREPARATION ·

Rolling out the base: On a lightly floured surface, roll out the pastry, turning it one-quarter turn after each roll, so that it becomes a neat circle about 26 cm/10 in diameter. The base will be 24 cm/9½ in diameter, so allow an extra couple of centimetres.

Decorating the base with the choux buns: Roll the pastry round the rolling pin, then unroll it onto a baking sheet which has been lightly brushed with cold water.

Using a *Pithiviers* marker or flan circle, cut out a 24 cm/9½ in pastry circle. Prick with the prongs of a fork.

Using the piping bag fitted with the 1.2 cm/½ in nozzle, pipe out the choux paste in a spiral shape, starting from the centre of the pastry base and pressing the nozzle down lightly onto the pastry. Stop piping about 3 cm/1¼ in from the edge of the pastry base.

Brush the exposed pastry border with eggwash, then pipe a 'crown' of choux paste all round the edge. This time, do not press down with the nozzle. Brush the 'crown' with eggwash, then leave to rest in a cool place for 30 minutes.

Lightly butter the other baking sheet, then pipe out 18

· EQUIPMENT ·

Wooden or *marble pastry board*

2 baking sheets

Piping bag

1 plain 1.2 cm/½ in nozzle

1 plain 0.5 cm/¼ in nozzle

1 St. Honoré nozzle, or a fluted 1.5-2 cm/¾ in nozzle

Wire rack

1 saucepan

1 × 24 cm/9½ in flan ring or Pithiviers marker

PICTURE PAGE 98

Serves 8

Preparation time: 35 minutes

Cooking time: 35 minutes for the base, 20 minutes for the choux buns

small choux buns, about 2 cm/¾ in diameter. Brush with eggwash and press lightly with the back of a fork.

· TO COOK ·

Preheat the oven to 220°C/425°F/gas 8.

Bake the buns and base for 10 minutes, then lower the temperature to 200°C/400°F/gas 7 and cook the small buns for a further 10 minutes and the base for a further 25 minutes.

Transfer the cooked buns and base to a wire rack and leave to cool at room temperature.

· ASSEMBLING THE ST. HONORE ·

In a saucepan, cook the sugar with 3 tbsp water until it turns pale amber.

Make a small hole in the bottom of the choux buns with the point of a knife. Insert the point of a small knife in the base of the buns and dip the tops into the caramelized sugar. Place on a baking sheet and leave to cool. As soon as they are cold, fill the buns through the hole in the bottom with the *crème Chiboust*, using the very small nozzle.

Arrange the filled buns evenly on top of the 'crown', sticking them down with a little caramel.

Using the special large nozzle, fill the centre of the *St. Honoré* with the *crème Chiboust*, piping it into an attractive pattern (see photo, page 98), or use the fluted nozzle to make rosettes, if you prefer.

· TO SERVE ·

Leave the *St. Honoré* in a cold place for at least 2 hours before serving. Serve on a round plate and cut it at the table. Garnish the dessert with a sugar or marzipan flower for a very pretty effect. A few wild strawberries or raspberries scattered over the cream just before serving are as good to look at as they are to taste.

· NOTES ·

You can use *crème Chantilly* (see page 66) instead of the *crème Chiboust*, but do not fill the choux buns, as the cream will melt the caramel when you stick them to the 'crown'.

1

After baking, invert the sponge and, when cool, peel off the paper.

2

Cut out 2 long bands the width of the flan rings.

3

Cut 1 circle the same diameter as the rings.

4

Place the circles on the cake boards inside the flan rings. Line each ring with a sponge band, cutting 1 band in half to fill the gaps.

5

After filling each mould one-quarter full of the mixture, scatter over a quarter of the fruit.

6

Pour in enough mixture to cover the fruit; it should come about two-thirds up the moulds. Scatter in the remaining fruit and top with more mixture.

7

Top with the daisy-shaped circles and press down gently.

8

After chilling, remove the ring and serve sliced.

CHARLOTTE AUX POIRES ET FRAISES DES BOIS
(Pear and wild strawberry charlotte)

· INGREDIENTS ·

400 g/14 oz fresh *or* canned pears in syrup, drained and cut into 7 mm/¼ in cubes

50 g/2 oz powdered milk

125 ml/4 fl oz milk

12 egg yolks

100 g/3½ oz sugar

3 quantities Sponge biscuit mixture (see recipe 2, page 53)

750 ml/1¼ pt whipping cream

200 ml/7 fl oz Sorbet syrup (see page 168)

400 ml/14 fl oz white pear liqueur

9 leaves of gelatine

1 quantity *Meringue italienne* (see page 58)

150 g/5 oz wild strawberries *or* raspberries

icing sugar, to serve

600 ml/1 pt red Fruit *coulis* (see page 71)

Makes 2 charlottes, each serving 10

Preparation time: 1 hour, plus 3-5 hours chilling

· PREPARATION ·

The crème anglaise: Purée 40 g/1½ oz of the pears and place in a saucepan with the powdered and fresh milk. Beat together lightly. Bring the mixture to the boil.

In a bowl, whisk together the egg yolks and sugar until they form a light ribbon.

Stirring constantly, pour on the boiling milk mixture, then pour the mixture back into the saucepan. Poach gently, stirring continuously, until the custard is thick enough to coat a wooden spoon, like a normal *crème anglaise*.

Pass the custard through a conical strainer into a bowl and set aside.

The sponge: Pipe out diagonally a sponge rectangle 60 × 40 cm/23½ × 16 in (see step-by-step instructions, opposite); this will make the 2 bases.

Pipe out 2 sponge rounds about the same diameter as the flan rings (20 cm/8 in), piping them in a sort of daisy shape. These will be the tops.

Cook the sponges; once cooked, they should be about 1.5 cm/½ in thick.

The cream: Beat until it forms a ribbon. Set aside.

Cutting out the sponge: Turn over the sponge rectangle. Carefully remove the greaseproof paper, then trim the edges with a serrated knife. Using the side of a flan ring as a guide, cut out 2½ bands from the long edge of the rectangle, then a circle the same diameter as the flan ring. With the serrated knife, slice the circle horizontally in half.

Place the 2 sponge bases on the cake boards and put the flan rings on top. Mix together the syrup and one-third of the pear liqueur and brush the sponge with this mixture. Brush the 2½ bands of sponge with the mixture.

Line each flan ring with a band of sponge, cutting the half band to fill the gaps.

Assembling the charlottes: Soak the gelatine leaves in very cold water for 15 minutes, then drain.

In a saucepan, heat the remaining liqueur until tepid. Drain the gelatine well, then stir it into the tepid pear liqueur with the pan off the heat.

Using a wire whisk, fold two-thirds of the *meringue italienne* into the whipped cream. Do not overwork. Do the same with the *crème anglaise*, which should be almost cold. Mix until completely homogenous. With a spatula, stir in the tepid pear

· EQUIPMENT ·

2 stainless steel flan rings, 20 cm/8 in diameter, 6 cm/2¼ in deep

1 saucepan

Conical strainer

2 × 22 cm/8½ in round cake boards

Piping bag, with a plain 1 cm/½ nozzle

liqueur and gelatine mixture.

Using a ladle, fill each flan ring one-quarter full of the mixture. Scatter a quarter of the pear cubes and the wild strawberries over each charlotte. Pour in enough mixture to cover the fruit; it should come about two-thirds up the moulds. Scatter in the rest of the fruit, fill up the moulds with mixture and place the 2 'daisy' circles on top, pressing down gently so that they stick to the *bavaroise* mixture.

Place in the fridge for 5 hours, or freeze for 3 hours before serving.

· TO SERVE ·

Carefully remove the flan ring. Sprinkle the top of the dessert with icing sugar. Serve very cold, in slices, accompanied by a red fruit *coulis*.

· STORAGE ·

The charlottes will keep for 2 or 3 days in the fridge or for up to a week in the freezer, wrapped in clingfilm.

· NOTES ·

It is always best to cook the sponge the day before so that it does not crumble when you cut it.

It is not really possible to reduce the quantities successfully for this recipe, which is why we suggest you make 2 charlottes, each for 10 people. You must also make a full quantity of *meringue italienne* and discard the remainder, or keep it for another use.

The wild strawberries are not absolutely essential, but they are wonderfully delicate and flavoursome. However, raspberries can be substituted.

OEUFS A LA NEIGE AUX COPEAUX DE CHOCOLAT
(Snow eggs with chocolate curls)

· INGREDIENTS ·

6 egg whites
340 g/11 oz sugar
250 ml/9 fl oz *Crème anglaise*, well-flavoured with vanilla (see page 70)
8 Chocolate curls (see page 242)
METHOD 1:
30 g/1 oz butter
1 tbsp oil, for greasing
METHOD 2:
1 lt/1¼ pt milk
60 g/2 oz sugar
1 tbsp oil, for greasing

Serves 4
Preparation time: 25 minutes
Cooking time: 6 minutes, plus making the caramel

This delicious dessert can be made even more delectable by serving some strawberries or raspberries in a separate bowl.

· PREPARATION ·

Beat the egg whites until soft peaks form, then, still beating, add 130 g/4 oz sugar and beat until very firm.

Method 1: Preheat the oven to 140°C/275°F/gas 2. To make attractive 'snowballs', pipe the beaten egg whites into the lightly buttered tartlet tins, using a piping bag without a nozzle. Smooth over the surface with a palette knife so that the balls are smooth and even. Cook in the preheated oven for 10 minutes, then carefully unmould the balls onto lightly greased foil or a greased baking sheet.

Method 2: In a shallow pan, heat the milk and 60 g/2 oz sugar to about 90°C/194°F. Keep at a very gentle simmer.

Using a large kitchen spoon, form the beaten whites into 4 *quenelles*, about the size of a large egg, smoothing the surface carefully with a palette knife. Gently lower each into the simmering milk, rinsing the spoon in cold water between each operation.

Poach for 3 minutes, then turn over the *quenelles* and poach for a further 3 minutes. With a slotted spoon, transfer the *quenelles* to drain on a tea towel. They should be just firm to the touch, but still light and delicate.

As soon as the *quenelles* have cooled and drained, arrange them on lightly greased foil or a greased baking sheet.

· CARAMELIZING THE 'SNOWBALLS' ·

Place the remaining 210 g/7 oz sugar in a saucepan or preserving pan and set over low heat, stirring continuously. As soon as the sugar caramelizes to a light golden colour, spoon it generously over the poached egg whites.

· TO SERVE ·

Divide the well-chilled *crème anglaise* between 4 shallow soup plates. Place 1 *quenelle* or 2 snowballs in each dish and arrange a chocolate curl at either edge.

· NOTES ·

Once they have been coated with caramel, the egg whites tend to become slightly moist and the caramel is no longer crunchy, so it is best to eat them within an hour or two.

· EQUIPMENT ·

Electric mixer, or mixing bowl and whisk
1 saucepan or preserving pan
Baking sheet or aluminium foil
METHOD 1:
Piping bag
8 tartlet tins, 7 cm/3 in at the top, 5.5 cm/2¼ in at the base, 1.5 cm/½ in deep
METHOD 2:
1 large shallow pan
1 large kitchen spoon, 10 cm/4 in long, 7 cm/2¼ in wide, 3 cm/1¼ in deep

PICTURE PAGE 106

TOP *Sablé aux fraises (page 137)*
BOTTOM *Oeufs à la neige aux copeaux de chocolat (page 105)*

TOP *Igloo douillet (page 108)*
BOTTOM *Palmerosa de mon ami Valentin*
(page 129)

IGLOO DOUILLET
(Cosy igloos)

PICTURE PAGE 107

· INGREDIENTS ·

1 quantity Sponge
biscuit mixture, recipe 1
(see page 53)

200 g/7 oz redcurrant
jelly

1½ leaves of gelatine

75 g/2½ oz sultanas

300 ml/11 fl oz white
dessert wine (preferably
Beaumes de Venise)

½ vanilla pod

3 egg yolks

10 g/1½ tsp custard
powder

Juice of ½ lemon

1 tbsp double cream

1 quantity *Meringue
italienne* (see page 58)

½ quantity *Crème
anglaise* (see page 70)

1 tbsp Marie Brizard
liqueur

Serves 8

Preparation time: 50
minutes·

Cooking time: about 6
minutes

· EQUIPMENT ·

1 baking sheet

1 saucepan

Conical strainer

8 hemispherical moulds,
preferably stainless steel,
9 cm/3½ in diameter,
5 cm/2 in deep, 4.5 cm/1¼ in
at the base

Greaseproof paper or baking
parchment

· PREPARATION ·

Preheat the oven to 220°C/425°F/gas 8.

The sponge biscuit: Spread the prepared mixture into a rectangular shape, 20 × 30 cm/8 × 12 in, on a baking sheet lined with baking parchment or greased greaseproof paper. It should be 3-5 mm/⅛-¼ in thick. Any remaining mixture (there should be about one-third left) can be used for making sponge fingers or small biscuits.

Bake in the preheated oven for about 6 minutes.

Cover with a tea towel and invert onto a flat surface. Peel off the paper and spread the redcurrant jelly over the sponge. Using the tea towel to help you, roll up the sponge like a Swiss roll, as small as possible, about 2 cm/¾ in diameter. Leave to settle in the fridge for several hours or place in the freezer, which will make it easier to slice.

The gelatine: Soak in very cold water for 15 minutes, then drain.

The sultanas: Blanch in boiling water, refresh, drain and place in a bowl. Pour over 50 ml/2 fl oz wine and leave the sultanas to macerate.

The wine custard: Put the remaining wine and the half vanilla pod in a saucepan and bring to the boil.

In a small bowl, combine the egg yolks and custard powder and beat with a small wire whisk until pale and frothy. Pour in the boiling wine, whisking continuously. Remove the vanilla.

Return the mixture to the saucepan and set over low heat, stirring continuously with a wooden spatula for 3-4 minutes, until the mixture is thick enough to coat the spatula.

Take the pan off the heat and stir in the drained gelatine. Immediately pass the custard through a conical strainer into a bowl. Set aside in a cool place, stirring from time to time to prevent a skin from forming.

Assembling the igloos: Cut the sponge roll into 3 mm/⅛ in slices and use them to line the moulds right to the top.

Stir in a few drops of lemon juice, the cream and half the *meringue italienne* into the wine custard (which should be barely lukewarm) and fill the moulds two-thirds full with this mixture. Divide the wine-soaked sultanas between the moulds, then fill to the top with custard.

Wrap each mould in clingfilm or greaseproof paper and chill in the fridge for several hours.

· TO SERVE ·

Unmould the igloos onto well-chilled serving plates. Flavour the *crème anglaise* with Marie Brizard and pour a few spoonfuls around each igloo. Enhance the presentation with some spun sugar Angel's Hair (see page 221) scattered over the igloos to look like fallen stalactites, or add a delicate, childlike note by floating a few flakes of rose-coloured meringue onto the *crème anglaise*.

· NOTES ·

Although you will use only two-thirds of the sponge biscuit mixture, you must make a full quantity in order to obtain a very light texture. The same applies to the *meringue italienne*. Keep the remaining half quantity for another use.

You can prepare this pudding at least 24 hours in advance, but unmould and garnish the igloos at the last moment.

PECHES AU CHAMPAGNE
(Peaches poached in champagne)

· INGREDIENTS ·

4 very ripe peaches, preferably white

500 ml/18 fl oz dry champagne

350 ml/12 fl oz Sorbet syrup (see page 168)

1 small vanilla pod

250 g/9 oz strawberries

150 g/5 oz sugar

250 ml/9 fl oz double cream

Juice of ½ lemon

4 small sprigs of fresh mint

Serves 4

Preparation time: 20 minutes

Cooking time: about 8 minutes

This very quick and easy dessert needs to be tasted to be fully appreciated.

· PREPARATION ·

The peaches: Make a very light incision all round the peach skins. Plunge the peaches into boiling water, then into cold water and peel. Place them in a shallow pan, pour over the champagne and syrup and add the vanilla pod. Bring slowly to the boil over low heat and poach the peaches at about 85°C/185°F. If the peaches are very ripe, they will be poached after 5 minutes.

Keep them in a cool place in the syrup, but do not refrigerate. Drain the peaches, reserving the poaching liquid.
The strawberries: Hull them and purée in a blender, or rub though a fine sieve set over a bowl. Stir the sugar into the purée.

Whip the cream until it forms a ribbon, then stir in the strawberry purée and the lemon juice.

· TO SERVE ·

Serve the peaches on round plates, or in glass dishes or small bowls. Line the bottom of the dishes with the strawberry cream and arrange a cooled but not chilled peach on top. Garnish each peach with a sprig of mint.

Serve the chilled poaching liquid separately in a sauceboat; it complements the strawberry cream beautifully.

· EQUIPMENT ·

1 shallow pan

1 *sieve* or *blender*

1 *bowl*

PICTURE PAGE 99

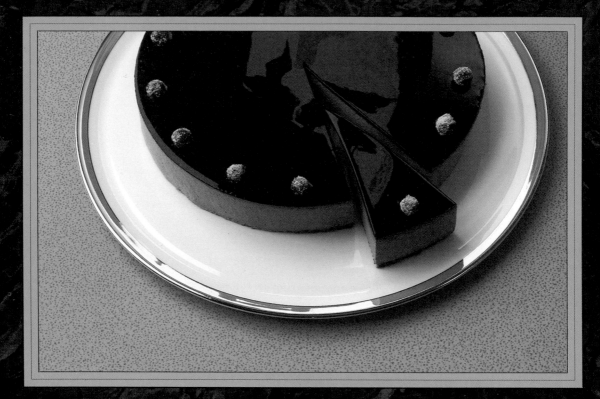

TOP LEFT *Délice au cassis (page 131)*
BOTTOM LEFT *Rozenn au parfum d'orange
mentholé (page 112)*
ABOVE *Délice aux fruits de la passion (page 132)*

ROZENN AU PARFUM D'ORANGE MENTHOLE
(Chocolate and orange Rozenn with mint-flavoured sauce)

PICTURE PAGE 110

· INGREDIENTS ·

1 quantity *Meringue italienne* (see page 58)

280 g/10 oz bitter *couverture* chocolate, plus 90 g/3 oz Menier chocolate *or*

370 g/13 oz good quality bitter chocolate

125 g/4 oz butter, softened

1 orange-flavoured Sponge biscuit, 22 cm/8½ in diameter (see page 56)

4 tbsp Sorbet syrup (see page 168)

4 tbsp Grand Marnier

400 ml/14 fl oz double cream

400 ml/14 fl oz whipping cream

TOPPING:

280 g/10 oz plain chocolate covering *or* bitter *couverture*

CREME ANGLAISE:

6 egg yolks

80 g/3 oz sugar

500 ml/18 fl oz milk

25 g/1 oz fresh mint sprigs

Makes 2 cakes, each serving 8

Preparation time: 1½ hours

· PREPARATION ·

Shred the *couverture* and break the Menier chocolate into a bowl. Place in a bain-marie or double boiler and melt the chocolate. Immediately stir in the butter with a spatula, a little at a time, until it has all melted.

Using a serrated knife, slice the sponge biscuit horizontally into 4 circles of equal thickness. Brush each circle with a mixture of the syrup and Grand Marnier.

Place the flan rings on the cake boards and place 1 sponge circle in each. Set aside.

The cream: Whip the 2 creams until thick.

The chocolate mousse: Using a balloon whisk, carefully fold 85 per cent of the meringue into the melted chocolate. Add about one-third of this mixture to the cream and beat lightly together. Using a spatula, fold the remaining chocolate mixture into the cream and mix very lightly until the mixture is just amalgamated. Do not overwork the mixture, or it may separate.

Assembling the Rozenns: Pour 40 per cent of the mixture into each flan ring and smooth the surface with a palette knife.

Top with a sponge circle and press down lightly with your fingertips.

Divide the remaining chocolate mixture between the 2 cakes and level the surface with a palette knife until very smooth. Slide the knife between the table and the cake board and jiggle it up and down to tap out any air bubbles. Smooth over the top again.

Place the cakes in the fridge for a minimum of 4 hours, or in the freezer for 2 hours.

· TO DECORATE ·

Using a cloth or sponge dipped in very hot water then squeezed almost dry, press it around the edges of the flan rings which will effectively loosen the cakes. Then carefully lift off the flan rings.

Smooth over the sides with a palette knife to cover any gaps if necessary. Slide the palette knife under the cakes and transfer them to a wire rack set over a shallow dish.

Melt the chocolate covering or *couverture* and ladle it over the cakes to coat them completely; do not leave any part uncovered. Smooth the edges with a small knife if necessary. Place the cakes briefly in the fridge to harden before serving.

· EQUIPMENT ·

Double saucepan or bain-marie

Electric mixer

2 flan rings, 22 cm/8½ in diameter, 3.5 cm/1½ in deep

2 × 24 cm/9½ in round cake boards

1 sieve

PICTURE PAGE 110

Continued on page 114

1

Shred the couverture with a knife.

2

Brush the sliced sponge circles with the mixture of syrup and Grand Marnier.

3

Carefully fold 85 per cent of the meringue into the melted chocolate.

4

Now add one-third of the chocolate meringue mixture to the cream, then the remainder.

5

Pour 40 per cent of the chocolate mousse into each flan ring and smooth the surface. Place a sponge circle in each ring and press down lightly with your fingertips.

6

Divide the remaining mousse between the 2 cakes.

7

After chilling for at least 4 hours, carefully lift off the ring.

8

Place the cakes on a rack set over a dish. Melt the couverture or cake covering and ladle it over the cakes, covering them completely. Smooth the edges; chill until hardened.

· TO SERVE ·

The sauce: Make the *crème anglaise* according to the method on page 70, but using the quantities given in this recipe. Infuse the mint in the milk instead of the vanilla pod. Pass through a strainer, chill and serve very cold.

The cake: Serve it whole at the table and cut individual slices for your guests, using a knife dipped in hot water and wiped dry between each slice. Pour a ribbon of sauce around each slice. This mint-flavoured sauce accompanies the *Rozenn* superbly.

· STORAGE ·

This dessert freezes very successfully; leave it inside the flan ring and wrap in clingfilm. Pour over the coating just before serving. Since you cannot make a smaller quantity of sponge biscuit mixture without spoiling the quality, it is better to prepare 2 cakes at the same time and freeze one of them. They will keep in the freezer for up to 1 week.

As with all desserts containing *meringue italienne*, you need to make the full quantity to obtain a successful mixture; discard the remaining 15 per cent, or keep it for another use.

LE FRAISIER
(Strawberry gateau)

· INGREDIENTS ·

Double quantity Genoise sponge, (see page 60)

1 tbsp butter, for greasing

Pinch of flour

2 kg/4 lb 4 oz medium-sized strawberries

250 ml/9 fl oz Sorbet syrup (see page 168)

150 ml/5 fl oz Kirsch

Double quantity *Crème mousseline* (see page 63)

320 g/11 oz confectioners' almond paste

Green food colouring

Pinch of icing sugar

2 tbsp Royal icing (see page 236)

· PREPARATION ·

The genoise: Prepare the sponge according to the method on page 60 and bake in the lightly buttered and floured mould or tin for about 1 hour.

The strawberries: Wash them if necessary. If they are not gritty, simply wipe them, so that they retain their full flavour and texture. Keep 8 or 10 of the best strawberries aside for decoration and hull the rest.

Filling the sponge: Using a serrated knife or ham slicer, cut the cake in half horizontally. Brush the cut side of each slice with a mixture of syrup and Kirsch.

Place the bottom half of the cake on the baking sheet and, using a palette knife, cover it with half the *crème mousseline*. Lay the strawberries over the cream, keeping them close together and making sure that those on the outer edge of the cake are pointing inwards towards the centre. Cover with the remaining *crème mousseline* and lay the top of the cake on this. Press down lightly with your fingertips, then refrigerate the cake for at least 8 hours, but not more than 24 hours.

Decorating the dessert: Add green food colouring to the almond paste to achieve the desired effect, then roll it out as

· EQUIPMENT ·

1 Genoise mould or cake tin, 36 × 30 cm/14 × 12 in, 5 cm/2 in deep

1 × 40 cm/16in square cake board

1 baking sheet

Round *or* rectangular doilies

PICTURE PAGES 116-7

Serves 40

Preparation time: 1 hour 45
minutes, plus 8 hours
chilling

Cooking time: 1 hour

evenly as possible on a surface lightly dusted with icing sugar. Roll it into a rectangle somewhat larger than the base of the cake (about 38 × 32 cm/15 × 12½ in). Roll the almond paste onto the rolling pin, then unroll it over the top of the cake. Trim the 4 sides with a serrated knife or ham slicer, taking care to wipe the blade each time. You should cut off about 1 cm/½ in all round, which will leave you with about 50 g/2 oz trimmings.

Use a large palette knife to slide the dessert onto the cake board base decorated with lace doilies.

Use a greaseproof cone to pipe out the word *Fraisier* in royal icing on top of the cake and pipe an attractive decorative border around the edge (see page 237).

· TO SERVE ·

The dessert is now ready to serve. Cut it into 5 slices widthways and 8 slices lengthways, giving 40 portions in all.

Garnish the cake with the reserved strawberries dipped in hard crack sugar or a red fruit *coulis*. (The recipe for the sugar is included in the *Croquembouche* recipe on page 126.)

· NOTES ·

Do not refrigerate the cake once it is coated with almond paste, as the paste will become moist.

If possible, bake the Genoise the previous day; it will then be easier to slice for filling.

This delicious dessert can be served with a red fruit *coulis* (see page 71). Allow 100 ml/3½ fl oz per person.

Le Fraisier (page 114)

NOUGAT GLACE AU MIEL ET AUX FIGUES DE PROVENCE

(Iced nougat with honey and figs)

· INGREDIENTS ·

40 g/1½ oz flaked almonds
60 g/2 oz sugar
THE MERINGUE:
30 g/1 oz sugar, plus a pinch for the egg whites
60 g/2 oz clear honey
15 g/½ oz glucose
3 egg whites
140 ml/5 fl oz double cream
60 g/2 oz assorted soft candied fruits, finely diced
6 very ripe fresh figs
1 tbsp oil, for greasing
THE CREME ANGLAISE:
500 ml/18 fl oz milk
6 egg yolks
60 g/2 oz sugar
65 g/2½ oz honey

Serves 6
Preparation time: 45 minutes
Freezing time: 2 hours

This creamy summer dessert, with its subtle hint of honey, will delight any gourmet.

· PREPARATION ·

Preheat the oven to 200°C/400°F/gas 7, or set the grill to high.
The nougatine: Spread the almonds on a baking sheet and place in the preheated oven or under the grill for 3-4 minutes, until lightly coloured. Do not let them brown too much or they will taste bitter.

Put the sugar in the pan and dissolve over medium heat, stirring continuously with a wooden spatula, until pale golden. Add the almonds, stir well and heat for 10 seconds. Pour onto a lightly oiled baking sheet and leave to cool for about 30 minutes. When the *nougatine* is completely cold, crush it with a rolling pin or the back of a large knife.

The meringue: In a very clean pan, combine the 30 g/1 oz sugar, the honey and the glucose. Set over low heat and dissolve, skimming the surface if necessary. Wash down the inside of the pan with a brush dipped in cold water, then increase the heat. Put in the sugar thermometer to check the temperature.

The egg whites: When the temperature of the sugar reaches 110°C/230°F, beat the egg whites until firm, add a pinch of sugar and beat until very stiff.

When the sugar temperature reaches 124°C/255°F (large ball), pour the cooked sugar onto the egg whites, still beating at medium speed. Once they are well mixed, continue to beat until the mixture is very smooth and has cooled to about 35°C/95°F. Set aside at room temperature.

The cream: Whip until it holds soft peaks.

Mixing the ingredients: Pour the meringue onto the cream, then add the candied fruits and *nougatine*. Mix carefully and thoroughly, using a spatula.

Divide the mixture between the moulds, cover with clingfilm and place in the freezer for at least 2 hours.

The crème anglaise: Prepare according to the method on page 70. Leave the custard to cool to room temperature, then chill in the fridge.

· TO SERVE ·

Unmould the ice creams onto well-chilled individual plates and pour a ribbon of chilled *crème anglaise* around each one.

· EQUIPMENT ·

1 baking sheet
1 sugar pan or a saucepan
Sugar thermometer
2 mixing bowls or an electric mixer
6 small cake tins or moulds, 8 cm/3¼ in diameter, 3 cm/1¼ in deep approx.

PICTURE PAGE 99

Halve the figs, slice into fan shapes and arrange them around the ice creams.

· STORAGE ·

The ice creams will keep in the freezer for up to 3 days; leave them in the moulds, covered with clingfilm.

PETITS COEURS DE FROMAGE BLANC AUX FRUITS ROUGES
(Little fromage blanc hearts with red fruits)

· INGREDIENTS ·

360 g/12 oz *fromage blanc or* curd cheese, drained (choose whichever fat content you prefer)

120 ml/4 fl oz double cream (optional)

12 strawberries

12 wild strawberries

16 gooseberries

4 bunches of redcurrants

4 bunches of white currants

Serves 4
Preparation time: 25 minutes

These little hearts are among the easiest of all desserts to make. The summer fruits give the dish a festive air but they can be replaced by any other fruits you choose, depending on the season.

For large gatherings, an attractively decorated large heart made in a mould for 6–8 people looks wonderful on a buffet.

· PREPARATION ·

Preparing the hearts: Put the *fromage blanc* in a bowl and beat well until it is completely smooth. You can add a little fresh cream when you beat the *fromage blanc* to make the texture slightly thicker.

Line the insides of the moulds with slightly dampened muslin or napkins.

Divide the *fromage blanc* between the moulds and tap them gently to eliminate any air bubbles. Wrap the overhanging muslin over the cheese, making sure it is well covered.

Chill in the fridge for at least 2 hours and up to 24 hours.

· TO SERVE ·

Serve the hearts on individual plates.

Unwrap the cheese and invert the mould onto the plate. Carefully lift off the mould and the muslin or napkin.

If you like, coat the hearts with double cream and arrange the fruits decoratively around the edge, perhaps in little bunches. Serve very cold.

· NOTES ·

If *fromage blanc* is not available, you can easily make your own. Combine in a blender or food processor equal quantities of cottage cheese and plain yoghurt, add lemon juice to taste and blend until very smooth and creamy.

· EQUIPMENT ·

4 coeur à la crème *moulds,*
9 × 8 cm/3½ × 3¼ in,
1.5 cm × ½ in deep

Butter muslin or small napkins

1 bowl

PICTURE PAGE 121

TOP LEFT *Alméria* (page 136)
BOTTOM LEFT *L'assiette des trois sablés* (page 138)
ABOVE *Petit coeur de fromage blanc aux fruits rouges* (page 119)

GATEAU AUX NOIX
(Walnut gateau)

· INGREDIENTS ·

250 g/9 oz walnuts *or*
pecans, hazelnuts etc

8 eggs

250 g/9 oz icing sugar

50 g/2 oz very fine
breadcrumbs

½ tsp vanilla essence

Juice of 1 lemon,
strained

50 g/2 oz butter, for
greasing

Serves 8

*Preparation time: about 15
minutes*

Cooking time: 55 minutes

We were given this recipe for this delicious, moist cake by our friends the Berkmans; Eva often delights us with this dessert. It is an excellent winter dish, which one can enjoy at any hour of the day.

· PREPARATION ·

Preheat the oven to 190°C/375°F/gas 6.

The nuts: Chop them very finely without reducing them to powder.

The egg yolks: Separate the eggs and put the yolks in a bowl with 200 g/7 oz of the icing sugar. Immediately whisk together until the mixture forms a ribbon. Using a flat slotted spoon or spatula, fold in 30 g/1 oz of the breadcrumbs, then the vanilla essence, lemon juice and lastly the nuts.

The egg whites: Beat in the mixer or with a whisk until well risen, then add the remaining sugar and beat at high speed for about 1 minute, until firm.

The mixture: Using a spatula, carefully fold one-third of the egg whites into the yolk mixture until completely amalgamated, then fold in the remaining whites; do not overmix.

· TO COOK ·

Generously butter the mould and coat with the remaining breadcrumbs. Pour in the mixture and bake in the preheated oven for 55 minutes. Carefully unmould the gateau onto a wire rack and give it a quarter turn every 10 minutes until completely cold, so that it does not stick to the rack.

· TO SERVE ·

Serve the gateau whole. If you like, sprinkle the top with icing sugar and draw a criss-cross pattern with the fine point of a knife or the prongs of a fork.

· STORAGE ·

Wrapped in clingfilm, it will keep at room temperature for 2 or 3 days.

· EQUIPMENT ·

2 bowls

Electric mixer

1 sponge tin or *a flan ring,
22 cm/8½ in diameter,
4 cm/1½ in deep*

BAVAROISE ENRUBANEE AU CHOCOLAT ET GRAND MARNIER

(Striped chocolate and Grand Marnier bavaroise)

· INGREDIENTS ·

1 quantity plain Sponge biscuit mixture (see recipe 2, page 53)

1 quantity chocolate-flavoured Sponge biscuit mixture, (see recipe 2, page 53), but made with 140 g/5 oz flour and 40 g/1½ oz sifted cocoa powder

100 ml/3½ fl oz Sorbet syrup (see page 168)

50 ml/2 fl oz Grand Marnier

FOR THE GRAND MARNIER BAVAROISE:

300 ml/11 fl oz milk

4 egg yolks

80 g/3 oz sugar

1½ leaves of gelatine

60 ml/2½ fl oz Grand Marnier

250 ml/9 fl oz double cream

FOR THE CHOCOLATE BAVAROISE:

100 g/4 oz bitter couverture or plain cooking chocolate

300 ml/11 fl oz milk

3 egg yolks

130 g/4 oz sugar

20 g/1 oz flour

1 leaf of gelatine

300 ml/11 fl oz double cream

Makes 2 charlottes, each serving 8

Preparation time: 1 hour 20 minutes, plus 1½ hours chilling

· PREPARATION ·

The sponge base: Using 2 separate piping bags, pipe out the plain and chocolate sponge mixtures diagonally onto a 60 × 40 cm/24 × 16 in baking sheet lined with buttered greaseproof paper, alternating the colours as in the step-by-step pictures (see page 124). You will have enough mixture left over for another quarter baking sheet.

Bake the striped sponge according to the method in Recipe 2 on page 53 and leave to cool.

Invert the baked sponge onto another baking sheet and carefully peel off the paper, starting from one edge. With a serrated knife, trim the edges of the sponge.

Working along the longer edge, cut out 3 bands the same width as the flan circles (ie, 3.5 cm/1½ in wide).

From the remaining sponge, use the point of a small knife to cut out 2 circles, each slightly smaller than the flan rings.

Mix together the syrup and Grand Marnier, then brush the sponge bands and circles with the mixture. Place the sponge circles on the cake boards and put the flan rings over the top.

Line each circle with a sponge band, syrup side inwards. Push the band well down so that the base touches the cake board. Cut a long enough strip from the remaining band to fit the gaps left in the flan rings.

The Grand Marnier bavaroise: Make a *crème anglaise* with the milk, egg yolks and sugar, following the method on page 70, and leave to cool to room temperature, but do not refrigerate.

Soak the gelatine in very cold water for 20 minutes, then drain well. Gently warm the Grand Marnier, then stir in the gelatine. Beat the cream until it forms a ribbon.

Stir the Grand Marnier mixture into the cooled *crème anglaise*, then delicately fold in the whipped cream with a balloon whisk.

The chocolate bavaroise: Soak the gelatine in very cold water for 20 minutes. Break the chocolate into pieces, then make a *crème pâtissière* with the chocolate, milk, egg yolks, sugar, and flour, following the method on page 61. Drain the gelatine well, then stir it into the *crème pâtissière*.

Leave to cool to room temperature, then beat the cream until it forms a ribbon.

· EQUIPMENT ·

2 baking sheets

2 × 24 cm/9½ in round cake boards

2 stainless steel flan rings, 22 cm/8½ in diameter, 3.5 cm/1½ in deep

Electric mixer or bowl and whisk

2 saucepans

2 piping bags, with plain 1 cm/½ in nozzles

Using a balloon whisk, carefully fold the whipped cream into the cooled *crème pâtissière*.

Assembling the charlottes: Divide the chocolate mixture between the 2 sponge-lined flan rings. Ladle over irregular quantities of the Grand Marnier mixture, letting it drop in spiral patterns to give a marbled effect. You must do this as soon as you have made the *bavaroises*, or the mixtures will set and you will not achieve the attractive marbling.

Place in the fridge for 4 hours, or in the freezer for 1½ hours.

· TO SERVE ·

Run a knife blade between the edge of the sponge and the inside of the flan ring and lift off the ring, rotating it slightly as you lift. Cut into slices with a knife dipped in hot water and serve very cold. A few chocolate curls (see page 242) make a pretty garnish for this dish, or accompany it with some Grand Marnier-flavoured *crème anglaise*, served in a sauceboat.

· STORAGE ·

If left in its flan ring and wrapped in clingfilm, one of the desserts can be kept in the fridge for 3 days, or for up to a week in the freezer.

1
After baking and cooling, invert the sponge and carefully peel off the paper, starting from one corner.

2
Cut out 3 long bands and 2 circles.

3
With the circles on the cake boards, line the rings with sponge bands, syrup side inwards. Cut strips from the third band to fill gaps. Trim the edges.

4
Pour the chocolate bavaroise into the rings, then quickly ladle in the Grand Marnier bavaroise to give a marbled effect.

Croquembouche (page 126)

CROQUEMBOUCHE

· INGREDIENTS ·

1.1 kg/2 lb 6 oz
Nougatine (see page 233)

2 tbsp peanut oil

2 tbsp Royal icing (see
page 236)

400 ml/14 fl oz Choux
paste (see below)

450 ml/16 fl oz double
cream, well chilled

950 g/2 lb *Crème
pâtissière* (see page 61)

50 ml/2 fl oz Kirsch
(optional)

750 g/1 lb 10 oz sugar

100 g/3½ oz glucose

10-12 sugar roses (see
pages 226-7) (optional)

CHOUX PASTE:

160 g/5½ oz butter

200 ml/8 fl oz water

200 ml/8 fl oz milk

¾ tsp fine salt

1½ tsp sugar

240 g/8 oz flour

7 × 70 g/size 1 eggs

Makes 1 Croquembouche
*60 cm/24 in high, made
with 110 choux buns
Serves 25-30*

A *Croquembouche* is the traditional centrepiece for christenings, first communions and weddings in France. You can make it more or less impressive, depending on the number of choux buns you use.

· PREPARATION ·

The nougatine: This must be divided into 4 pieces of the following weights: 770 g/1 lb 11 oz, 130 g/4 oz, and 2 pieces each of 100 g/3½ oz, but only take and work 1 piece at a time from the mass. Immediately roll out the first piece on a warm baking sheet or plastic board, keeping the rest of the *nougatine* warm in the oven or under a lamp.

First shaping: Roll out the 130 g/4 oz piece of *nougatine* to a thickness of 0.5 cm/¼ in. With a large knife, cut out 20 triangles 4 cm/1½ in at the base and 5 cm/2 in high. Before they harden, drape them over the *tuile* shaper or the small rolling pin, so that they become slightly rounded. You will be left with about 30 g/1 oz trimmings.

Place the shaped triangles on a lightly oiled pastry sheet as soon as they have cooled.

Second shaping: Roll out one of the 100 g/3½ oz pieces of *nougatine* to a thickness of 0.5 cm/¼ in. Using the larger pastry cutter, cut out 5 half moons, 2.5 cm/1 in wide, and place them on the pastry sheet with the triangles.

You will be left with about 25 g/1 oz trimmings.

Third shaping: Roll out the second 100 g/3½ oz piece of *nougatine* to a thickness of 0.5 cm/¼ in and cut out one 11 cm/4½ in circle and one 7 cm/2¾ in circle with the pastry cutters. Place on the pastry sheet with the other shapes.

You will be left with about 45 g/1½ oz trimmings.

Fourth shaping: Roll the largest piece of *nougatine* into a circle 1 cm/⅓ in thick. Line the lightly oiled flan ring or sponge tin with this circle.

With a small, sharp knife, trim off the excess *nougatine* from the top of the mould, so that the edge is very smooth and even. As soon as the *nougatine* base has cooled, carefully unmould it and place it on the pastry sheet with the other shapes.

Take particular care with this shape, as it will form the base for the *Croquembouche*.

You will be left with about 120 g/4 oz trimmings

Decoration: Using a paper cone, decorate each shape with royal icing (see photo, page 237).

Set the *nougatine* base upside down on the cake board. Decorate all round the base with royal icing to hide any gaps

· EQUIPMENT ·

3 baking sheets

1 non-stick plastic board

*Rolling pin, weighted or
made from heavy hardwood*

*Small rolling pin or tuile
shaper*

*2 plain or fluted pastry
cutters, 1 × 11 cm/4½ in
diameter, 1 × 7 cm/2¾ in
diameter*

*1 flan ring or sponge tin,
25 cm/10 in diameter,
5 cm/2 in deep*

Greaseproof piping cornet

*1 cake board,
27 cm/11 in diameter*

*Piping bag, fitted with a
plain 5 mm/¼ in nozzle*

1 bowl

1 copper sugar pan

1 Croquembouche *mould*

Sugar thermometer

Sugar lamp (optional)

PICTURE PAGE 125

and to anchor the base onto the cake board.

The choux paste: Prepare and bake according to the recipe (page 46), using the piping bag fitted with a plain nozzle to pipe out 110 choux buns, about 2.5 cm/1 in diameter.

The light cream: Beat the double cream until it forms a ribbon, then fold in the *crème pâtissière*. Beat lightly until the creams are amalgamated, then flavour with Kirsch if required.

The sugar: Pour 250 ml/9 fl oz water into the sugar pan and add the sugar. Stir lightly with a skimmer and, when the sugar begins to dissolve, set the pan over moderate heat until the sugar has dissolved completely and begins to boil. Skim the surface, and brush down the inside of the pan, dipping the brush in cold water each time. Add the glucose and cook until the temperature reaches 160°C/320°F (very hard crack). It should be a very clear amber.

The choux buns: Using a small knife, make a small hole in the base of each bun. One by one, dip the tops into the sugar, to cover about one-third of each bun. Place on a lightly oiled baking sheet to cool. When the buns are quite cold, use the piping bag to fill them with the cream mixture.

Assembling the choux buns: This can be done 4–6 hours before serving.

Lightly oil the inside of the *Croquembouche* mould. Place one bun in the bottom of the mould, with the sugared side against the cone. Spear one bun with the point of a small knife and dip one-fifth of one edge in the sugar; place this bun against one side of the first bun, arranging it so that the sugared side is against the wall of the mould. The hot sugar will stick this bun to the first one.

Continue to add more buns in the same way, making only one row at a time, so that the rows remain straight.

The *Croquembouche* is assembled when all the buns have been used or the mould is full. Leave it for a few moments until the sugar is completely cold. Check that the mould is not sticking to the *Croquembouche* by rotating it slightly with your hand.

The finishing touches: Carefully invert the mould onto the *nougatine* base and remove the mould to reveal the pile of choux buns.

Using a little of the cooked sugar, stick the *nougatine* triangles around the base, arrange the half moons and circles at the top, and finish with the sugar roses.

Nougatine can be rather difficult to work, so you may find it easier to omit the triangles and other shapes, but the base is indispensable.

A few extra roses placed around the base will help to anchor the choux buns to the *nougatine*, and make the *Croquembouche* more stable. The sugar roses can be replaced by marzipan

1

PALMEROSA DE MON AMI VALENTIN

1
With a flexible knife, slice the
peeled grapefruit into segments
between the membranes. Squeeze
the juice from the peel and pith,
dice the flesh, and sprinkle over
the sugar.

2
Cut the biscuit joconde in circles,
place on a wire rack and brush
with vanilla syrup.

2

3

3
Set the bowl of meringue in a
bowl of crushed ice. Lightly
whisk in the grapefruit juice
mixture, then stir in the whipped
cream.

4
Carefully fold in the diced
grapefruit, taking care to separate
the dice.

4

5

5
Stand the moulds in crushed ice.
Spoon one-third of the grapefruit
mixture into the moulds and
spread it up the sides.

6
Cut a small triangle out of 8
sponge rounds, then make two
cuts from the opposite side almost
to the centre. Press one round into
each mould.

6

7

7
Top the filled moulds with a
sponge round. Smooth the surface
and scrape off any excess mixture.
Wrap in clingfilm and chill for
4 hours.

8
Unmould the chilled palmerosas
and spoon over the strawberry
glaze. Serve very cold.

8

flowers, which are easier to make — or even by coloured *dragées* placed here and there; these can look very pretty.

· TO SERVE ·

Using a knife with a rigid blade, first remove the *nougatine* 'crown', put it on a plate, and break it into 6 or 8 more or less equal pieces.

Starting from the top of the *Croquembouche*, slide the knife blade between the choux buns and serve 3 or 4 on to each plate. When everyone has been served, use the knife to break up part of the *nougatine* base, especially the decorative triangles. Pass around the plate of *nougatine* pieces for your guests to help themselves.

· NOTES ·

If the sugar cools and thickens while you are assembling the buns, heat it very gently over a low flame from time to time, but do not overheat it.

PALMEROSA DE MON AMI VALENTIN

· INGREDIENTS ·

5 grapefruit, preferably pink

50 g/2 oz sugar

1 baked *Biscuit joconde* (see page 55)

5 tbsp Sorbet syrup (see page 168), flavoured with vanilla

4½ leaves of gelatine

50 ml/2 fl oz Grand Marnier

350 ml/12 fl oz double cream, chilled

1 quantity *Meringue italienne* (see page 58)

FOR THE GLAZE:

3 leaves of gelatine

300 g/10 oz strawberries

150 g/5 oz sugar

½ quantity red *Fruit coulis* (see page 71)

48 raspberries

This recipe was given to me by a good friend and famous *pâtissier*, Monsieur Valentin. It takes a long time to prepare, but its subtle, sweet flavour and refreshing tang make it worthwhile.

· PREPARATION ·

The grapefruit: Using a supple-bladed knife, pare off the peel and pith, then cut the flesh into segments between the white membranes. Squeeze out all the juice from the peel and pulp into a bowl. Cut the grapefruit segments into medium dice, sprinkle over the sugar and mix gently. Place in a strainer set over the bowl containing the grapefruit juice and leave to drain for 30 minutes. Measure the resulting juices into a jug; you should have not more than 200 ml/7 fl oz. Strain the juices.

The biscuit joconde: Cut out sixteen 8 cm/3¼ in circles. Arrange them on a wire rack and brush lightly with the vanilla syrup.

The gelatine: Soak in very cold water for 15 minutes. Drain and place in a saucepan, together with one-third of the grapefruit juice and the Grand Marnier. Set over gentle heat to dissolve the gelatine; do not let the mixture boil. Stir in the

· EQUIPMENT ·

1 sieve

1 conical strainer

Crushed ice

1 small saucepan

1 pastry cutter, 8 cm/3¼ in diameter

8 round moulds or dishes, preferably stainless steel, 9 cm/3½ in diameter, 5 cm/2 in deep, 4.5 cm/1¼ in at the base

Wire rack

PICTURE PAGE 107

Serves 8

Preparation time: 1¼ hours

remaining grapefruit juice and set aside.

The cream: Whip until it forms a ribbon.

The grapefruit mixture: Put two-thirds of the *meringue italienne* in a bowl and set in a dish of crushed ice (see note below). Pour in the grapefruit juice mixture and mix lightly with a wire whisk. Stir in the whipped cream, a little at a time, then, using a spatula, carefully fold in the diced grapefruit taking care to separate the dice.

Assembling the moulds: Stand the moulds in a dish of crushed ice. Using one-third of the grapefruit mixture, divide it between the moulds. Using a soup spoon, spread the mixture up the sides of the moulds to line them.

Take 8 biscuit rounds and, using scissors, carefully cut out a small triangle and make 2 cuts from the opposite side, almost to the centre. Press one into each mould. Fill up the moulds with the remaining grapefruit mixture and top with a whole biscuit round. Flatten the surface with a palette knife and scrape off any excess mixture.

Wrap the moulds in clingfilm and leave to set in the fridge for 4 hours, or freeze for 2 hours before serving.

The strawberry glaze: Soak the 3 leaves of gelatine in very cold water for 15 minutes. Drain.

Rub the strawberries through a sieve into a saucepan, stir in the sugar and bring to the boil. Take the pan off the heat and stir in the well-drained gelatine. Skim the surface if necessary, then leave to cool until the glaze is half-set.

· TO SERVE ·

Dip the base of the moulds in very hot water for a few seconds. Hold the moulds over a wire rack and press one side with your fingers so that the *Palmerosa* slips towards the other side. It will then slide easily out of the mould. Place on the rack and, using a spoon, coat each *Palmerosa* with strawberry glaze.

Use a palette knife to transfer them to individual serving plates. Pour a ribbon of fruit *coulis* around each one and decorate each plate with 6 raspberries or substitute strawberries for the decorative raspberries if you prefer. Serve very cold.

· STORAGE ·

The *Palmerosas* will keep in a cold fridge for at least 48 hours, and can be frozen for up to a week. Refrigerate or freeze them in the mould and glaze just before serving.

As with all desserts containing *meringue italienne*, you must make the full quantity to obtain a successful mixture; discard the remaining one-third, or keep it for another use.

DELICE AU CASSIS
(Blackcurrant delight)

· INGREDIENTS ·

350 g/11 oz blackcurrants

150 ml / 6 fl oz Sorbet syrup (see page 168), divided into 3 equal quantities

4 leaves of gelatine

12 g/2 tsp powdered milk

¼ vanilla pod

3 egg yolks

25 g/1 oz sugar

1 round Sponge biscuit (see recipe 2, page 53), 20 cm/8 in diameter, sliced into a circle 5 mm/¼ in thick

200 ml/7 fl oz *Crème de cassis*

1 quantity *Meringue italienne* (see page 58)

400 ml/14 fl oz double cream

Granulated sugar, to decorate

Serves 8

Preparation time: 45 minutes

Cooking time: 10 minutes

· PREPARATION ·

The blackcurrant purée: Set aside 14 blackcurrants for the decoration. Purée the rest in the blender with 50 ml/2 oz syrup, then pass the purée through a conical strainer.

The blackcurrant custard: Soak 2 gelatine leaves in cold water for 15 minutes, then drain. Reserve 2 tbsp blackcurrant purée and put the rest in a saucepan. Add the powdered milk and vanilla and bring to the boil.

Combine the egg yolks and sugar in a bowl and whisk until they form a ribbon.

Pour the boiling blackcurrant purée onto the egg mixture, whisking continuously, then pour this custard back into the pan and set over low heat, stirring continuously with a spatula until the custard is thick enough to coat the spatula. Do not allow it to boil.

Take the pan off the heat and stir the drained gelatine into the custard. Discard the vanilla, then pass the custard through a conical strainer into a bowl and leave to cool, stirring occasionally to prevent a skin from forming.

The sponge: Place the sponge circle on the cake board. Mix together 50 ml/2 fl oz syrup and 1 tbsp of the reserved blackcurrant purée and brush this mixture over the sponge. Place the flan ring around the sponge.

The blackcurrant mousse: When the custard is lukewarm, gently fold in one-sixth of the *meringue italienne*, then the *crème de cassis*, using a balloon whisk. Beat the cream until it forms a ribbon and, with a wooden spatula, gently fold it into the mixture. You must now assemble the dessert immediately, before the gelatine causes the mousse to set.

Assembling the délice: Fill the flan ring with blackcurrant mousse and carefully smooth over the surface with a palette knife. Place in the freezer or a very cold fridge for several hours.

To glaze: Soak the 2 remaining gelatine leaves in cold water for 15 minutes, then drain well.

You can glaze the dessert with the flan ring in place, which will give you a neat, drip-free border, or remove the ring first if you prefer. To remove it, heat the outside of the ring over a gas flame for a few seconds, then slide the ring upwards, rotating it slightly.

Mix together the remaining syrup and blackcurrant purée and stir in the well-drained gelatine. Leave to cool, then use it to glaze the top of the dessert. Keep the *délice* in the flan ring and glaze just before serving.

· EQUIPMENT ·

Blender or food processor

1 saucepan

1 mixing bowl

1 × 24 cm/10 in round cake board

1 flan ring, 22 cm/8½ in diameter, 3.5 mm/1½ in deep

Conical strainer

PICTURE PAGE 110

· TO SERVE ·

If you have not already done so, remove the flan ring by sliding a knife blade dipped in hot water between the dessert and the ring. Roll the reserved blackcurrants in granulated sugar and decorate the top of the *délice*.

Serve the dessert whole, and slice it at the table with a knife dipped in hot water before cutting each slice.

· STORAGE ·

Unglazed and in the flan ring, the *délice* will keep in the fridge for several days, or for 2 weeks in the freezer.

· NOTES ·

Since it is difficult to divide the recipe for *meringue italienne*, you may prefer to prepare two of these *délices* at the same time and keep one for another occasion.

DELICE AUX FRUITS DE LA PASSION
(Passion fruit delight)

· INGREDIENTS ·

9 passion fruit

450 ml/16 fl oz sieved passion fruit pulp (from about 45-50 fruits)

7 leaves of gelatine

100 ml/3½ fl oz milk

40 g/1½ oz powdered milk

½ vanilla pod, split

10 egg yolks

70 g/2½ oz sugar

1 round Sponge biscuit, 20 cm/8 in diameter (see recipe 2, page 53)

150 ml/5 fl oz Sorbet syrup (see page 168)

100 ml/3½ fl oz vodka

1 quantity *Meringue italienne* (see page 58)

675 ml/24 fl oz double cream

Juice of 1 orange, strained

· PREPARATION ·

The passion fruit: Cut a thin slice off both ends of 8 of the passion fruit, so that they will stand firmly, then cut them in half horizontally. Using a small spoon, scoop out about one-third of the pulp from each shell into a saucepan. Wrap the passion fruit shells in clingfilm and place in the fridge.

The passion fruit custard: Soak 6 of the gelatine leaves in very cold water for 20 minutes, then drain well.

In a saucepan, combine 350 ml/12 fl oz sieved passion fruit pulp, the milk, powdered milk and the split vanilla pod and bring to the boil. Put the egg yolks and sugar in a bowl and immediately whisk to a ribbon consistency.

Take the pan off the heat and pour the boiling milk mixture onto the yolks, stirring continuously. Set over low heat and cook, stirring continuously with a spatula, until the custard is thick enough to coat the spatula; do not let the custard boil. Take the pan off the heat and stir in the well-drained gelatine.

Remove the vanilla pod, then, when the gelatine has dissolved completely, pass the custard through a conical strainer and leave to cool, stirring from time to time.

The sponge: Cut the sponge horizontally into 2 circles, each about 5 mm/¼ in thick. You will have about half the sponge left over. Place a sponge circle on each cake board and brush with a mixture of 50 ml/2 fl oz syrup, 100 ml/4 fl oz sieved

· EQUIPMENT ·

2 saucepans

2 bowls

1 conical strainer

2 × 24 cm/10 in round cake boards

2 flan rings, 22 cm/8½ in diameter, 3.5 cm/1½ in deep

PICTURE PAGE 111

Continued on page 134

DELICE AU CASSIS

1

Cut a slice 5 mm/⅛ in thick from the sponge biscuit for the base and place on the cake board.

1

2

Brush with a mixture of syrup and blackcurrant purée for moistness and flavour.

2

3

Gently fold the meringue into the cooled blackcurrant custard, using a wire whisk.

3

4

With a wooden spatula, carefully fold the whipped cream into the mixture until well blended.

4

5

Immediately pour this mousse over the sponge base and fill up the flan ring. This must be done quickly before the mousse sets.

5

6

Smooth the surface of the mousse with a palette knife to make it completely level. Chill in the fridge or freezer for several hours.

6

7

To glaze: pour the cooled glaze over the top of the mousse, starting at the centre and spreading the glaze to the edges with a palette knife.

7

8

With the point of a knife, immediately prick out any air bubbles from the glaze. If the flan ring is still in place, slide a knife between it and the délice and slide off

8

Makes 2 desserts, each to serve 8

Preparation time: 45 minutes

Cooking time: 10 minutes

passion fruit pulp and 50 ml/2 fl oz vodka. Place the flan rings around the sponges.

The passion fruit mousse or bavaroise: When the custard has cooled to lukewarm, stir in the remaining vodka, then carefully fold in half the meringue, using a wire whisk.

Whip the cream until it forms a ribbon, then fold it into the custard with a wooden spatula. You must now use the mousse immediately, as the gelatine will cause it to set quite quickly.

Assembling the délices: Fill the flan rings with the mousse and carefully smooth over the tops with a palette knife. Place in the freezer or a very cold fridge for several hours.

The glaze: Soak the remaining gelatine leaf in cold water for 15 minutes, then drain well.

You can glaze the desserts either with the flan rings in place, which will give you a neat edge, without the glaze running down the sides, or you can remove the rings first. To do this, heat the outside edges of the ring over a gas flame for a few seconds, then slide the rings upwards, rotating them slightly, and lift them off.

Add the remaining syrup and the orange juice to the reserved passion fruit pulp in the saucepan and bring to the boil. Take the pan off the heat and stir in the drained gelatine. When it has dissolved, pass the glaze through a conical sieve and leave until almost cold before glazing the desserts.

· TO SERVE ·

If you left the flan rings in place to glaze the desserts, remove them by running a knife blade dipped in hot water between the inside of the ring and the desserts, then lift off.

Just before serving, decorate the top with the remaining passion fruit seeds; this makes a simple, natural decoration. Serve the dessert whole, or cut into slices and garnish with the passion fruit shells, which gives a more fruity flavour.

· NOTES ·

The *délices* can also be served as individual desserts. Use 20 small flan rings, 6.5 cm/2½ in diameter, 4 cm/1½ in deep. Bake a rectangular sponge, 5 mm/¼ in thick instead of the round one, and cut out 20 6 cm/2⅜ in circles. The given quantity of mousse is enough for 20 desserts. Apple jelly (see page 71) can be substituted for the passion fruit glaze. Since a smaller quantity of *meringue italienne* cannot be made successfully, we suggest that you make two *délices*; they will keep in the fridge for several days and can be frozen for up to 2 weeks. Keep them in the flan rings and glaze shortly before serving. Discard the remaining meringue, or keep it for another use.

MOUSSE D'ABRICOT A LA FINE CHAMPAGNE, SAUCE ORANGE

(Apricot and brandy mousse with orange sauce)

· INGREDIENTS ·

½ quantity Sponge biscuit mixture (see recipe 1, page 53)

Butter, for greasing

Pinch of flour

2 leaves of gelatine

30 ml/1 fl oz brandy

400 g/14 oz canned apricot halves, drained *or* 8 whole fresh apricots, poached

50 ml/2 fl oz apricot liqueur

Juice of 4 oranges

Juice of ½ lemon

250 ml/9 fl oz double cream, well chilled

100 ml/3½ fl oz Sorbet syrup (see page 168)

Serves 8

Preparation time: 50 minutes

· PREPARATION ·

Preheat the oven to 220°C/425°F/gas 8.

The sponge biscuit: Place a sheet of baking parchment or buttered and floured greaseproof paper on a baking sheet and spread the mixture into a rectangle, as for a Swiss roll, 5 mm/¼ in thick.

Cook according to the method on page 53. Remove from the oven, leave to cool, then cut out eight 8.5 cm/3¼ in biscuit rounds with the pastry cutter. Set aside.

The gelatine: Soak in very cold water for 15 minutes. Drain, then place in a saucepan with the brandy. Heat very gently to dissolve the gelatine; do not boil. Keep at room temperature.

The apricots: Place 8 apricot halves in the blender or food processor, together with the apricot liqueur and purée for 2 minutes. Rub the purée through a fine sieve or pass through a conical strainer. Finely dice 4 apricot halves and set aside.

Cut 4 more apricot halves into 8 segments and set aside.

The orange and lemon juice: Put the orange juice into a saucepan and, over medium heat, reduce by half. Add the lemon juice and immediately take the pan off the heat. Pass through a strainer into a bowl and leave to cool, then refrigerate immediately.

The apricot mousse: Whip the chilled cream with the syrup until it forms a ribbon. Stir in the apricot purée, then fold in the gelatine mixture.

Assembling the moulds: Half fill them with apricot mousse. Using a teaspoon, divide the diced apricots between the moulds, then fill to the top with the remaining mousse.

Place a biscuit round on top of each one and refrigerate for 4 hours, or place in the freezer for 2 hours.

· TO SERVE ·

Dip the base of the moulds in very hot water for a few seconds. Unmould the mousses directly onto serving plates. Arrange 4 apricot segments like a flower on top of each mousse and pour the orange sauce around the edge. As an extra decoration, scatter crushed sugar and almond *nougatine* (see page 233) over the mousses and between the apricot segments.

Serve very cold.

· NOTES ·

Serve the sponge trimmings with jam as a tea-time treat.

· EQUIPMENT ·

Greaseproof paper *or* baking parchment

1 baking sheet

8.5 cm/3¼ in pastry cutter

Blender *or* food processor

Conical strainer

1 saucepan

8 circular moulds, 8.5 cm/3¼ in diameter, 3 cm/1¼ in deep, 7 cm/2¾ in at the base

ALMERIA

· INGREDIENTS ·

Treble quantity of
Orange sponge biscuit
(see page 56)

50 g/2 oz butter, plus a
pinch of flour, for the
mould

500 ml/18 fl oz double
cream, well chilled

Double quantity *Crème
pâtissière* (see page 61),
well chilled

350 ml/12 fl oz Sorbet
syrup (see page 168)

150 ml/5 fl oz Grand
Marnier

20 g/³⁄₄ oz candied
orange peel, finely
chopped

Pinch of icing sugar

550 g/1 lb 2 oz marzipan

700 g/1 lb 8 oz fondant

Yellow food colouring

100 g/3½ oz plain
chocolate, melted, for
decoration

Serves 36

*Preparation time: about 1½
hours*

*Cooking time: 1 hour (for
the sponge), to be made 24
hours in advance*

This is a marvellous dessert for a special occasion buffet — a real treat to look at and to eat.

· PREPARATION ·

Preheat the oven to 180°C/350°F/gas 5.

The sponge: Lightly butter and flour the Genoise mould or flan ring and fill it with the sponge mixture. Bake in the preheated oven for 1 hour.

You must bake the sponge at least 24 hours before using, so that it will be easier to split and fill.

The cream: In a bowl, whip the cream until it forms a ribbon, then stir it into the chilled *crème pâtissière*, a little at a time.

Filling the sponge: Using a ham slicer or serrated knife, cut the sponge horizontally into 4 equal slices. Brush the cut sides with a mixture of syrup and Grand Marnier.

Using a large palette knife, place the bottom slice on the smaller cake board. With another palette knife, spread about one-quarter of the cream over the sponge and scatter over one-third of the finely chopped orange peel in an even layer. Top with a second sponge circle. Make 2 more layers in the same way, finishing with the top of the sponge.

With the palette knife, thinly coat the top and sides of the filled sponge with cream; there should be about 100 ml/3½ fl oz cream left over. Place the sponge in the fridge for several hours (but not more than 24 hours).

Icing and decorating the dessert: Do not do this more than 2 or 3 hours before serving.

On a marble or wooden surface lightly dusted with icing sugar, roll out the marzipan, as evenly as possible, into a 55-60 cm/21½-23½ in circle, about 2-3 mm/¹⁄₁₂ in thick. Roll it onto the rolling pin, then unroll it over the cake so that it covers the top and sides completely. Make sure that the marzipan is quite smooth, with no creases or air bubbles. Using a sharp knife, cut away any excess from the base. You will have about 100 g/3½ oz trimmings.

Place the cake on a wire rack set over a baking sheet or fondant tray. Put the fondant into a saucepan or fondant pan, set over low heat and stir with a spatula. The fondant is ready when it reaches a temperature of 35-40°C/95-104°F (lukewarm) and has a light ribbon, almost liquid consistency. If the fondant seems too thick, thin it with a little sorbet syrup. Add a few drops of yellow food colouring.

Quickly pour the fondant over the middle of the cake and down the sides. Using the palette knife, spread it over the top

· EQUIPMENT ·

1 Genoise mould or *flan ring, 35 cm/14 in diameter, 5 cm/2 in deep*

1 large bowl

2 cake boards, 1 × 35 cm/14 in diameter, 1 × 40 cm/16 in diameter

Wooden or *marble pastry board*

1 baking sheet or *fondant tray*

1 saucepan or *fondant pan*

Wire rack

Paper doilies

PICTURE PAGE 120

with a circular motion, so that the entire cake is covered with fondant. Gently tap the rack on the tray so that the excess fondant falls into the tray. You will be left with about 150 g/ 5 oz fondant in the tray, which can be re-used.

Leave to cool for about 15 minutes.

Dip the blade of a small, sharp knife into hot water and neaten the bottom edge of the cake between the wire rack and the cake board. Dip the blade into hot water between each operation.

Cover the larger cake board with paper doilies, then, using the large palette knife, transfer the entire dessert (board and all) to the larger cake board.

Pipe out the word *Alméria* with melted chocolate on top of the cake and pipe a pretty border around the edge (see examples, page 237).

· TO SERVE ·

Serve the *Alméria* whole and cut it at the table, using a knife dipped in hot water for each slice, in the following way: Cut an 8 cm/3¼ in border round the edge of the cake and cut this into slices, then slice the centre in the usual way. Add a touch of artistry with some pretty sugar or marzipan roses.

SABLE AUX FRAISES
(Strawberry shortbread)

PICTURE PAGE 106

· INGREDIENTS ·

680 g/1 lb 8 oz *Pâte sablée* (see recipe 1, page 47)

Pinch of flour

800 g/1 lb 12 oz strawberries

600 ml/1 pt red Fruit *coulis* (see page 71)

50 g/2 oz icing sugar

Serves 6

Preparation time: 25 minutes

Cooking time: 8 minutes

· PREPARATION ·

Preheat the oven to 200°C/400°F/gas 7.

The pastry bases: Divide the *pâte sablée* into 2 equal pieces to make rolling out easier.

On a lightly floured surface, roll out both halves of the dough to a thickness of about 2 mm/¹⁄₁₆ in. Cut out 9 circles from each piece, using the pastry cutter, and arrange them on a baking sheet. Bake in the preheated oven for 8 minutes, until they are pale golden. Use a palette knife to slide the circles onto a wire rack and leave in a cool place.

The strawberries: Just before filling the bases, wash the strawberries if necessary, hull them and cut in half or leave whole, depending on their size. Roll them in two-thirds of the *coulis* and leave to macerate in the fridge.

· TO SERVE ·

Put a pastry base on each plate. Arrange a few macerated strawberries on top, then add another circle, with more strawberries, and top with a third pastry circle, which you have sprinkled generously with icing sugar. Use wild strawberries

· EQUIPMENT ·

Wooden or marble pastry board

Plain or fluted round pastry cutter, 10 cm/4 in diameter

1 or 2 baking sheets

or raspberries in season instead of the strawberries.

As a finishing touch, you can top the *sablés* with a fine strawberry dipped in *coulis*. Serve the remaining *coulis* in a sauceboat, or poured in a ribbon around the *sablés*.

· NOTES ·

This recipe can be prepared well in advance, but do not assemble the *sablés* until just before serving, as the *coulis* will soften the pastry and it will lose its wonderful crumbly texture.

L'ASSIETTE DES TROIS SABLES
(Trio of shortbreads)

· INGREDIENTS ·

| 200 g/7 oz *Pâte sablée* (see page 47) |
| Pinch of flour |
| 32 wild strawberries |
| 28 raspberries |
| 16 clusters of redcurrants |
| 30 g/1 oz icing sugar |
| 8 small sprigs of mint |
| 200 ml/7 fl oz red Fruit *coulis* (see page 71) |
| 3 tbsp double cream |

| Serves 4 |
| Preparation time: 25 minutes |
| Cooking time: 4 minutes |

· PREPARATION ·

Preheat the oven to 200°C/400°F/gas 7.

The pastry bases: On a lightly floured surface, roll out the pastry to a thickness of about 2 mm/$\frac{1}{16}$ in.

Cut out 24 circles with the pastry cutter and, using a palette knife, place them on a baking sheet, taking care not to spoil the shape. You will have about 80 g/3 oz trimmings.

Bake in the preheated oven for 4 minutes until pale golden. Use a palette knife to transfer the circles to a wire rack and leave in a cool place.

The fruit: Just before filling the *sablés*, hull the wild strawberries and raspberries, keeping them separate. De-stalk the redcurrants, reserving 4 clusters for the garnish.

· TO SERVE ·

Place 3 *sablé* bases on each serving plate and top each one with a different variety of fruit (5 raspberries on one, 6 strawberries on the second and about 16 redcurrants on the third).

Sprinkle the remaining circles generously with icing sugar and place on top of the fruit. Top each with an appropriate berry (raspberry on the raspberry *sablé* etc). If you like, arrange an appropriate berry and mint sprig next to each *sablé*. Pour a tablespoon of *coulis* between each *sablé* and pipe a spiral of cream on top. You can also make it into a spider's web by drawing the point of a sharp knife or a cocktail stick through the cream.

· NOTES ·

Assemble and garnish the *sablés* just before serving, or they will lose their delicious crumbliness.

The berries suggested here can be replaced by other fruits in season (see *Sablés aux poires*, opposite).

· EQUIPMENT ·

| Wooden or marble pastry board |
| 1 fluted pastry cutter, 5 cm/2 in diameter |
| 1 baking sheet |
| Wire rack |

PICTURE PAGE 120

SABLES AUX POIRES ET AUX MYRTILLES
(Pear and bilberry sablés)

· INGREDIENTS ·

6 very ripe fresh pears

300 g/10 oz canned bilberries in syrup, drained, *or* fresh bilberries, poached in syrup and drained

1 lemon, cut in half

500 ml/18 fl oz water

500 g/18 oz sugar

1 vanilla pod, split

680 g/1 lb 8 oz *Pâte sablée* (see page 47)

Pinch of flour

1 egg yolk, beaten with 1 tbsp milk, to glaze

600 ml/1 pt strawberry *or* raspberry *Coulis* (see page 71)

SABAYON SAUCE:

1 leaf of gelatine

1 whole egg

2 egg yolks

60 g/2 oz sugar

300 ml/11 fl oz double cream

100 ml/3 fl oz pear liqueur

Serves 6

Preparation time: 45 minutes

Cooking time: 8 minutes

· PREPARATION ·

Preheat the oven to 200°C/400°F/gas 7.

The pears: Peel them and rub with the cut lemon.

In a large saucepan, make a syrup with the water, sugar and split vanilla pod and bring to a simmer. Put in the pears, cover with greaseproof paper and simmer gently for about 15 minutes, depending on the size and ripeness of the fruit. The pears are cooked when you can insert the point of a very fine knife without meeting any resistance. Set aside in their syrup in a cool place.

When the pears have cooled completely, cut them in half, core them, then cut each half into 8 or 10 very fine slices. Lay them on absorbent paper and place in the fridge.

The pastry bases: Divide the pastry into 2 equal pieces to make rolling easier.

On a lightly floured surface, roll out both pieces of dough to a thickness of about 2 mm/$\frac{1}{16}$ in. Cut out 9 circles from each piece, using the pastry cutter, and arrange them on the baking sheet. Brush 6 of the pastry circles with the glaze and decorate with lines made with the back of a fork or the point of a sharp knife. Bake in the preheated oven for 8 minutes, until they are pale golden. Use a palette knife to transfer the cooked circles to a wire rack and leave in a cool place.

The sabayon sauce: Soak the gelatine leaf in cold water for 15 minutes, then drain.

Put the whole egg and the yolks in the bowl of the mixer. Add the sugar and place the bowl in a bain-marie set over high heat.

Immediately whisk the mixture until it forms a ribbon. Use your finger to test that the temperature does not rise above 60°/140°C, or the mixture will curdle.

Add the well-drained gelatine, then return the bowl to the mixer and beat at medium speed until cold.

Beat the cream until it forms a ribbon, then gently fold it into the cold *sabayon*, being careful not to overwork the mixture. Flavour with the pear *eau de vie* and place in the fridge.

Assembling the sablés: Using a spatula, carefully fold the pears into the *sabayon* sauce. Place one unglazed pastry base on each serving plate and top with a good spoonful of *sabayon* mixture. Cover with a second unglazed pastry circle, then a spoonful of *sabayon* and finally top with a glazed and decorated pastry circle. Pour the strawberry or raspberry *coulis*

· EQUIPMENT ·

1 large saucepan

Wooden *or* marble pastry board

Plain *or* fluted pastry cutter, 10 cm/4 in diameter

1 *or* 2 baking sheets

Electric mixer

Bain-marie

in a ribbon around each *sablé* and garnish with 4 coffee spoons of bilberries, either arranged in little heaps or sprinkled over the *coulis*.

· NOTES ·

You can substitute tinned pears in syrup for the fresh pears, but what you gain in time, you will lose in quality.

The cold poaching syrup can be served as a refreshing drink, as a fruit cocktail or in a fresh fruit salad.

You can prepare this recipe well in advance of your guests' arrival, but do not assemble the *sablés* until 5 minutes before serving, or the pastry will lose its crumbly texture.

SAVARINS AUX FRUITS DE SAISON
(Savarins with seasonal fruits)

· INGREDIENTS ·

1 quantity *Pâte à savarin* (see page 34)

30 g/1 oz butter, for greasing

2.5 lt/4½ pt Sorbet syrup (see page 168)

400 g/14 oz apricot jam, sieved

500 ml/18 fl oz rum

40 g/1½ oz flaked almonds

100 g/3½ oz glacé cherries, halved

400 g/14 oz of each of 8 kinds of seasonal fruit (total weight 3.2 kg/7 lb)

1.2 kg/2 lb 8 oz *Crème Chantilly* (optional) (see page 66)

Makes 2 savarins, each serving 16

Preparation time: 1 hour 15 minutes

Cooking time: 50 minutes

· PREPARATION ·

Preheat the oven to 220°C/425°F/gas 8.

Baking the savarins: Brush the insides of the moulds with butter and fill with the prepared *savarin* dough. Smooth the top of the dough with your fingertips to ensure that it is uniformly thick all round.

Leave to rise in a warm (24-26°C/75-79°F), draught-free place for about 40 minutes.

Place the moulds on a baking sheet and bake in the preheated oven for 30 minutes. Reduce the temperature to 200°C/400°F/gas 7 and bake for a further 15 minutes.

Remove the *savarins* from the oven, unmould them and place upside down on the same baking sheet. Immediately return them to the oven and bake for about 5 minutes longer to ensure that they are evenly cooked; the inside of the crown always cooks more slowly than the outside.

Place on a wire rack and leave to cool for at least 1 hour.

Soaking the savarins: Pour the 30° Beaume sorbet syrup into the shallow or preserving pan, add 2.5 lt/4½ pt water, which will give you a 15° Beaumé syrup, and bring to the boil.

Take the pan off the heat and let the syrup cool to 90°C/194°F.

Place one of the round wire racks in the bottom of the pan and lay one of the *savarins* upside down on the rack. Place the other rack on top of the *savarin* and weight it with a weight which is just heavy enough to keep the *savarin* immersed in the syrup without crushing it.

Leave the *savarin* to soak in the syrup for 10 minutes, then

· EQUIPMENT ·

2 × 21 cm/8 in savarin moulds

1 baking sheet

2 round 24 cm/10 in wire racks

1 shallow pan or a preserving pan, 26 cm/10½ in diameter

1 deep tray or a roasting pan with a rack

1 saucepan

Piping bag with a 1 cm/½ in decorative nozzle (optional)

Sugar thermometer

remove the weight and the top rack and dislodge the *savarin* by sliding a fish slice under the supporting rack. Place on the rack of the deep tray or roasting pan.

The *savarin* is now two-thirds soaked in syrup.

Reheat the syrup until it reaches 90°C/194°F and soak the second *savarin* in the same way as the first. Place on the rack with the first *savarin*.

Reheat the syrup to 90°C/194°F and spoon or ladle it over the *savarins* for 10 minutes, so that they absorb as much syrup as possible and are thoroughly soaked and very moist in the centre. You will have about 1 lt/1¾ pt of syrup left over.

Glazing and decorating the savarins: Put the apricot jam in a saucepan and boil for 2 minutes.

Sprinkle the two *savarins* with equal quantities of rum, leave for 1 minute, then repeat the operation.

Brush the top of the *savarins* with the hot jam and decorate the tops with little flower shapes made from the almonds and halved cherries.

The fruit: Peel, stone and wash it as necessary and cut into slices, rounds or quarters.

· TO SERVE ·

Carefully place the prepared *savarins* on 2 round shallow dishes and fill the centre of the crowns with the fruit.

If you like, pipe a pretty border of *crème Chantilly* between the fruit and the *savarin* and serve the rest of the cream in a sauceboat.

· NOTES ·

Once the *savarins* are cooked, they can be kept unsoaked for about 3 days, which means that you can prepare well in advance for a large party.

The same recipe can be used to make small rum babas. Use individual moulds and soak and cook them for a shorter time — the exact time will depend on the size of the babas. The given quantity of dough makes about 32-36 babas.

Although the small babas are perfect to serve to a number of friends, the large *savarins* really come into their own when they are artistically displayed on a buffet at a large reception.

LA TRUFFE:
SAUCE ANGLAISE AU CAFE
(Chocolate truffle cake with coffee custard)

· INGREDIENTS ·

1 x 20 cm/8 in Genoise
sponge (see page 60),
made with 160 g/5½ oz
flour and 80 g/3½ oz
cocoa powder

50 ml/2 fl oz Sorbet
syrup (see page 168)

2 tbsp Cognac

475 g/17 oz bitter
couverture or plain
chocolate

475 ml/17 fl oz double
cream

10 g/1 tsp cocoa powder,
to decorate

500 ml/18 fl oz
coffee-flavoured *Crème
anglaise* (see page 70)

Serves 8

*Preparation time: 25
minutes*

We were given this quick and easy recipe by a colleague, Jean Masson, who prepared it at a seminar of the *Maîtres Pâtissiers de France* some 10 years ago. Since then, it has proved one of our most popular desserts.

· PREPARATION ·

The chocolate sponge base: Slice a 5 mm/¼ in thick circle off the top of the sponge and keep the rest in the fridge or freezer to use another time. Place the circle on the cake board and brush with a mixture of syrup and Cognac.

Set the flan ring around the sponge.

The truffle mixture: Roughly chop the *couverture* or chocolate and put in a bain-marie. Melt the chocolate gently, without letting it reach more than 35°C/95°F.

Put the cream in a bowl and whip until it forms a light ribbon. Pour half the melted chocolate into the cream and mix well with a whisk, but do not overwork the mixture. Add the remaining chocolate and beat very lightly until the mixture is homogenous, but stop before it separates. Pour the mixture into the flan ring, and with a palette knife push it outwards from the centre towards the edges, taking care not to leave any little gaps. Smooth the surface with the palette knife.

Place in the fridge for at least 30 minutes, until the truffle mixture has set.

· TO SERVE ·

To remove the flan ring, heat the outside of the ring over a gas flame for a few seconds, or dip the blade of a fine knife into boiling water and run it between the inside of the ring and the dessert, then rotate the circle slightly and lift it off.

Sprinkle the top with cocoa and serve.

Some *crème anglaise*, flavoured to taste with instant coffee, makes a superb accompaniment to this dessert. Serve it separately in a sauceboat.

· STORAGE ·

This truffle cake will keep well, still in the flan ring, for 2 days in the fridge, or 2 weeks in the freezer.

· EQUIPMENT ·

*1 flan ring, 22 cm/8½ in
diameter, 3.5 cm/1½ in deep*

*1 × 24 cm/10 in round cake
board*

1 bowl

Bain-marie

HOT SWEETS AND DESSERTS

*I*n winter, more than in any other season, one longs for a hot pudding. Special favourites at this bleak time of year include hot fruit fritters, plain or souffléd *crêpes* flavoured with vanilla, orange blossom water or Grand Marnier and *gratins* of fresh fruits.

Everyone is impressed by a soufflé, which testifies to a great deal of time and effort on the part of the hostess. Actually, the soufflé base (called *l'appareil*) can be prepared well in advance of the meal and kept at room temperature. Then, at the last moment, you need only beat the egg whites, fold them in to the *appareil*, pour the mixture into the soufflé dishes and cook at once.

CREPES DANIEL PINAUDIER

· INGREDIENTS ·

250 g/9 oz flour
30 g/1 oz sugar
Pinch of salt
4 eggs
650 ml/22 fl oz milk, boiled and cooled
200 ml/7 fl oz double cream
Flavouring of your choice
30 g/1 oz clarified butter

Serves 10
Preparation time: 10 minutes, plus at least 1 hour resting time
Cooking time: 1-2 minutes for each crêpe

· PREPARATION ·

Combine the flour, sugar and salt in a bowl and add the eggs, 2 at a time, mixing well with a spatula. Stir in one-third of the milk until you have a smooth, homogenous batter. Pour in the cream and the rest of the milk and leave to rest in a cool place for at least an hour before cooking the *crêpes*.

· TO COOK ·

Stir the batter and add your chosen flavouring.

Brush the frying pans or *crêpe* pan with clarified butter and heat them. Ladle in a little batter and cook for 1 or 2 minutes on each side, turning the *crêpe* with a palette knife or tossing it.

· TO SERVE ·

Roll or fold the *crêpes* into half or four and eat them as soon as they are cooked. Choose your own favourite flavouring — vanilla, orange blossom water, lemon zest or Grand Marnier, for example, or serve the *crêpes* plain; they are delicious sprinkled with sugar or served with jam or apple jelly (see page 70).

· EQUIPMENT ·

1 bowl
1 or 2 round frying pans, 30 cm/12 in diameter or a crêpe pan, 12 cm/5 in diameter

CHRISTMAS PUDDING

· INGREDIENTS ·

550 g/18 oz raisins
375 g/13 oz sultanas
375 g/13 oz currants
200 g/7 oz chopped almonds
400 g/14 oz finely grated suet
Zest and juice of 1 orange
Zest and juice of 1 lemon
1 apple, unpeeled, cored and grated
1 carrot, peeled and grated
250 g/9 oz fresh white breadcrumbs *or brioche* crumbs
250 g/9 oz flour
400 g/14 oz raw Demerara sugar
6 eggs
½ tsp salt
½ tsp ground cinnamon
1 heaped tsp ground mixed spice
110 g/4 oz candied mixed peel, finely chopped
110 g/4 oz glacé cherries, finely diced
1 glass brandy, plus 160 ml/5 fl oz for after the puddings are cooked
1 bottle (340 ml/12 fl oz) of Guinness or stout
150 g/5 oz clarified butter, for greasing
BRANDY SAUCE (for 10 people):
500 ml/18 fl oz double cream
70 g/2½ oz sugar
8 g/1 tsp potato flour, mixed with 1 tbsp milk
70 ml/3 fl oz brandy

Christmas pudding is divine, particularly this recipe, which Albert was given more than 30 years ago by Mrs. Bradbrook, a superb English cook. At the beginning of every year, we make our Christmas pudding for family and friends to enjoy the following Christmas; they also make a wonderful present. And we keep a few from previous years so that we can enjoy the indescribably glorious taste of a 3- or 4-year-old Christmas pudding.

· PREPARATION ·

Combine all the ingredients in a mixing bowl, except 160 ml/5 fl oz brandy and the clarified butter. Mix well.

Press a piece of greaseproof paper firmly over the mixture and place in the fridge for 48 hours.

Moulding the puddings: Preheat the oven to 150°C/300°F/gas 2.

Stir the pudding mix once more with a spatula, then divide the mixture between the 4 basins. Press down firmly with a spoon so that the puddings are very compact. Wipe the inside rim and the outsides of the basins with a damp cloth.

Cut out four 18 cm/7 in circles of greaseproof paper and brush with a little clarified butter. Place the circles over the puddings and press down firmly so that the paper sticks and makes a steamproof seal.

· TO COOK ·

Lay a circle of slightly dampened muslin over each basin, stretch tautly and tie the muslin tightly with string under the rim.

Place the puddings in a roasting pan lined with greaseproof paper and pour in enough boiling water to come halfway up the sides of the basins. Cover the pan with foil and cut a hole about 5 cm/2 in wide in the centre, making sure that it is not immediately above a pudding.

Cook in the preheated oven for 8 hours, checking the water level every 2 hours; it should always come halfway up the sides of the basins. Top up with boiling water when necessary.

· TO COOL ·

Take the puddings out of the roasting pan and put in a cool place for 24 hours.

· STORAGE ·

Remove the butter muslin, wash it and leave to dry. Leave the

· EQUIPMENT ·

1 large mixing bowl
4 × 850 ml/1½ pt china pudding basins, which must be scrupulously clean
Greaseproof paper
4 circles of butter muslin, 28 cm/11 in diameter
Kitchen string
1 roasting pan, at least 8 cm/3¼ in deep
Aluminium foil
1 saucepan
1 pressure cooker or steamer

Continued on page 146

Christmas pudding

Makes 4 puddings, each serving 10

Preparation time: 2 hours, to be done 1-5 years in advance

Cooking time: 8 hours, plus 2½ hours heating

greaseproof paper in place. Carefully clean the inside rims and outsides of the basins.

Lift up one edge of the greaseproof paper and sprinkle each pudding with one-quarter of the brandy, then replace the paper to make an airtight seal.

Stretch the washed muslin over the basins and tie tightly with string. Brush with clarified butter to make them more or less watertight. Keep in the fridge until next Christmas, or even longer. . .

· THE BRANDY SAUCE ·

Put the cream and sugar in a saucepan, bring to the boil, then lower the heat and reduce gently by a quarter. Stir in the potato flour and boil for 1 minute. Add the brandy.

Keep the sauce hot without letting it boil.

· TO HEAT THE PUDDING ·

Place the pudding in a pressure cooker without the valve, or in a steamer and steam for 2½ hours.

· TO SERVE ·

Remove the cloth and greaseproof paper and unmould the pudding into a shallow dish. Decorate the top with a sprig of holly and bring the pudding to the table. If you like, flame with a little warmed brandy before serving. Serve the brandy sauce separately in a sauceboat, or serve the pudding with brandy butter made with creamed, softened butter, sifted icing sugar and brandy to taste.

FEUILLETES TIEDES AUX RAISINS, SABAYON AU KIRSCH

(Warm feuilletés with grapes and Kirsch-flavoured sabayon)

· PREPARATION ·

Preheat the oven to 220°C/425°F/gas 8.

The grapes: Peel them and scoop out the pips with a small spoon, leaving the grapes whole and taking care not to spoil the shape. Place in a bowl and sprinkle over a little Kirsch. Set aside.

The feuilletés: On a lightly floured surface, roll out the pastry to a thickness of about 5 mm/¼ in. Using the larger pastry cutter, cut out 4 circles and place on a baking sheet lightly brushed with cold water. Leave to rest in the fridge for at least 30 minutes before baking. Glaze the tops of the pastry circles

· INGREDIENTS ·

400 g/14 oz white grapes

150 ml/5 fl oz Kirsch

Pinch of flour

350 g/12 oz Puff pastry
(see pages 42-3)

Eggwash, made with
1 tbsp milk and 1 egg
yolk

40 g/1½ oz icing sugar

120 g/4 oz sugar

100 ml/4 fl oz water

6 egg yolks

4 small sprigs of mint

Serves 4

Preparation time: 40
minutes

Cooking time: 12 minutes

with eggwash, then press down the smaller pastry cutter onto the pastry to mark out a lid. Use the point of a knife to mark criss-crosses on the lids.

· TO COOK ·

Bake the *feuilletés* in the preheated oven for 10 minutes, then remove from the oven, sprinkle with icing sugar and return to the oven for a further 2 minutes to give them a beautiful glaze. Transfer to a wire rack.

Run the point of a knife round the marked edge of the lids and lift off. Keep the baked pastry cases and lids warm.

The sabayon: Combine the sugar and water in a small saucepan, bring to the boil, then leave to cool.

Add the egg yolks and 100 ml/4 fl oz Kirsch, set over low heat and whisk continuously until you have a smooth, rich mousse. Increase the heat and continue to whisk until the sauce has a ribbon consistency. Stir in the remaining Kirsch and take the pan off the heat.

· TO SERVE ·

Gently warm the grapes. Place the *feuilletés* on individual plates and put a spoonful of *sabayon* in each. Drain the grapes well, then divide most of them between the *feuilletés*, reserving a few for the garnish. Fill the *feuilletés* with another spoonful of *sabayon* and pour the rest in a ribbon around each *feuilleté*. Prop the lids at an angle against the *feuilletés*, with one side on the edge of the plate. Garnish the *sabayon* with the reserved grapes and a sprig of mint.

· NOTES ·

To keep the pastry crisp and light, do not fill the *feuilletés* until just before serving. Make the *sabayon* at the last moment and use it immediately, or the lightness will be spoilt.

· EQUIPMENT ·

1 bowl

1 plain round pastry cutter,
9 cm/3½ in diameter

1 plain round pastry cutter,
7 cm/2¼ in diameter

1 baking sheet

Wooden or marble pastry
board

1 small saucepan

PICTURE PAGE 149

ABOVE *Les gaufres* (page 166)
TOP RIGHT *Pêche rôtie au caramel noisetine*
(page 162)
BOTTOM RIGHT *Feuilleté tiède aux raisins, sabayon au
Kirsch* (page 146)

SOUFFLES CHAUDS AUX FRAMBOISES
(Hot raspberry soufflés)

· INGREDIENTS ·

500 ml/18 fl oz milk
520 g/1 lb 2 oz sugar
6 egg yolks
50 g/2 oz flour
30 g/1 oz butter
1.1 kg/2 lb 6 oz raspberries, fresh or frozen
2 tbsp *framboise eau de vie*
1 lt/1¾ pt water
Juice of 1 lemon
60 g/2 oz butter, melted
10 egg whites
12 vanilla-flavoured Macaroons (see page 204)
50 g/2 oz icing sugar, to serve

Serves 6

Preparation time: 25 minutes

Cooking time: 8-10 minutes

· PREPARATION ·

Preheat the oven to 220°C/425°F/gas 8.

The crème pâtissière: Combine the milk and 80 g/3 oz sugar in a saucepan and bring to the boil. Put the egg yolks in a bowl, add 45 g/1½ oz sugar and beat immediately with a wire whisk for several minutes. Stir in the flour and beat until the mixture is very smooth. Pour on the boiling milk, whisking continuously.

Pour the custard back into the pan, set over high heat and boil for about 3 minutes, stirring continuously. Flake 30 g/1 oz butter and dot it over the surface to prevent a skin from forming. Keep in a warm place.

The raspberries: Pick out 18 nice berries and put them in a bowl with 1 tbsp *framboise*. Cover with a saucer and set aside.

Put the rest of the raspberries in a saucepan with 300 g/10 oz sugar and 1 lt/1¾ pt water. Set over high heat, bring to the boil and cook for 5 minutes. Purée in the blender or food processor, then rub through a sieve.

Return two-thirds of the purée to the pan, set over high heat and cook gently until it has the consistency of jam. Set aside. Add the lemon juice to the remaining *framboise* and purée to make a *coulis* and keep warm in a bain-marie.

Assembling the soufflés: Brush the insides of the dishes with the melted butter. Put 70 g/2½ oz sugar into one dish and rotate the dish so that the inside is well coated with sugar. Tip the excess sugar into the next dish and repeat until all the dishes are coated with sugar. Fold the raspberry 'jam' into the custard and pour the mixture into a wide-mouthed bowl.

Beat the egg whites until slightly foamy, then add 25 g/1 oz sugar and beat until soft peaks form. Using a wire whisk, quickly mix one-third of the egg whites into the custard, then, with a spatula, gently fold in the rest. Half-fill the prepared dishes with the mixture, then put in 3 of the reserved raspberries and 2 lightly crushed macaroons. Fill up the dishes with soufflé mixture, smooth the surface with a palette knife and push the mixture away from the edge of the dishes with the point of a knife.

· TO COOK ·

Cook in the preheated oven for 8-10 minutes. Dust the soufflés with icing sugar and serve at once. Serve the warm raspberry *coulis* separately in a sauceboat.

· EQUIPMENT ·

2 saucepans
Blender or food processor
1 fine sieve
6 small soufflé dishes, 10 cm/4 in diameter, 6 cm/2¼ in deep
Electric mixer or a bowl and whisk

PICTURE PAGE 152

SOUFFLES TIEDES AUX POIRES, SAUCE CHOCOLAT
(Warm pear soufflés with chocolate sauce)

· INGREDIENTS ·

450 g/1 lb pears in syrup, drained weight

150 g/5 oz sugar, plus a pinch for the egg whites

10 g/4 tsp cornflour

30 ml/1 fl oz pear eau de vie

100 g/3½ oz butter, melted

6 egg whites

60 g/2 oz *Nougatine* (see page 233), chopped

300 ml/11 fl oz Chocolate sauce (see page 67)

6 small sprigs of mint

Serves 6

Preparation time: 25 minutes

Cooking time: 3 minutes

· PREPARATION ·

Preheat the oven to 220°C/425°F/gas 8.

The soufflé mixture: Purée 350 g/12 oz well-drained pears in the food processor and put in a saucepan. Cook over low heat for about 20 minutes, stirring frequently with a spatula. Keep warm.

In the sugar pan or saucepan, combine 100 g/3½ oz sugar with 50 ml/2 fl oz water and cook gently until the sugar dissolves completely. Wash down the inside of the pan with a brush dipped in cold water each time, and insert the sugar thermometer.

When the temperature reaches 160°C/320°F, immediately pour the cooked sugar onto the puréed pears, stirring with a spatula.

Mix together the cornflour and pear *eau de vie*, pour into the mixture and boil for 2 minutes. Pour the mixture into a bowl, cover with a plate and keep at room temperature.

The pears: Cut out of the remaining pears 6 ovals, 2 cm/¾ in long and 5 mm/¼ in thick, and slice each one into a fan shape. Dice the remaining pears and set aside.

Assembling the soufflés: Generously brush the insides of the ramekins with melted butter. Put the remaining sugar into one ramekin and rotate the dish so that it is well coated with sugar. Tip the excess sugar into the next ramekin and repeat until all the ramekins are coated with sugar.

Whisk the egg whites in the mixer, add a pinch of sugar and beat until well risen. Mix one-third into the pear purée, using a wire whisk, and mix until completely incorporated. Carefully fold in the rest of the whites with a spatula.

Use the spatula to half-fill the ramekins, then pile in the *nougatine* like little nests. Fill the ramekins with the mixture, then smooth the edges with a palette knife and push the mixture away from the edge with the point of a knife.

· TO COOK ·

Preheat the baking sheet for 5 minutes, then arrange the soufflés on the sheet and cook for 3 minutes.

· TO SERVE ·

Carefully unmould the soufflés onto warmed plates and quickly pour a ribbon of chocolate sauce around the edge.

Arrange the diced pears on the chocolate sauce and garnish

· EQUIPMENT ·

Food processor or blender

Electric mixer

1 saucepan

1 sugar pan or saucepan

Sugar thermometer

1 bowl

6 small ovenproof ramekins, 7 cm/2¾ in at the top, 5 cm/2 in at the base, 6 cm/2¼ deep

1 baking sheet

PICTURE PAGE 153

Continued on page 154

ABOVE *Soufflé chaud aux framboises (page 150)*
TOP RIGHT *Soufflé tiède aux poires, sauce chocolat (page 151)*
BOTTOM RIGHT *Soufflé tiède aux pêches (page 158)*

each soufflé with a pear fan and a mint sprig.

If you prefer, use 3 larger china soufflé dishes (10 cm/4 in diameter, 6 cm/2¼ in deep) and do not unmould the soufflés. Cook for 6 minutes, then arrange the diced pears and fans on top of the soufflés and serve the chocolate sauce separately in a sauceboat.

Serve immediately; this is a very delicate and fragile soufflé, which cannot be kept waiting.

SOUFFLES CHAUDS AUX MIRABELLES
(Hot mirabelle plum soufflés)

· INGREDIENTS ·

400 ml/14 fl oz milk
110 g/4 oz sugar, plus a pinch for the egg whites
50 g/2 oz flour
10 egg yolks
8 egg whites
550 g/1 lb 4 oz mirabelles in syrup, drained and syrup reserved
25 g/1 oz butter
100 ml/3½ fl oz mirabelle *eau de vie*
For the soufflé dishes:
30 g/1 oz melted butter
70 g/2½ oz sugar
Icing sugar, to serve

Serves 6
Preparation time: 30 minutes
Cooking time: 10 minutes

Mainly grown in Alsace, mirabelles are small yellow plums with a very distinctive flavour. They are relatively unfamiliar in this country, but are regarded as a delicacy by plum lovers.

· PREPARATION ·

Crème pâtissière: Combine the milk and two-thirds of the sugar in a saucepan and bring to the boil.

Place 6 egg yolks and the remaining sugar in a bowl and work together with a wooden spoon for several minutes. Add the flour and beat until the mixture is very smooth. Pour in the boiling milk, whisking continuously.

Return the mixture to the pan, set over high heat and boil, stirring continuously, for 3 minutes.

Pour the custard into a bowl. Flake a little butter over the surface or dust lightly with icing sugar to prevent a skin from forming. Leave at room temperature.

The mirabelles: Place the reserved syrup from the mirabelles in a pan and boil vigorously until reduced by half. Lower the heat, add 450 g/1 lb mirabelles and cook gently for 10 minutes, then rub through a sieve; the purée should have a softish consistency. If it seems too liquid, reduce over medium heat, whisking continuously. Set aside at room temperature. Place the remaining mirabelles in a bowl, pour over half the *eau de vie* and leave to macerate.

The soufflé dishes: Using a pastry brush, coat the insides of the dishes with melted butter.

Pour the sugar into one dish and rotate it so that the whole surface is well coated with sugar. Pour the excess sugar into the next dish and repeat the process with each dish.

Place a baking sheet in the oven and preheat to 220°C/425°F/gas 8.

· EQUIPMENT ·

2 saucepans
1 fine sieve
Electric mixer
1 baking sheet
6 individual soufflé dishes, 10 cm/4 in diameter, 6 cm/2¼ in deep

1

Gently fold one-third of the beaten egg white into the mirabelle mixture, then fold in the rest with a spatula.

2

Fill the dishes one-third full with the soufflé mixture.

1

3

Divide the halved mirabelles between the dishes. Fill with the remaining soufflé mixture and smooth the surface. Run the point of the knife around the edge of the mixture to help the soufflés rise.

2

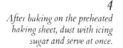

3

4

After baking on the preheated baking sheet, dust with icing sugar and serve at once.

4

The soufflé mixture: Whisk the mirabelle purée into the *crème pâtissière*, then the remaining egg yolks and *eau de vie*.

Beat the egg whites until frothy, add a pinch of sugar and beat until soft peaks form.

Using the whisk, quickly beat one-third of the egg whites into the mixture, then, with a spatula, gently fold in the rest of the egg whites.

Spoon the mixture into the soufflé dishes so that they are one-third full. Cut the alcohol-soaked mirabelles in half and divide them between the dishes.

Fill to the top with the remaining mixture and smooth over the surface with a palette knife. Run the point of a knife around the edge of the mixture; this will help the soufflés to rise. (You should always do this for any hot soufflé.)

· TO COOK ·

Arrange the soufflés on the preheated baking sheet and cook for 10 minutes.

Serve immediately, dusted with icing sugar..

· NOTES ·

There will be sufficient mixture left to make an extra soufflé, so you can be generous with your servings.

ABOVE *Crêpe soufflée à l'orange et au Grand Marnier (page 159)*
RIGHT *Pithiviers (page 160)*

SOUFFLES TIEDES AUX PECHES
(Warm peach soufflés)

· INGREDIENTS ·

1 passion fruit
Small selection of fruits (eg, peach, banana, kiwi), finely diced
2 tbsp Kirsch
360 g/12 oz peaches in syrup, drained weight, drained with syrup reserved
150 g/5 oz sugar, plus a pinch for the egg whites
7 g/1 tbsp cornflour
100 g/3½ oz butter, melted
6 egg whites
18 wild strawberries to garnish (optional)
6 small sprigs of mint

Serves 6

Preparation time: 35 minutes

Cooking time: 3 minutes

· PREPARATION ·

Preheat the oven to 220°C/425°F/gas 8.

The diced fruit: Open the passion fruit and scoop the flesh into a bowl. Add the diced fruit. Finely dice 50 g/2 oz peaches and add one-third to the bowl. Place the rest in a ramekin and pour over 1 tbsp Kirsch.

The soufflé mixture: Purée the remaining peaches in the food processor and put in a saucepan. Cook over low heat for 20 minutes, stirring occasionally with a spatula. Keep warm.

In the sugar pan or saucepan, combine 100 g/3½ oz sugar with 50 ml/2 fl oz water and cook gently until the sugar dissolves completely. Wash down the insides of the pan with a brush dipped in cold water each time, and insert the sugar thermometer. When it reaches 160°C/320°F, pour the cooked sugar onto the puréed peaches, stirring with a spatula.

Mix together the cornflour and the rest of the Kirsch, pour into the mixture and boil for 2 minutes. Transfer the mixture to a bowl, cover with a plate and keep at room temperature.

Assembling the soufflés: Generously brush the insides of the ramekins with melted butter. Put the remaining sugar into one ramekin and rotate so that the inside is well coated with sugar. Tip the excess sugar into the next ramekin and repeat until all the ramekins are coated with sugar.

Whisk the egg whites in the mixer, add a pinch of sugar and beat until well risen. Mix one-third into the peach purée, then carefully fold in the rest with a spatula. Half-fill the ramekins with the mixture, then spoon in the diced peaches in Kirsch. Fill the ramekins with soufflé mixture, smooth the edges with a palette knife and push the mixture away from the edge of the dishes with the point of a knife.

· TO COOK ·

Preheat the baking sheet for 5 minutes, then arrange the soufflés on the sheet and cook for 3 minutes.

· TO SERVE ·

Divide the diced fruit between 6 plates and spoon 1 tbsp reserved peach syrup over each. Carefully unmould the soufflés onto the plates. Decorate each soufflé with 3 wild strawberries and a sprig of mint and serve at once.

If you prefer, use 3 larger china soufflé dishes (10 cm/4 in diameter, 6 cm/2¼ in deep) and do not unmould the soufflés. Cook for 6 minutes, then arrange the diced fruits on top of the soufflés and omit the syrup.

· EQUIPMENT ·

Food processor or blender
1 saucepan
1 sugar pan or saucepan
Sugar thermometer
2 bowls
6 small ovenproof ramekins, 7 cm/2¼ in at the top, 5 cm/2 in at the base, 6 cm/2¼ in deep
Electric mixer
1 baking sheet

PICTURE PAGE 153

CREPES SOUFFLEES A L'ORANGE ET GRAND MARNIER

(Souffléd crêpes with oranges and Grand Marnier)

· INGREDIENTS ·

4 oranges

140 g/5 oz *Crème pâtissière* (see page 61)

4 egg whites

Pinch of sugar

50 ml/2 fl oz Grand Marnier

4 *Crêpes Daniel Pinaudier* (see page 143), 12-14 cm/4-6 in diameter, cooked until barely coloured

20 g/³⁄₄ oz icing sugar

Serves 4

Preparation time: 30 minutes

Cooking time: 2½ minutes

These souffléd, filled crêpes make a most delicious, light, winter dessert.

· PREPARATION ·

Preheat the oven to 220°C/425°F/gas 8.

The oranges: With a flexible knife, peel 2 oranges, removing all the pith and membranes, and cut into segments. Set aside.

Squeeze the membranes into a saucepan to extract all the juice, and add the juice of the 2 remaining oranges.

Set over low heat and reduce the juice by half, then strain into a bowl and keep at room temperature.

The soufflé mixture: Put the *crème pâtissière* in a bowl and heat gently in a bain-marie.

Beat the egg whites with a pinch of sugar until soft peaks form. Take the *crème pâtissière* off the heat, whisk in the Grand Marnier and beat for a few seconds, then add one-third of the egg whites. Mix well, then carefully fold in the rest with a spatula.

Filling the crêpes: Lay them flat on the baking sheet and put a spoonful of soufflé mixture in the middle of each one. Put 2 orange segments on the mixture and gently fold the *crêpes* in half, without applying any pressure. Pipe in the rest of the mixture, piping a pretty border at the opening of each *crêpe*. Make sure that they are all well filled.

If you prefer, fold the *crêpes* into 4 before filling, then pipe the mixture into the cavities, finishing with an attractive border.

· TO COOK ·

Preheat the grill to high.

As soon as the *crêpes* are filled, cook in the preheated oven for 2½ minutes. Immediately sprinkle them generously with icing sugar and place under the hot grill for about 30 seconds, so that the sugar melts and becomes partly caramelized.

· TO SERVE ·

Use a palette knife to slide each *crêpe* onto a plate. Pour some of the reduced orange juice around each one and arrange 5 or 6 orange segments on the juice. If you like, arrange a few strands of candied orange zest on the orange segments (see recipe for lime zests in *Gratin de fruits de saison*, page 163). Serve at once.

· EQUIPMENT ·

1 saucepan

1 bowl

Electric mixer

1 non-stick baking sheet or a lightly greased baking sheet

Bain-marie

Piping bag with a decorative 1 cm/½ in nozzle

Conical strainer

PICTURE PAGE 156

PITHIVIERS

· **PREPARATION** ·

The pastry: Cut the pastry into 2 parts, one weighing 350 g/ 12 oz and the other 250 g/9 oz.

First make the base: on a lightly floured surface, roll out the smaller piece of dough, turning it frequently by one-quarter turn until you have a circle about 28 cm/11 in diameter and 2 mm/¹⁄₁₆ in thick. Roll it loosely onto the rolling pin, then

1

1
Spoon the filling into the centre of the pastry base and brush the edges with eggwash.

2

2
Unroll the top over the base and press the edges together.

3

3
After chilling, mark the pattern and cut the overhanging edge into a scallop shape.

4

4
Mark curved 'sunray' lines from the centre to the edge of the cake.

5

5
Glazed and marked ready for baking.

6

6
Bake, then sprinkle with icing sugar and bake again.

· INGREDIENTS ·

600 g/1 lb 5 oz Puff
pastry (see pages 42-3)

Pinch of flour

300 g/10 oz Almond
cream (see page 65)

60 g/2 oz *Crème
pâtissière* (see page 61)
(optional)

1 tbsp white rum
(optional)

1 egg yolk, lightly
beaten with 1 tbsp milk

30 g/1 oz icing sugar

Serves 8

*Preparation time: 15
minutes, plus 30 minutes
resting time*

Cooking time: 40 minutes

unroll onto a baking sheet lightly brushed with cold water.

Next make the top: roll out the larger piece of dough in exactly the same way and to a circle of the same diameter; it should be about 3 mm/⅛ in thick.

To assemble: Mix together the almond cream and the *crème pâtissière* and stir in the rum if you are using it. (It is not essential to add *crème pâtissière* to the almond cream for the filling, but it makes it beautifully moist.) Spoon the mixture into the centre of the pastry base, then spread it with a palette knife to within 3-4 cm/1½ in of the edge. Glaze the exposed edge with eggwash.

Place the second circle on top and press the edges of the 2 circles firmly together so that they are well sealed.

Chill in the fridge for 30 minutes.

Marking out the pattern: Press down a *Pithiviers* marker, or a flan ring or shallow plate 24 cm/9½ in diameter on top of the *Pithiviers*. With a small sharp knife, cut the overhanging dough into a scallop-shaped border. Remove the marker.

Glaze with eggwash, then, with the point of a knife, mark out faint lines from the centre of the cake to the edge, like sunrays, in the shape of a rosette. Mark the scalloped edges with diagonal lines.

· TO COOK ·

Preheat the oven to 240°C/475°F/gas 10. Bake the *Pithiviers* for 10 minutes, then lower the oven temperature to 200°C/400°F/gas 7 and cook for a further 25 minutes.

Increase the oven temperature to 220°C/425°F/gas 8. Sprinkle the *Pithiviers* with the icing sugar and bake for a final 5 minutes to give the cake a beautiful glaze.

· TO SERVE ·

Serve the *Pithiviers* warm with no further adornment; it will be wonderful. You can, if you wish, make a sauce to hand round separately in a sauceboat. Some apricot *coulis* or *crème anglaise* will enhance the flavour of the almond cream.

· STORAGE ·

To freeze the *Pithiviers*, assemble the cake, then freeze it unbaked, unglazed and unpatterned. To serve, remove from the freezer for 30 minutes, then glaze and mark the top. Bake while still frozen, allowing an extra 10 minutes cooking time.

It will keep in the freezer for up to a week.

· EQUIPMENT ·

Wooden or *marble pastry
board*

1 baking sheet

*1 Pithiviers marker or flan
ring, 24 cm/9½ in diameter*

PICTURE PAGE 157

PÊCHES RÔTIES AU CARAMEL NOISETTINE
(Peaches in nutty caramel)

· INGREDIENTS ·

50 g/2 oz sugar

75 g/3 oz butter

Juice of ½ lemon, strained

Few drops of grenadine (optional)

4 white *or* yellow peaches

60 g/2 oz flaked hazelnuts

20 g/¾ oz unsalted pistachios, skinned

Serves 4

Preparation time: 20 minutes

Cooking time: about 10 minutes

This delicious, ravishingly pretty dessert can be served either warm or hot and is very quick and easy to prepare. The combination of hazelnuts, pistachios, caramel and peaches is divine.

· PREPARATION ·

The caramel: Place the sugar and butter in a shallow pan set over low heat and cook, stirring continuously with a spatula, until the mixture becomes pale golden. Remove from the heat, stir in the lemon juice and a drop or two of grenadine, if you are using it, and keep in a warm place.

The peaches: Preheat the oven to 240°C/475°F/gas 10.

Bring a saucepan of water to the boil. Plunge in the peaches for a few seconds, then skin them. Arrange them in the roasting tin. Pour over the caramel and scatter over the hazelnuts. Cook in the hot oven for about 10 minutes. (If the peaches are very ripe, they will only need 7–8 minutes.)

Baste them with the caramel 3 or 4 times during cooking to glaze as they cook.

The pistachios: Split the nuts in half. Two minutes before the peaches are cooked, add half the pistachios to the caramel and hazelnut mixture and reserve the rest.

· TO SERVE ·

Place each peach in a shallow dish. Divide the caramel-nut mixture between the dishes, spooning it generously over the peaches. Stud the top of the peaches with the remaining pistachios.

· EQUIPMENT ·

1 shallow pan

1 saucepan

1 roasting tin, large enough to hold the 4 peaches

PICTURE PAGE 149

GRATIN DE FRUITS DE SAISON
(Gratin of fresh fruits)

· INGREDIENTS ·

6 different kinds of fruit,
total weight 600 g/1 lb
4 oz (eg, cherries,
peaches, wild
strawberries, pears,
oranges, lychees)

2 limes

450 ml/16 fl oz water

75 g/2½ oz sugar

4 egg yolks

2 tbsp Kirsch

1 tbsp double cream

Serves 4

Preparation time: 35
minutes

Cooking time: about 12
minutes

Any fruit can be used for this recipe, which is delicious at any time of year and is very simple to prepare.

· PREPARATION ·

Preheat the grill to high.

The limes: Wash them and peel off the zests with a vegetable peeler, taking care to leave behind any bitter white pith. With a large knife, slice the zests into fine, even *julienne* strips.

Blanch the zests in 300 ml/11 fl oz water and, as soon as the water boils, refresh in cold water and drain.

Return the zests to the pan, add 25 g/1 oz sugar and 150 ml/5 fl oz water and simmer very gently over low heat for 8–10 minutes, until almost all the syrup has evaporated; there should be about 1 teaspoon left. Drain the zests in a sieve or strainer, spreading them out well so that they do not stick together as they cool. Keep in a warm place.

The fruit: Peel, deseed, hull and finely slice the fruit as necessary and divide it between the *gratin* dishes. Keep in a warm place.

The sabayon: Combine the egg yolks, 2 tablespoons cold water, the remaining sugar and 1 tablespoon Kirsch in a saucepan.

Set over low heat and whisk until the mixture emulsifies and reaches a temperature of 65–70°C/150–160°F. Do not overheat, or the yolks will coagulate.

Take the pan off the heat and stir in the cream and the rest of the Kirsch. Immediately pour the *sabayon* over the fruit and place the dishes under the hot grill for 1 or 2 minutes, until golden brown.

· TO SERVE ·

Scatter the candied lime zests over the *gratins* and serve at once.

· EQUIPMENT ·

2 small saucepans

Fine sieve or strainer

4 small china or coppered
gratin dishes

FARANDOLE DE BEIGNETS AU COULIS DE FRUITS DE SAISON
(Medley of fresh fruit fritters)

· INGREDIENTS ·

7 g/1 tsp fresh yeast

75 ml/3 fl oz milk

130 g/4½ oz flour

60 ml/2 fl oz lager or light ale

1 egg yolk

Pinch of salt

2 tbsp groundnut oil

500 g/1 lb 1 oz fresh fruit (banana, apple, 2 slices pineapple, pear, cherries, carefully stoned, but with the stalks left on, strawberries, figs and apricots) – all should be ripe but firm

100 g/4 oz sugar

60 ml/2 fl oz Kirsch

Juice of 1 lemon

1½ egg whites

Oil for deep frying

300 ml/11 fl oz red Fruit *coulis* (see page 71) (optional)

Serves 6

Preparation time: 20 minutes

Cooking time: 2-3 minutes

Resting time: 2-3 hours

This lovely dish 'like Granny made' will delight everyone at the table. We give a finer but less velvety recipe for fritter batter in our book *New Classic Cuisine*.

· PREPARATION ·

The batter: With a whisk, beat together the yeast with half the milk. Put the flour in the mixing bowl, then, whisking continuously, beat in the rest of the milk, the lager, egg yolk and salt. Beat until the mixture is very smooth, with no lumps.

When the mixture is smooth, pour in the yeast mixture and the 2 tbsp oil. Mix well.

Cover the bowl with a plate or flan tin and leave to rest at room temperature for 2 or 3 hours.

The fruit: Peel the banana, apple, pear and pineapple, removing its central core. Cut all the fruit into slices or quarters, removing the seeds or stones where necessary.

Place the fruit in a bowl with 50 g/2 oz sugar, the Kirsch and lemon juice and leave to macerate for 30 minutes.

Preparing and cooking the fritters: Beat the egg whites until stiff, then fold in the remaining sugar. As soon as they are firm, fold them delicately into the batter. Place a few pieces of prepared fruit in the batter.

· TO COOK ·

Heat the deep frying oil to 180-200°C/356-392°F, until it gives off a slight haze.

Make sure the pieces of fruit are well coated in the batter, then, using a fork, transfer them to the deep fryer. Fry for 2—3 minutes, until pale golden. The fritters will rise to the surface when they are cooked. Use the prongs of a fork to turn them over carefully so that they are browned on both sides. Drain the fritters, then place them on absorbent paper or a cloth. Keep warm.

Fry the remaining fritters in the same way, in several batches.

· TO SERVE ·

Sprinkle the fritters generously with sugar and serve very hot, arranged on a large platter lined with frilly paper, or better still, a napkin. You may like to serve the fritters with fresh red fruit *coulis* or redcurrant *coulis* and let your guests help themselves.

· EQUIPMENT ·

Deep fat fryer

Electric mixer or *bowl and whisk*

Absorbent paper

1

Make the batter and set aside at room temperature for 2-3 hours.

2

Meanwhile, prepare the fruit. Put a few pieces in the batter and coat well. Spear with a fork and lower into the preheated oil.

1

3

Deep fry for 2-3 minutes, until pale golden. The fritters will rise to the surface when cooked. Turn with a fork to brown on both sides.

4

Drain the fritters on absorbent paper. Fry the remaining fritters in several batches. Sprinkle with sugar and serve very hot.

3

2

4

LES GAUFRES
(Waffles)

· INGREDIENTS ·

250 g/9 oz flour

25 g/1 oz sugar

Large pinch of salt

75 g/3 oz butter, melted
and cooled

3 eggs, separated

400 ml/14 fl oz milk

Flavouring of your
choice (eg orange
blossom, rum, Grand
Marnier, lemon zest)

TO GARNISH: (OPTIONAL)

500 g/1 lb 1 oz
strawberries

300 ml/11 fl oz *Crème
Chantilly* (see page 66),
whipped to soft peaks

*Makes 12 single waffles or 6
doubles, to serve 6*

*Preparation time: 10
minutes, plus 15 minutes
resting*

Cooking time: 3-4 minutes

Waffles remind us vividly of our childhood when, after a walk in the Bois de Vincennes, our mother would always take us to buy some at a waffle stall. This is a really 'grandmotherly' dessert, very simple and easy to prepare.

· PREPARATION ·

Place the flour in a bowl and make a well in the centre. Put in the sugar (reserving a pinch for the egg whites), salt, melted butter and the egg yolks. Gradually add the milk, beating all the time with a whisk until the mixture is very smooth.

Cover the bowl with a plate or clingfilm and leave at room temperature for at least 15 minutes.

· TO COOK ·

Plug in the electric waffle iron, or heat it over a flame if you have an old-fashioned model.

Beat the egg whites until stiff, add a pinch of sugar and beat well. Fold the beaten whites into the waffle mixture; do not overwork.

Lightly brush the inside of the waffle iron with butter. Ladle in just enough batter to cover the grid. Close the lid and cook for 3-4 minutes. (If you are using a non-electric model, turn it over after 2 minutes.) Cooking time will depend on whether you prefer your waffles dry and crunchy or soft and pale. Open the lid and check the progress of your waffles after 3 minutes.

Make the remaining waffles in the same way; it is not necessary to grease the grid again before cooking the other waffles.

Transfer the cooked waffles to a wire rack and serve as soon as possible.

· TO SERVE ·

Wrap the waffles in a napkin and serve on a plate, or simply pile them up on a large plate. Sprinkle over a little caster sugar, or serve with vanilla ice cream. When they are in season, serve your waffles with strawberries and *crème Chantilly* — what a feast! They are also delicious with quince or redcurrant jelly.

· EQUIPMENT ·

1 bowl

Electric mixer or *mixing
bowl and whisk*

Waffle iron

PICTURE PAGE 148

ICE CREAMS AND SORBETS

Of all desserts, these get everyone's vote. This is not a new phenomenon. According to gastronomic historians, it was the Chinese who first discovered the art of making iced sweets; the Italians followed suit in the seventeenth century and brought the vogue for ice cream across to France and the rest of Europe.

All ice creams and sorbets are sublime, whether they be based on milk, eggs, cream or fruit, flavoured with alcohol or spices, bitter, sweet or sugary, or absolutely plain. Nowadays, ice cream lovers do not have to rely on the professionals — they whip up their own confections as easily as they would a cocktail and churn them in a domestic ice cream maker. These are becoming increasingly simple to use and, technically speaking, more and more efficient and less and less expensive.

· TO MAKE SUCCESSFUL ICE CREAM ·

Churn ice cream only a short time before you eat it; it will have a softer, creamier texture and a more subtle flavour. Avoid keeping stocks of home-made ice cream in the freezer, for, once churned, it will rapidly lose its quality if stored for any length of time.

It is vitally important to be aware that pathogens can be supported by ice cream unless it is treated by either pasteurization or sterilization. Government regulations require that ice cream for commercial sale be treated in three specific ways. We suggest one of these for domestic use. To achieve pasteurization the mixture should be heated to a temperature of 79.4°C/175°F and kept at this temperature for 15 seconds. Note that custard-based ice creams should not be churned for at least twenty-four hours after having made the custard. Keep it in the fridge, stirring occasionally, so that the taste and texture mature and develop.

Churning during the freezing process introduces air into the mixture and produces a fine, silky, light-textured ice cream. Over-freezing, or freezing for too long, can adversely affect flavour and consistency, while insufficient freezing yields a thick, heavy ice cream, which is low in volume.

The recipes in this chapter are intended only for domestic and not for commercial use. For this reason, they contain no stabilizing or preserving ingredients or other additives, which do nothing for the flavour in any case.

SIROP A SORBET
(Sorbet or 30° Beaumé syrup)

· INGREDIENTS ·

750 g/1 lb 10 oz sugar

650 ml/22 fl oz water

90 g/3 oz glucose

Makes about 1.4 lt/2½ pt

Preparation time: 5 minutes

Cooking time: 20 minutes

This syrup is used for all sorbets and for soaking sponge biscuits and Genoise sponges.

· PREPARATION ·

Combine all the ingredients in a saucepan and bring to the boil, stirring occasionally with a wooden spatula. Boil for about 3 minutes, skimming the surface if necessary. If you have a saccharometer, the reading should be 30° Beaumé or 1.2624 on the density scale.

Pass the syrup through a conical strainer and leave until completely cold before using.

· STORAGE ·

The sorbet syrup will keep in the fridge for up to 2 weeks covered with clingfilm or in an airtight container.

· EQUIPMENT ·

1 saucepan

1 conical strainer

Beaumé scale saccharometer (optional)

SORBET AUX FIGUES ET PORTO
(Fig and port sorbet)

· INGREDIENTS ·

750 g/1 lb 8 oz very ripe fresh figs

100 g/4 oz sugar

250 ml/9 fl oz port

Juice of ½ lemon

12 mint leaves (optional)

Serves 6

Preparation time: 15 minutes

Cooking time: 5 minutes

Churning time: 10-20 minutes

This fig and port sorbet goes very well with an apricot sorbet and presents a delightful contrast of colour and flavour.

· PREPARATION ·

Poaching the figs: With a sharp knife, peel the figs, then cut them into 4 or 6, depending on their size.

Combine the sugar, port and figs in a saucepan and bring to the boil over high heat. As soon as the mixture bubbles, lower the heat and simmer gently for 5 minutes. Transfer to a bowl and leave at room temperature.

The mixture: When the figs are cold, place them in the blender together with their poaching liquid. Add the lemon juice and blend for 2 minutes to obtain a purée. Rub this through a sieve.

To churn: Place the mixture in the ice cream maker and churn until it is completely smooth.

· TO SERVE ·

Using an ice cream scoop or 2 soup spoons, form the sorbet into small ovals and serve in glass dishes or on shallow plates.

If you like, arrange a few mint leaves on the sorbet to enhance the flavour, or you can place a few thin slices of fig around the edge.

· EQUIPMENT ·

1 saucepan

Blender or food processor

Sieve

Ice cream maker

SORBET A LA TOMATE
(Tomato sorbet)

PICTURE PAGE 175

· INGREDIENTS ·

12 medium-sized
tomatoes

250 ml/9 fl oz Sorbet
syrup (see page 168)

500 ml/18 fl oz fresh *or*
canned tomato juice

1 drop of Tabasco

Salt and freshly ground
pepper

12 small sprigs of basil

12 cherry tomatoes, plus
100 ml/4 fl oz Sorbet
syrup (optional)

Juice of ½ lemon,
strained

Serves 4

*Preparation time: 10
minutes*

*Churning time: 10–20
minutes*

· EQUIPMENT ·

Ice cream maker

2 saucepans

2 bowls

1 ice cream scoop (optional)

This sorbet can be served as a starter or a dessert; taste it first to see which you prefer.

· PREPARATION ·

The tomatoes: Plunge the medium-sized tomatoes into boiling water for a few seconds, then into cold water. Skin them and cut a thin slice off the bases so that they stand firmly. Cut one-third off the top and discard.

Scoop out the seeds and cores and sprinkle the insides with salt and pepper. Place on a tray, upside down and keep in the fridge.

Bring 100 ml/4 fl oz syrup to the boil, plunge in the cherry tomatoes and immediately pour them into a bowl, together with the syrup. Keep in a cool place.

· CHURNING ·

In a bowl, mix the tomato juice with 250 ml/9 fl oz syrup, then add the Tabasco and season to taste with salt and pepper. Whisk well so that the mixture is very smooth.

Pour into the ice cream maker and churn for 10–20 minutes, depending on the machine. This sorbet should have a firmer texture than a fruit sorbet, but should still be velvety and smooth.

· TO SERVE ·

Fill the tomato shells with a spoonful of sorbet and decorate the tops with a sprig of fresh basil.

Put 3 tomatoes on each chilled serving plate. If you are using the cherry tomatoes, skin them just before serving and arrange 3 decoratively on each plate.

· NOTES ·

The cherry tomatoes are not essential, but they do look very pretty and add a deliciously sweet note to the sorbet.

EXOTIC FRUIT SORBETS

Presented in their shells: **1** *Prickly pear,*
2 *tamarillo or tree-tomato,* **3** *lime,* **4** *kumquat,*
5 *passion fruit,* **6** *rambutan,* **7** *pineapple, and*
8 *kiwi fruit (page 173).*

TIERCE DE SORBETS SUR SA FEUILLE DE MERINGUE
(Trio of sorbets on a meringue leaf)

· INGREDIENTS ·

1 quantity *Meringue française* (see page 57)

50 g/2 oz flaked almonds

3 types of sorbet of your choice (eg, champagne, (see page 176) strawberry, apricot)

16 bunches of redcurrants (optional)

½ quantity *Crème anglaise* (optional)

50 g/2 oz crystallized violets

16 sprigs of mint

30 g/1 oz butter, for greasing

Serves 16

Preparation time: 20 minutes

Cooking time: 1 hour 45 minutes

· PREPARATION ·

Preheat the oven to 100–120°C/200–225°F/gas ¼–½.

Cut out a template of the leaf-shaped diagram (right) and, using it as a model, very lightly draw 16 leaf shapes on a sheet of baking parchment or greased greaseproof paper. Pipe the prepared meringue around the outline of the leaves. Press 3 flaked almonds into the base of each stem.

Bake in the preheated oven for 1 hour 45 minutes, until the bottom of the leaves are as dry as the top. Leave to cool for about 45 minutes.

Slide the blade of a palette knife between the paper and the meringue leaves, keeping it very flat, and carefully transfer them to a wire rack.

· TO SERVE ·

Place a meringue leaf on each serving plate and fill the cavities in the leaves with a *quenelle* of each type of sorbet, shaping them with 2 spoons dipped in hot water between each operation. Fill the stem with a small bunch of redcurrants.

Coat the edges of the meringue with *crème anglaise* and decorate with crystallized violets. Arrange a sprig of mint in the centre of the 3 sorbets.

· NOTES ·

You cannot successfully make the meringue if you use a smaller quantity, which is why we suggest making 16 leaves. These will keep very well for several days in an airtight container.

You can use other fruits to decorate the stems, but they should be delicately flavoured, like wild strawberries, bilberries etc. Not everyone likes *crème anglaise*, so it can be omitted. We use it mainly to take the edge off the frozen sorbets.

· EQUIPMENT ·

1 baking sheet

Piping bag fitted with a 1 cm/½ in decorative nozzle

Baking parchment or greaseproof paper

Wire rack

PICTURE PAGE 174

SORBETS AUX FRUITS DE SAISON OU EXOTIQUES

(Sorbets made with seasonal or exotic fruits)

· INGREDIENTS ·

750 ml/25 fl oz fruit pulp

250-500 ml/9-18 fl oz
Sorbet syrup (see
page 168), depending on
the acidity of the fruit

Juice of 1 lemon,
depending on the fruits
(optional)

Serves 4

Preparation time: depends
on the fruits used

Churning time: 10-20
minutes

With these sorbets, you can present a veritable palette of rainbow colours. The sorbets can be made with practically any kind of fruit, and may be served with fresh sliced fruit, either presented in the dish or served separately.

· PREPARATION ·

The fruits: Depending on which fruits you choose, peel or deseed them, taking care not to spoil the shell or skin, which you will need for serving.

Press or purée the pulp and rub through a sieve or pass through a conical strainer into a bowl. Add as much syrup as you need — the precise quantity will depend on the acidity of the fruit. If possible, measure the density of the mixture, which should be 16° Beaumé. If you have no saccharometer, taste to see whether the mixture is sufficiently sweetened.

If the fruits lack flavour or are not ripe enough, add the lemon juice to enhance the flavour.

· CHURNING ·

Pour the mixture into the ice cream maker and churn for 10-20 minutes, depending on the machine. The correct texture depends on which fruits you use.

Serve the sorbet at once, or keep in the freezer.

· TO SERVE ·

If you have made several different kinds of sorbet, you could serve them on a meringue leaf (see *Tierce de sorbets*, page 172). Otherwise, serve the sorbets in the fruit shell or skins, which will heighten their flavour. Fill the shells by spooning in the sorbet or piping it in with a piping bag fitted with a ridged 1 cm/½ in nozzle. Both shells and piping bag should be well chilled in the fridge before use.

Each fruit sorbet is served in its own shell, which stands on a base of moulded ice decorated with flower petals. To make a moulded ice base, see page 241.

· EQUIPMENT ·

Ice cream maker

1 or more bowls

Blender or food processor

Beaumé scale saccharometer
(optional)

Fine sieve or conical strainer

PICTURE PAGES 170-1

Tierce de sorbets sur sa feuille de meringue
(page 172)
LEFT *Champagne*, CENTRE *Strawberry, and*
RIGHT *Mango*

TOP LEFT *Sorbet à la tomate (page 169)*
TOP RIGHT *Glace amandine, sauce chocolat*
(page 177)
BOTTOM LEFT *Granité de poires au vin de*
Brouilly (page 185)
BOTTOM RIGHT *Petits vacherins glacés aux pistils*
de safran (page 186)

SORBET AU CHAMPAGNE OU SAUTERNES
(Champagne or Sauternes sorbet)

· INGREDIENTS ·

½ egg white

300 ml/11 fl oz Sorbet syrup (see page 168)

750 ml /1 bottle dry champagne, preferably pink

Juice of ½ lemon

Serves 6

Preparation time: 10 minutes

Churning time: 10-20 minutes

· PREPARATION ·

Beat the egg white very lightly with a fork.

Put the syrup in a bowl, pour over the champagne and stir with a spatula. Add the lemon juice, then the egg white and mix well.

Churn the mixture in the ice cream maker; depending on the model, it will take between 10 and 20 minutes. The sorbet should be smooth but very light.

· TO SERVE ·

Serve the sorbet in well-chilled glass dishes and decorate with wild strawberries in season.

· NOTES ·

Use pink champagne if possible as, once churned, it has a lovely, more delicate colour than white champagne.

The sorbet should be eaten as soon as it is churned to preserve its smoothness and light texture. It may be served as a dessert or in the middle of a meal.

You can use 750 ml/1 bottle Sauternes instead of the champagne; use only 250 ml/9 fl oz syrup to a bottle of Sauternes. This sorbet makes a superb accompaniment to *foie gras*.

· EQUIPMENT ·

1 bowl

Ice cream maker

GLACE AU MIEL
(Honey ice cream)

· INGREDIENTS ·

100 ml/4 fl oz double cream

FOR THE CREME ANGLAISE:

6 egg yolks

75 g/2½ oz sugar

500 ml/18 fl oz milk

150 g/5 oz honey

· PREPARATION ·

The custard: Boil the milk with the honey, then make a *creme anglaise* following the method on page 70. Use only 75 g/2½ oz sugar, as the honey is very sweet.

· CHURNING ·

When the custard is cold, pass it through a conical strainer into the ice cream maker and churn for about 10 minutes, so that the ice cream is still fairly soft. Add the cream and churn for a further 20 minutes, depending on the machine, until the ice cream is firm.

Serve at once or keep in the freezer until needed — but only for a short time.

· EQUIPMENT ·

Ice cream maker

Conical strainer

· TO SERVE ·

Everyone will enjoy this honey ice cream. To serve it in a really original way, put a spoonful of ice cream into a chilled coffee cup and pour over some very hot coffee. Do this at the table so that your guests can immediately taste and enjoy this delectable contrast of the very hot and the very cold.

GLACE AMANDINE, SAUCE CHOCOLAT
(Hazelnut praline ice cream)

· INGREDIENTS ·

60 g/2 oz whole hazelnuts

60 g/2 oz sugar

1 tsp peanut oil

1 tsp instant coffee powder

½ quantity *Crème anglaise*, made without vanilla (see page 70)

50 ml/2 fl oz double cream

CHOCOLATE SAUCE

150 g/5 oz bitter chocolate *or* plain couverture

150 ml/6 fl oz double cream

25 g/1 oz butter

Serves 4
Preparation time: 15 minutes
Churning time: 10–20 minutes

· PREPARATION ·

Preheat the oven to 240°C/475°F/gas 10.

The hazelnuts: Spread the nuts on a baking tray and place in the preheated oven or under the grill for 5 minutes, until the skin blisters and the hazelnuts turn golden brown. Rub with a cloth to remove the skins and keep the nuts in a warm place.

Caramelizing the nuts: Put the sugar in a heavy-based pan and heat, without any added liquid, stirring continuously, until it has dissolved completely and is a lovely pale gold. Throw in the hazelnuts and cook for 1 minute. Pour the mixture onto a lightly oiled baking sheet and leave to cool at room temperature for about 20 minutes. When the praline is completely cold, crush with a rolling pin and keep at room temperature.

To churn: Combine the coffee powder and the cold *crème anglaise* in a bowl and whisk together. Stir in the double cream and pour the mixture into the ice cream maker.

Depending on the model, it will take between 10 and 20 minutes. When the ice cream is ready, stir in the cold praline. Serve immediately or keep in the freezer.

The chocolate sauce: Make the sauce according to the recipe on page 67, allowing about 50 ml/2 fl oz per person. Serve the hot sauce separately in a sauceboat.

· NOTES ·

Ice creams should be eaten as soon as they are churned; their texture and flavour will be much better. Never keep them in the freezer for more than a few hours.

· EQUIPMENT ·

1 baking sheet

1 sugar pan *or* saucepan

Ice cream maker

PICTURE PAGE 175

LEFT *Soufflé glacé aux fraises (page 184)*
ABOVE *Melon en surprise (page 181)*

GLACE AUX MARRONS
(Chestnut ice cream)

· INGREDIENTS ·

½ quantity *Crème anglaise*, made with only 100 g/4 oz sugar and without the vanilla (see page 70)

150 g/5 oz sweetened chestnut purée

50 ml/2 fl oz double cream

30 ml/2 tbsp rum

75 g/2½ oz chestnuts in syrup *or marrons glacés*, whole or in pieces

---

Serves 6

Preparation time: 15 minutes

Cooking time: about 8 minutes

Churning time: about 30 minutes

· PREPARATION ·

The chestnut custard: Make the *crème anglaise* by boiling the milk with the chestnut purée, then beat together the sugar and egg yolks. Use only 100 g/4 oz sugar, as the chestnut purée is very sweet. Make the custard following the method on page 70. Leave until almost cold, then stir in the rum.

· CHURNING ·

Pass the chestnut custard through a conical strainer directly into the ice cream maker and churn for about 10 minutes so that the ice cream is still fairly soft. Add the cream and churn for about 20 minutes, depending on the machine, until the ice cream is firm. Serve at once or keep in the freezer until needed — but only for a limited time.

· TO SERVE ·

Serve the ice cream in dishes, topped with *marrons glacés*, or for a special occasion serve this ice cream with hot chocolate sauce (page 67) and some small French meringues (page 57). Delicious!

· EQUIPMENT ·

Ice cream maker

Conical strainer

GLACE A LA CANNELLE
(Cinnamon ice cream)

· INGREDIENTS ·

½ quantity *Crème anglaise*, made without the vanilla (see page 70)

8 cinnamon sticks (about 40 g/1½ oz)

100 ml/4 fl oz double cream

Serves 6

Preparation time: 15 minutes

Cooking time: about 8 minutes

Churning time: about 30 minutes

This cinnamon ice cream is delicious served on its own or with a spoonful of chocolate sauce (see page 67). It also tastes divine served on a delicate, barely warm apple tart.

· PREPARATION ·

The custard: Make the *crème anglaise* according to the method on page 70, but substitute the cinnamon sticks for the vanilla. Leave them in the custard while it is cooling, until you churn the ice cream.

· CHURNING ·

Pass the custard through a conical strainer directly into the ice cream maker and churn for about 10 minutes so that the ice cream is still fairly soft. Add the cream and churn for about 20 minutes more, depending on the machine, until the ice cream is firm.

Serve at once or keep in the freezer for a short time only.

· EQUIPMENT ·

Ice cream maker

Conical strainer

MELON EN SURPRISE
(Melon surprise)

· INGREDIENTS ·

4 × 400 g/14 oz melons, preferably Charentais or Cavaillon

16 strawberries

24 wild strawberries

16 raspberries

500 ml/18 fl oz apricot sorbet (see Fruit sorbet recipe, page 173)

500 g/18 oz crushed ice, to serve, (optional)

4 small sprigs of mint

Serves 4

Preparation time: 20 minutes

· EQUIPMENT ·

1 bowl

1 melon baller

1 ice cream scoop (optional)

PICTURE PAGE 179

This is a particularly attractive way of serving melon. It makes a lovely summer dessert which will tempt you even if you are not hungry.

· PREPARATION ·

The melon: Using a very fine, long-bladed knife, cut off the top of the melon in a zigzag pattern, starting about two-thirds of the way up and cutting diagonally to the centre (see photo, page 179). Discard the melon seeds. Scoop out little balls of flesh from the inside of the 'lid' and place in a bowl.
The soft fruits: If absolutely necessary, wash them as carefully as possible, hull them and place with the melon balls.

· TO SERVE ·

Set the melon in a bowl or dish two-thirds filled with crushed ice. Arrange the fruits in the cavity and top with a scoop of apricot sorbet, using an ice cream scoop or 2 soup spoons to make a *quenelle* shape. Garnish the sorbet with a little sprig of mint and serve at once.

· NOTES ·

You can substitute other fruit sorbets for the apricot; try passion fruit or yellow peach.

LEFT, TOP TO BOTTOM *Petit toast au fromage blanc et aux câpres, Petit choux au fromage, Petit toast aux oeufs durs et cerfeuil, Croustade d'oeuf de caille, sauce cocktail.*
FAR RIGHT *Blini au caviar and* RIGHT *Blini au caviar (salmon roe).* TOP RIGHT *Petite bouchée au fenouil (pages 190–3)*

S O U F F L E G L A C E A U X F R A I S E S
(Iced strawberry soufflé)

PICTURE PAGE 178

· INGREDIENTS ·

1 kg/2 lb 2 oz
strawberries

730 ml/25 fl oz double
cream

420 g/15 oz sugar

3 egg whites

Juice of 1 small lemon

750 ml/26 fl oz red Fruit
coulis (see page 71)

Serves 8

Preparation time: 25
minutes

Freezing time: 5 hours

· EQUIPMENT ·

Blender or *food processor*

Electric mixer

Conical strainer

1 soufflé dish,
17 cm/7 in diameter,
10 cm/4 in deep

Greaseproof paper

· PREPARATION ·

To prepare the dish: Fold a sheet of greaseproof paper lengthways in three and tie it around the edge of the dish to form a collar, which should come 5 cm/2 in above the rim of the dish.

The strawberries: Rinse in cold water, hull and reserve 200 g/7 oz in the fridge. Purée the rest in the blender or food processor for a few moments, then pass through the strainer and keep the purée in the fridge.

The cream: Whip until it forms a ribbon, then place in the fridge.

The egg whites: Beat with 1 tbsp sugar until stiff peaks form.

Assembling the soufflé: With a balloon whisk, fold the sugar into the strawberry purée. Stir in the lemon juice and whipped cream, then carefully fold in the beaten egg whites.

Pour the mixture into the prepared dish; the mousse will come about 3 cm/1¼ in above the rim of the dish — hence the paper collar. Freeze the soufflé for 5 hours at a minimum temperature of –15°C/5°F.

· TO SERVE ·

Quarter the reserved strawberries and mix them into the fruit *coulis*. Carefully peel away the paper collar from the soufflé.

Spoon out 5 or 6 tbsp of mousse from the centre of the soufflé, which should be half frozen. Fill the cavity with the strawberry and *coulis* mixture, then replace a little of the mousse and smooth over the top with a palette knife.

Arrange the soufflé on a round dish decorated with a folded napkin or a doily and serve at once. You can enhance the appearance of this soufflé with whole, unhulled strawberries dipped in hard crack sugar; leave to cool, then arrange them around the edge, or top the soufflé with plain strawberries. Complement the flavour with some light, delicate orange *tuiles* (see page 194).

· NOTES ·

The soufflé can be made with other fruits, such as raspberries, peaches, pineapple or blackcurrants. You can also use the mixture to make individual soufflés; freezing time will be 1½ hours. Be careful not to freeze this soufflé for too long, or it will lose its soft consistency.

If you want to freeze the soufflé for longer, substitute a half quantity of *meringue italienne* (see page 58) for the egg whites in the recipe and reduce the amount of sugar accordingly.

GRANITE DE POIRES AU VIN DE BROUILLY

(Pears with granita of Brouilly)

· INGREDIENTS ·

4 William *or* Comice pears, *or* 8 small pears

1 bottle Brouilly *or* any good Beaujolais

150 g/5 oz sugar

¼ cinnamon stick

1 clove

Small strip dried orange zest

½ lemon

Fresh mint leaves, to garnish

Serves 4

Preparation time: 20 minutes

Cooking time: 15-25 minutes, depending on the size and ripeness of the pears

Freezing time: 1½ hours

One advantage of granita is that it is less sweet than a sorbet and can thus be served in the middle of a meal. Pear granita goes very well before a game dish.

· PREPARATION ·

The wine: Pour into a saucepan and add the sugar, cinnamon stick, clove and orange zest. Bring to the boil over high heat, stirring with a spatula, so that the sugar dissolves completely. As soon as the mixture boils, remove from the heat.

The pears: Peel them, leaving a band of peel around the stalks. Cut round the edges of the peel to make a pretty frilly 'collar'. Rub the pears with the cut lemon to prevent discolouration.

Place the pears in the saucepan with the Brouilly, cover with greaseproof paper and poach for 15-25 minutes; the pears should still be firm. The exact cooking time will depend on the type of pears and how ripe they are. They are ready when the point of a very fine knife inserted into the middle of the pears meets a slight resistance.

Transfer everything to a bowl and leave in a cool place.

When the pears are cold, discard the cinnamon, clove and orange zest. If the pears are large, cut off the tops, following the indented lines of the 'collars'. Using a teaspoon, carefully scoop out the cores without spoiling the shape of the fruit. (If the pears are small, leave them whole and drain them.)

Strain the poaching liquid through a conical strainer. It should be at 12-14° Beaumé. Pour into a shallow dish and freeze for 1½ hours at -15°C/5°F, stirring the mixture 2 or 3 times so that it becomes 'slushy'.

· TO SERVE ·

If the pears are large, place in the freezer for 10 minutes, then spoon the granita into the cavity. If they are small, arrange 2 on each well-chilled plate with a scoop of granita in front, decorated with fresh mint leaves.

· NOTES ·

You can churn the granita in an ice cream maker if you like, but do not do this more than a few minutes before serving or the grainy texture will be spoilt and you will lose the attractive granular effect.

· EQUIPMENT ·

1 saucepan

1 conical strainer

Greaseproof paper

Beaumé scale saccharometer

PICTURE PAGE 175

PETITS VACHERINS GLACES AUX PISTILS DE SAFRAN
(Meringue nests with saffron ice cream)

· INGREDIENTS ·

8 nectarines or small
peaches

1 bottle red wine
(preferably Burgundy)

250 g/9 oz sugar

1 quantity *Meringue
française* (see page 57)

60 g/2 oz cocoa butter or
clarified butter, for
greasing the moulds

50 g/2 oz crystallized
violets, finely chopped

½ quantity *Crème
anglaise*, made without
vanilla (see page 70)

Pinch of saffron threads

100 ml/4 fl oz double
cream

30 g/1 oz butter, for
greasing

Serves 16

Preparation time: 1 hour

Cooking time: 1 hour 45
minutes for the meringue,
5-10 minutes for the fruit

Churning time: 10-20
minutes

This lovely dessert with its heavenly colours and glorious flavour is simple to make, but is truly luxurious.

· PREPARATION ·

Preheat the oven to 100-120°C/200-225°F/gas ¼-½.

The nectarines or peaches: Make a small incision in the skins and plunge the fruit into boiling water for 1 minute, then refresh at once in cold water. Peel the fruit and immediately place in a saucepan with the wine and sugar. Cover with a circle of greaseproof paper the same size as the inside of the pan and cut a small hole in the centre. Poach very gently for about 5 minutes; cooking time will depend on the ripeness of the fruit. Transfer the fruit and poaching liquid to a bowl and cover with clingfilm.

Piping out the meringue nests: On a sheet of buttered greaseproof paper or baking parchment, pipe out 16 circles of meringue, 5 cm/2 in diameter, in a spiral, using the decorative nozzle. Pipe another coil on top of the outside edges to make little nests and finish with 5 small 'legs' (see photo, page 175). Set aside.

The meringue cups: Thoroughly wash and dry the moulds, then turn them upside down and grease the outsides with cocoa butter or clarified butter. Place in the fridge for 5 minutes so that the butter hardens.

Using the other piping bag fitted with the smaller nozzle, or a paper cone, pipe the meringue over the outside of the moulds in a pretty, lacy pattern. Seal any joins with an extra dot of meringue. Sprinkle the top of the lacy cups with the chopped violets.

Cooking the nests and cups: Cook in the very low oven for 45 minutes, then remove the cups and leave in a very dry place at room temperature. Cook the nests for a further hour, until the bottoms are as dry as the tops. Set aside with the meringue cups.

After about 45 minutes, when the nests are completely cold, carefully slide a palette knife between the meringue and the paper, keeping the blade very flat, and transfer the nests to a wire rack. Very carefully lift the lacy cups off the moulds and place on the rack. As the cups are extremely fragile, we suggest that you make more than you need (at least 20) in case of breakages.

The ice cream: Make the *crème anglaise*, then pass through a

· EQUIPMENT ·

1 saucepan

1 large bowl

Clingfilm

Baking parchment or
greaseproof paper

1 piping bag with a
decorative 1 cm/½ in nozzle

1 piping bag fitted with a
plain 2-3 mm/⅛ in nozzle
or a paper cone

20 small moulds with
slightly rounded bases,
4 cm/1½ in diameter approx.
(eg plain tartlet tins)

Wire rack

Ice cream maker

PICTURE PAGE 175

conical strainer and immediately add the saffron threads. Leave to cool, stirring from time to time.

Pour the cooled custard into an ice cream maker and churn for 10-20 minutes, depending on the machine. About 5-8 minutes before the end of churning, add the cream and continue to churn.

When the ice cream is half frozen lift off, with a spoon, any saffron threads that have stuck to the paddle and mix them into the ice cream.

The syrup: When the fruit has cooled completely, pour the poaching liquid into a saucepan and reduce over high heat for about 30 minutes, until syrupy. Leave the fruit in the bowl, covered with clingfilm. Set the reduced syrup to cool in a bed of crushed ice.

· TO SERVE ·

Place the meringue nests on individual plates and fill with a neat scoop of saffron-flavoured ice cream. Arrange the lacy cups over the ice cream. Be careful when you do this — they are very fragile. Slice each fruit into 10 segments and arrange 5 around each meringue nest. Pour a ribbon of syrup around each *vacherin* and serve at once.

· NOTES ·

Since you cannot successfully make a smaller quantity of meringue, we suggest that you make 16 nests and 20 cups; any remaining meringue shapes can be kept for several days in an airtight container.

If you make the custard for the ice cream the day before, or several hours before churning, it will taste even better.

CHAPTER
· 4 ·

CANAPES AND
PETITS FOURS

*E*legant little mouthfuls, *petits salés* herald the start and finish of a meal. As they are intended as a foretaste of what is to come, they should not be too substantial or filling. They must be light and delicate — a tasty accompaniment to a pre-dinner drink — and they should whet the appetite for the meal, without blunting it.

Like the *petits salés*, the petits fours served after a meal should not make you feel bloated, but should be so light and appealing that they are irresistible.

PETITS SALES

Since we also make the little savoury cases and bases for *petits salés* in our patisserie, we decided to devote a short chapter to this subject. They can be made from puff pastry, shortcrust, white bread or *brioche* dough; the subject is so wide and varied that it really deserves an entire book devoted to *amuse-gueules*.

There are certain basic rules for *petits salés:* they should always be well-seasoned; be generous with the spices. They must be light and not too rich or indigestible.

Above all, they must be crisp and fresh; garnish the bases at the last moment. Choose your flavours and fillings with care — *petits salés* are intended to awaken and prepare the tastebuds for what is to come. Do not offer too many or too much choice, or you will spoil your appetite for the meal.

We offer our guests a very small but carefully chosen selection of *amuse-gueules*; here are our recipes for some of them.

SAUCE MAYONNAISE
(Mayonnaise)

· INGREDIENTS ·

1 egg yolk
1 tsp Dijon mustard
Pinch of salt
Freshly ground white pepper
250 ml/9 fl oz vegetable oil
1 tsp white wine vinegar or juice of ¼ lemon
1 tsp double cream

Makes 250 ml/9 fl oz
Preparation time: 10 minutes

Mayonnaise is the starting point for all manner of delicious sauces and goes well with many of our canapés.

· PREPARATION ·

Combine the egg yolk, mustard, salt and pepper in a bowl and mix with a wooden spoon or wire whisk.

Gradually pour on the oil in a thin, steady stream, beating continuously. Stir in the vinegar or lemon and finally the cream.

· STORAGE ·

Do not refrigerate this sauce, but keep it at room temperature.

· EQUIPMENT ·

1 bowl

PETITS TOASTS
AUX OEUFS DURS ET CERFEUIL
(Canapés with hard-boiled eggs and chervil)

· INGREDIENTS ·

24 small rounds of white bread or *brioche* (see page 32), 4 cm/1½ in diameter, 1 cm/½ in thick

3 hard-boiled eggs (cooked for 10 minutes)

4 tbsp Mayonnaise (see page 189)

1 tbsp snipped chervil

Salt and freshly ground pepper

24 sprigs of chervil

Makes 24

Preparation time: 10 minutes

Cooking time: 10 minutes

These canapés appeal to both children and adults.

· PREPARATION ·

Preheat the oven to 220°C/425°F/gas 8.

Arrange the rounds of bread on the baking sheet and cook for 10 minutes, turning them over after 5 minutes. They should be very dry and light golden. Transfer to a wire rack and leave at room temperature.

· TO GARNISH ·

Shell the eggs, chop them with a knife and place in a bowl. Mix in the mayonnaise and snipped chervil and season to taste. Place a teaspoonful of the mixture on each toast round, moulding it into a neat dome. Garnish with a sprig of chervil.

· TO SERVE ·

Arrange the canapés on a silver plate or platter and serve as soon as they are garnished so that they remain crunchy.

· EQUIPMENT ·

1 baking sheet

1 bowl

Wire rack

PICTURE PAGE 182

PETITS CHOUX AU FROMAGE
(Little cheese-filled choux buns)

· INGREDIENTS ·

½ quantity *Choux* paste (see page 46)

20 g/¾ oz butter

20 g/¾ oz flour

250 ml/9 fl oz milk

1 egg yolk

2 tbsp double cream

45 g/1½ oz Gruyère, grated

Salt and freshly ground pepper

Eggwash, made with 1 egg yolk and 1 tbsp milk (optional)

· PREPARATION ·

The mornay sauce: Melt the butter in a saucepan and stir in the flour. Cook for 5 minutes, stirring continuously with a whisk. Pour in the milk and boil for 3 minutes, stirring all the time.

Take the pan off the heat and immediately stir in the egg yolk, then the cream and 35 g/1 oz Gruyère. Mix well and season to taste. Pour the sauce into a bowl and keep at room temperature.

The choux paste: Pipe out 24 small choux buns, about 3 cm/1¼ in diameter and bake according to the method on page 46. If you like, glaze the buns with eggwash and sprinkle over the remaining cheese before baking.

Filling the buns: With the fine point of a knife, make a small hole in the side of each bun. Pipe in the mornay sauce, which should be cool or cold, and leave the buns on a baking sheet or wire rack until ready to use.

· EQUIPMENT ·

1 saucepan

1 bowl

1 baking sheet

Piping bag with a plain 1 cm/½ in nozzle

PICTURE PAGE 182

Makes 24 choux buns

Preparation time: 25
minutes

Cooking time: 18 minutes

· TO SERVE ·

Preheat the oven to 140°C/275°F/gas 2.

Heat the filled buns for 5 minutes, until the sauce is hot. Arrange on a silver plate or dish and serve immediately.

· STORAGE ·

The given quantity of choux paste will make 48 buns; you can freeze the rest, which will save a lot of preparation on another occasion.

· NOTES ·

These choux canapés are particularly nice in winter.

PETITES BOUCHEES
AU FENOUIL
—*(Little bouchées with fennel)*—

· INGREDIENTS ·

360 g/12 oz Puff pastry
(see pages 42-3)

Pinch of flour

Eggwash, made with
1 egg yolk and
1 tbsp milk

450 g/1 lb fennel bulb
(trimmed weight 250 g/
9 oz)

30 g/1 oz butter

100 ml/4 fl oz double
cream

Salt and freshly ground
pepper

24 small sprigs of fennel
leaves

Makes 24

Preparation time: 35
minutes

Cooking time: 15 minutes

· PREPARATION ·

The bouchées: Preheat the oven to 240°C/475°F/gas 10.

On a lightly floured wooden or marble surface, roll out the pastry to a thickness of about 5 mm/¼ in.

Using the larger pastry cutter, cut out 24 circles and arrange them on a lightly dampened baking sheet. Place in the freezer for 5 minutes, or in the fridge for 10 minutes.

Cooking the bouchées: Glaze the pastry circles with eggwash and press the smaller pastry cutter onto the surface to mark out the lids. Bake in the preheated oven for 15 minutes.

Cut round the marked edge with a sharp knife and lift out the lids. Keep the *bouchées* at room temperature.

The fennel: Quarter, wash and peel the fennel bulb, then chop finely. Sweat in a saucepan with the butter until soft. Add the cream and reduce for 4 or 5 minutes. Season to taste.

· TO SERVE ·

Preheat the oven to 150°C/300°F/gas 3.

Use a teaspoon to fill the *bouchées* with the fennel mixture and warm for 5 minutes, until the fennel is heated through.

Arrange a sprig of fennel on top of each one and serve at once on a warmed silver plate or platter.

· NOTES ·

The fennel can be replaced by mushrooms or a mixture of diced red peppers and courgettes.

· EQUIPMENT ·

Wooden or marble pastry
board

1 plain round 4 cm/1½ in
pastry cutter

1 plain round 2 cm/¾ in
pastry cutter

1 saucepan

1 baking sheet

PICTURE PAGE 183

CROUSTADES D'OEUF DE CAILLE, SAUCE COCKTAIL

(Tartlets with quails' eggs and cocktail sauce)

· INGREDIENTS ·

200 g/7 oz Puff pastry trimmings (see page 42-3) or *Pâte brisée* (see page 31)

Pinch of flour

9 tbsp Mayonnaise (see page 189)

1 tbsp tomato ketchup

Dash of brandy

Salt and freshly ground pepper

24 quails' eggs

300 g/10 oz smoked salmon trimmings, finely diced

1 tbsp snipped chives

Makes 24

Preparation time: 40 minutes

Cooking time: 7 minutes

· PREPARATION ·

Preheat the oven to 220°C/425°F/gas 8.

On a lightly floured surface, roll out the pastry as thinly as possible. Arrange 24 tartlet tins on a baking sheet so that they are touching. Roll the pastry on to the rolling pin, then unroll it over the tins.

Using a small ball of floured pastry, gently press the pastry into the tins, then roll the rolling pin over the top to cut off the excess pastry. You will be left with about 80 g/2½ oz trimmings.

Place another tin on top of each mould and lay the wire rack over the top. Put the weight on the rack and chill in the fridge for 10 minutes before baking.

· TO COOK ·

Bake in the preheated oven for 7 minutes. As soon as the tartlets are cooked, remove the rack and weight and carefully neaten the edges of the pastry with a sharp knife. Take the tartlets out of the tins and transfer to a wire rack.

The cocktail sauce: In a bowl, mix together the mayonnaise, ketchup and brandy and season to taste.

The quails' eggs: Soft-boil them for about 2 minutes, refresh in cold water, then shell them, taking care not to break them.

Filling the tartlets: Mix 3 tablespoons cocktail sauce with the smoked salmon dice and divide this mixture between the tartlet cases. Top with an egg. Cover the eggs with the remaining sauce, allowing exactly 1 teaspoon per egg. Sprinkle over the snipped chives.

· TO SERVE ·

Serve on a plate or platter.

As these *croustades* are so fragile, they should be filled only a very short time before serving. To enjoy them at their best, they should be eaten as soon as they are ready.

· EQUIPMENT ·

Wooden or marble pastry board

48 tartlet tins, 4.5 cm/1¾ in diameter, 2.5 cm/1 in at the base, 1 cm/½ in deep

1 baking sheet

Wire rack

500 g/1 lb weight

1 bowl

PICTURE PAGE 182

BLINIS AU CAVIAR
(Blinis with caviar)

PICTURE PAGE 183

· INGREDIENTS ·
50 g/2 oz clarified butter

½ quantity Blinis batter
(see page 34)

300 g/10 oz caviar *or*
salmon roe

Makes 36 × 4 cm/1½ in
blinis

Preparation time: 5 minutes

Cooking time: 1 minute
each

· PREPARATION AND COOKING ·

Brush the pan with clarified butter and heat well. Put in 6 or 8 good teaspoons of batter, leaving plenty of space between them so that they do not stick together. Cook the blinis for 30 seconds on each side, turning them over with a palette knife. Drain on kitchen paper. Cook the remaining blinis in batches of 6 or 8 and serve immediately.

· TO SERVE ·

Arrange the blinis on warmed serving plates or silver dishes and garnish each one with a teaspoon of caviar or salmon roe. The blinis are succulent even served plain, but, needless to say, we prefer to be tempted by the caviar!

· EQUIPMENT ·
1 crêpe *or* blinis pan

PETITS TOASTS AU FROMAGE BLANC ET AUX CAPRES
(Little canapés with fromage blanc and capers)

· INGREDIENTS ·
24 small rounds of white
bread or *brioche* (see
page 32) 4 cm/1½ in
diameter, 1 cm/½ in
thick

80 g/3 oz *fromage blanc*

6 tbsp double cream

10 g/2 tbsp snipped
chives

Salt and freshly ground
pepper

½ tsp paprika

24 capers

Makes 24

Preparation time: 20
minutes

Cooking time: 10 minutes

These savoury little canapés are quick and easy to prepare and are always popular.

· PREPARATION ·

Preheat the oven to 220°C/425°F/gas 8.

Arrange the rounds of bread on a baking sheet and cook for 10 minutes, turning them over after 5 minutes. They should be very dry and light golden. Transfer to a wire rack and leave at room temperature.

· TO GARNISH ·

In a bowl, combine the *fromage blanc*, cream and chives. Season to taste. Pipe the mixture into an attractive dome on the toast rounds and sprinkle with paprika. Cut a cross in the top of the capers and open them out slightly to form a flower shape. Place 1 on each canapé.

· TO SERVE ·

Arrange the canapés on a silver plate or platter and serve as soon as they are garnished so that they remain crisp.

· EQUIPMENT ·
1 baking sheet

1 bowl

Wire rack

Piping bag with a plain
1 cm/½ in nozzle

PICTURE PAGE 182

P E T I T S   F O U R S

*P*etits fours (literally 'little ovens') are small biscuits, prettily decorated cakes and sweetmeats designed to be served with desserts or after-dinner coffee. Originally, they were cooked at low temperature in an oven which had cooled down after the *pâtissier* had baked his large cakes — hence their name.

Present a good selection of petits fours; they should be small and attractive, light, delicate, crisp and fresh, and designed to be swallowed in a single mouthful.

Petits fours come in many varieties, from tiny cakes iced with fondant to realistic-looking marzipan fruits and crisp little biscuits (delicious with ice cream), and many other delicacies which combine pastry and fruit. There are three distinct categories — *frais, fruits déguisés* and *secs* (fresh, glazed fruits and dried).

Petits fours frais include mini choux buns, éclairs, tartlets, *nougatine* bites etc. *Fruits déguisés* are nice, too: cherries in *eau-de-vie* dipped in fondant or hard crack sugar, dates and glacé pineapple chunks, or grilled hazelnuts, completely or partially wrapped in a thin pastel-tinted marzipan coating, then dipped into hard crack sugar to give them a brilliant sheen.

Needless to say, these creamy-textured choux buns or *sablés* filled with fresh or poached fruits, these crunchy sugary creations which stick to the teeth, must be accompanied by long, fruity drinks or cocktails, or perhaps just champagne.

The last category is the *petits fours secs* which mainly accompany ice cream and sorbets and especially the coffee. These are the petits fours we generally serve. Among these recipes are *tuiles, friands,* macaroons, *allumettes, palmiers,* pastry cigarettes etc — all are light and crumbly and none will detract from the taste of fine coffee. Indeed, they are the perfect complement to a good dinner.

T U I L E S   D E N T E L L E S
A   L ' O R A N G E
(Lacy orange tuiles)

· INGREDIENTS ·

100 g/4 oz nibbed almonds

100 g/4 oz icing sugar, sifted

30 g/1 oz flour

250 ml/9 fl oz orange juice

Grated zest of ½ orange

70 g/3 oz butter, melted, at room temperature

30 g/1 oz butter, for greasing

These delicious petits fours look like lace. But, pretty as they look, remember that they are terribly fragile. *Tuiles* make a delicious accompaniment to all sorbets and taste perfect with a cup of coffee.

· PREPARATION ·

The mixture: Combine the nibbed almonds, icing sugar and flour in a bowl and mix together with a spatula. Stir in the orange juice and grated zest.

Work in the cooled melted butter. Cover the bowl with clingfilm or a plate and set aside in a cold place or refrigerate for at least 2 hours.

· EQUIPMENT ·

1 bowl

Grater

1 baking sheet, 40 × 60 cm/16 × 24 in

1 smaller baking sheet

1 savarin *mould or a rolling pin or* tuile *shaper*

PICTURE PAGES 202-3

Makes 22-24

Preparation time: 10 minutes, plus 2 hours resting time

Cooking time: 8 minutes

· TO COOK ·

Preheat oven to 200°C/400°F/gas 7.

Generously grease the baking sheets. Using a soup spoon, spoon out 18 small, even mounds of the mixture onto the baking sheet, spacing them out evenly.

If your baking sheet is not as large as the given size, do not attempt to cram the *tuiles* into a limited space, but spoon the excess onto the smaller baking sheet.

Dip a fork into a glass of cold water and press down lightly on each mound with the back of the fork to make a sort of very thin pancake, about 7 cm/2¾ in diameter and of even thickness. Dip the fork into the water for each *tuile*.

Bake in the preheated oven for about 5 minutes, until the outside of the *tuiles* are a delicate golden colour and the centres are a little paler. Remove from the oven and leave for 1 minute before lifting them off the baking sheet.

Slide a palette knife or metal scraper between a *tuile* and the baking sheet and gently lift off the *tuile*. Do this very carefully, as they are fragile. Turn the *tuiles* over and place them in the *savarin* mould or *tuile* shaper, or drape them loosely over a rolling pin. Leave for 5 minutes without touching them.

· TO SERVE ·

Slide the *tuiles* directly onto a platter or serving dish. On no account move them from one plate to another, as they are very fragile and will break. Sprinkle with icing sugar just before serving.

· NOTES ·

This recipe can be divided to make fewer *tuiles*, just halve all the ingredients.

Do not make *tuiles* too far in advance, or they will lose their crispness. It is best to make them just an hour or two before serving. If you prefer a more orangey colour, a drop of red food colouring can be added.

MADELEINES AU MIEL
(Honey madeleines)

· INGREDIENTS ·

2 × 60-70 g/size 2 eggs

75 g/2½ oz sugar

10 g/1 tbsp dark soft brown sugar

Small pinch of salt

90 g/3 oz flour

2.5 g/1 tsp baking powder

Vanilla essence (optional)

90 g/3 oz melted butter, cooled

10 g/1 tbsp clear honey

30 g/1 oz melted butter, cooled, for greasing

Makes 14 large or 40 small madeleines

Preparation time: 20 minutes

Cooking time: 10 minutes for the larger madeleines, 5 minutes for the small ones

This recipe comes from our friend Denis Ruffel. It is easy to make and will fill your kitchen with good smells and delight all your friends.

· PREPARATION ·

Preheat the oven to 220°C/425°F/gas 8.

Combine the eggs, both kinds of sugar and the salt in a bowl and work lightly with a spatula until the mixture begins to turn light in colour. Sift together the flour and baking powder and fold them gently into the mixture, together with the vanilla, if you are using it. Do not overwork the mixture.

Lastly, pour in the cooled melted butter and the honey and mix until completely amalgamated. Cover the bowl with clingfilm and leave to rest in a cool place for about 30 minutes.

· TO COOK ·

Brush the insides of the madeleine tray with melted butter.

Pipe the mixture into the cavities in the tray, forming it into evenly-shaped domes.

Bake in the preheated oven for about 5 minutes for the small madeleines and 10 minutes for the larger ones. On no account overcook them, or they will not be moist.

As soon as they are cooked, invert the tray directly onto a wire rack. Be careful not to let the tray fall onto the madeleines, or it will crush them.

Serve the madeleines just as they are when they have barely cooled; they are sheer perfection.

· TO SERVE ·

If you want to gild the lily, you can dip either the top or the base of the madeleines in plain chocolate *couverture* or melted chocolate; leave to cool completely before serving.

· EQUIPMENT ·

1 mixing bowl

1 madeleine tray (either for the larger 8 × 4.5 cm/3¼ × 1¼ in madeleines, or for the smaller 4 × 3 cm/1½ × 1¼ in madeleines)

Piping bag fitted with a plain 1 cm/½ in nozzle

Wire rack

PICTURE PAGES 202-3

CREME GANACHE
' POUR TRUFFES '
(Chocolate truffle cream)

PICTURE PAGES 68-9

This truffle cream can also be used to fill such delicacies as thin, layered biscuits, like a *condé*. It is extremely rich, so serve only tiny quantities. Made into truffles and served with coffee, they are a true gourmand's delight!

· PREPARATION ·

The chocolate couverture: Roughly chop the chocolate and melt it in a double boiler.

The cream: Put the cream in a saucepan and boil it for 2 minutes. Set in a cool place until it has cooled to 35–40°C/95–104°F.

Pour the cooled cream onto the melted chocolate, whisking continuously, and beat until the mixture is completely homogenous. Keep in a cool place until it has cooled to about 20°C/68°F.

The butter: Place the butter in a bowl and beat with a whisk for 3 minutes, until very light.

Still beating, incorporate the cooled chocolate-cream mixture, a little at a time, then add the alcohol of your choice. When the mixture is very smooth and shiny, it is ready to use.

· MOULDING THE TRUFFLES ·

Shape the mixture into balls of the appropriate size and place on a sheet of greaseproof paper. Either use the piping bag, or use 2 teaspoons to form the mixture into little egg-shaped *quenelles*. Place in the fridge for about 2 hours, until set.

· COATING THE TRUFFLES ·

Melt the chocolate covering, then spear each truffle with a fork and quickly dip it into the melted chocolate. This must be done extremely rapidly, or the truffles will melt. Quickly roll the coated truffles in the cocoa and place on a wire rack.

· TO SERVE ·

Once the truffles have been rolled in the cocoa, they should be kept in a cool place, then refrigerated for 1 hour before serving.

· INGREDIENTS ·

600 g/1 lb 4 oz plain chocolate or *couverture*

200 g/7 fl oz double cream

300 g/10 oz butter, at room temperature

50 ml /2 fl oz alcohol of your choice – eg whisky, rum, Kirsch (optional)

FOR THE COATING:

About 300 g/10 oz plain *couverture* or chocolate covering

About 500 g/1 lb 2 oz cocoa powder

Makes about 1.15 kg/ 2 lb 8 oz

Preparation time: 30 minutes, plus cooling

· EQUIPMENT ·

Double saucepan

1 saucepan

1 bowl and whisk

Piping bag fitted with a plain 1 cm/½ in nozzle

Greaseproof paper

ALLUMETTES GLACEES
(Iced puff pastry 'matchsticks')

· INGREDIENTS ·

140 g/5 oz Puff pastry
(see pages 42-3)

Pinch of flour

2 tbsp Royal icing (see
page 236)

Makes 24

Preparation time: 30
minutes

Cooking time: 10 minutes

· PREPARATION ·

Preheat the oven to 200°C/400°F/gas 7.

On a lightly floured surface, roll out the pastry as thinly as possible into a 13.5 × 19 cm/5½ × 7½ in rectangle. Slide it onto a baking sheet and leave to rest in the freezer for 20 minutes.

Take the pastry out of the freezer and, with a palette knife, spread over the royal icing in a thin, even layer. Trim the edges of the pastry rectangle with a chopping knife, dampened to prevent the icing from sticking to the blade. You should be left with about 10 g/⅓ oz trimmings and a 12 × 18 cm/5 × 7 in pastry rectangle. Still using the dampened knife, cut the pastry into 3 equal strips, 12 × 6 cm/5 × 2⅜ in. Cut each strip into 8 small 'matchsticks', 1.5 cm/½ in wide. You should now have 24 matchsticks.

Arrange them on a lightly dampened baking sheet.

· TO COOK ·

Bake in the preheated oven for 10 minutes, then transfer to a wire rack.

· TO SERVE ·

Serve the *allumettes* by themselves or with other *petits fours secs* as an accompaniment to coffee. The sooner they are served after baking, the better they will be. For a creamy yet crunchy treat, split the *allumettes* lengthways and fill with a touch of *crème mousseline* flavoured with Grand Marnier (see page 63).

· EQUIPMENT ·

Wooden or *marble pastry board*

2 baking sheets

Wire rack

PICTURE PAGES 202-3

PALMIERS

· INGREDIENTS ·

100 g/3½ oz icing sugar, sifted

250 g/9 oz Puff pastry (see pages 42-3), turned 4 times

50 g/2 oz butter, for greasing

Makes 50 small palmiers

Preparation time: 25 minutes

Cooking time: 8-10 minutes

Albert is a past master at making these marvellous, classic *petits fours secs.*

· PREPARATION ·

Preheat the oven to 220°C/425°F/gas 8.

Rolling and shaping the pastry: Sprinkle the work surface generously with some of the icing sugar, then give the pastry its last 2 turns, so that it has had 6 turns in all. Place on a plate or baking sheet and put in the freezer for 10 minutes, or in the fridge for 20 minutes.

When the pastry is chilled, sprinkle the surface with icing sugar and roll the pastry into a 35 cm/13½ in square, about 3 mm/⅛ in thick. Trim the edges and cut the square in the middle to give 2 strips, each about 35 cm/13½ in long and 17.5 cm/7½ in wide.

Bring the 2 ends of the strip together towards the centre and fold them over lengthways, so that you have a band of 4 thicknesses (see the diagram right).

Repeat the operation with the other strip.

Place on a baking sheet and put in the freezer for 5 minutes, or in the fridge for 15 minutes to harden.

Cut each band of pastry into thin strips, 5mm/¼ in wide by 9cm/3½ in across. Lay them on a lightly buttered baking sheet in staggered rows, placing them about 6cm/2½ in apart.

· TO COOK ·

Bake in the preheated oven for 8-10 minutes, turning the *palmiers* nearest to the corners of the baking sheet after 5 or 6 minutes. As soon as the *palmiers* are cooked, transfer them to a wire rack, taking great care not to place one on top of another, or they will stick together.

· TO SERVE ·

Serve these crisp biscuits on the day they are made.

· EQUIPMENT ·

Wooden or *marble pastry board*

2 baking sheets

Wire rack

PICTURE PAGES 202-3

NOISETTES CARAMELISEES AU CHOCOLAT
(Caramelized hazelnuts with chocolate)

· INGREDIENTS ·

100 hazelnuts

60 g/2½ oz sugar

25 ml/1 fl oz water

1 tsp butter

Oil, for greasing

24 × 3.5 cm/1¼ in *Nougatine* triangles (see page 233), each weighing about 2 g/¹⁄₁₂ oz, 2 mm/¹⁄₁₂ in thick (remember that you will have to allow for the trimmings, so the total weight should be 60 g/2½ oz)

200 g/7 oz *couverture or* Menier chocolate

Makes 24

Preparation time: 1 hour

Although these marvellous and original petits fours are fiddly to make, you will be amply rewarded by the overwhelming compliments you will receive from your guests!

· PREPARATION ·

Preheat the oven to 240°C/475°F/gas 10, or the grill to very hot.

Roasting the nuts: Roast or grill the hazelnuts for about 3 minutes, until the skin begins to peel off and they turn pale golden. Place them in a tea towel, bring up the four corners together and rub until the skins come off completely. You can also remove the skins without a cloth by rubbing and rolling them in a coarse sieve.

Set aside the prepared nuts in a bowl.

Cooking the sugar: Put the sugar in a heavy-based pan with the water and cook until the temperature reaches 115°C/240°F on a sugar thermometer.

Sugaring the nuts: Immediately plunge the nuts into the cooked sugar, take the pan off the heat and stir with a wooden spatula. Still stirring gently, return the pan to a medium heat and reheat the sugar and nuts. At this point, the sugar will seem to crystallize and will then become opaque and hard before it starts to melt again with the heat. This process is called *sabler* and it will occur 3 or 4 minutes after you have put the nuts into the sugar.

The sugar will become golden and then turn a lovely caramel colour at a temperature of about 165°C/320°F.

Take the pan off the heat, add the butter and stir until it is completely absorbed.

Assembling the nut clusters: Pour the sugar and nut mixture onto the lightly oiled baking sheet. Turn the mixture a few times with a palette knife so that the sugar coats the nuts; this will take about 2 minutes. With your fingertips, separate the nuts and arrange 3 on each nougatine base, then place one more on top to make a little pyramid. If the mixture starts to harden before you have finished assembling the clusters, place the baking sheet in a moderate oven to soften the caramel until it is workable again. Set the clusters aside in a cool place for a few minutes before coating with chocolate.

Coating the nuts: Arrange the nut clusters on a wire rack set over a shallow dish.

· EQUIPMENT ·

1 small, thick-bottomed saucepan

1 baking sheet or flan tin, lightly greased

1 wire rack

Sugar thermometer

PICTURE PAGES 202-3

1

1
Roast or grill the nuts until the skin begins to peel and they turn pale golden. Rub in a tea towel to remove all the skin.

2
Cook the sugar and water until the temperature reaches 115°C/240°F. Lightly oil a baking tray.

2

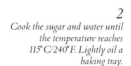

3
Add the nuts to the cooked sugar, take the pan off the heat and stir. Return to medium heat; in 3-4 minutes, the sugar will seem to crystallize.

4
Continue cooking until the sugar caramelizes and turns golden (165°C/320°F). Off the heat, stir in the butter until absorbed. Pour on to the baking tray.

3

4

5
Turn for about 2 minutes with a palette knife, so that the sugar coats the nuts. Over a wire rack, arrange 3 nuts on each nougatine base; place 1 on top to form a pyramid. Cool briefly.

6
Spoon over the melted chocolate to cover the nuts and bases.

5

6

Melt the chocolate, then spoon it over the pyramids, making sure that the hazelnuts and nougatine bases are well covered.

· STORAGE ·

These petits fours can be prepared up to 2 days in advance before being coated with the chocolate, if kept in a dry place. After coating they can be stored for up to 3 days if kept cool and dry.

MAIN PICTURE, TOP TIER *Noisettes caramelisées au chocolat;* CENTRE TIER *Tuiles dentelles à l'orange;* BOTTOM TIER *(clockwise) Allumettes glacées, Madeleines au miel, Truffes au chocolat, Macarons and Palmiers. (See pages 194–204)* OPPOSITE, TOP TO BOTTOM *Palmier, Truffe au chocolat, Allumette glacée, Tuile dentelle à l'orange.* BELOW LEFT *Noisette caramelisée au chocolat,* and BELOW *Madeleine au miel.*

MACARONS
(Macaroons)

PICTURE PAGES 202-3

· INGREDIENTS ·

225 g/8 oz icing sugar

125 g/4 oz ground almonds

4 egg whites

25 g/1 oz sugar

Flavourings:

½ tsp vanilla essence, *or*

½ tsp raspberry essence, plus a few drops red food colouring (optional) *or* 20 g/¾ oz sifted cocoa powder

Makes about 36

Preparation time: 15 minutes

Cooking time: 10 minutes

· EQUIPMENT ·

Electric mixer

Piping bag and plain 1 cm/½ in nozzle

4 baking sheets

Greaseproof paper

Wire rack

These are some of the most delicate petits fours, both to make and to eat. They should be shiny and smooth and, above all, very moist in the centre.

· PREPARATION ·

The icing sugar and ground almonds: Sift the icing sugar, then sift again with the ground almonds and the cocoa powder, if you are making chocolate macaroons. Keep the mixture on a sheet of greaseproof paper.

The egg whites: Beat until half-risen, then add the sugar and beat until stiff. Add the chosen flavouring, then increase the speed to high and beat for 1 minute, until very firm.

The macaroon mixture: Sprinkle the icing sugar and almond mixture over the egg whites and fold in gently with a spatula. Mix together until they are thoroughly blended and the mixture is very smooth.

Piping the macaroons: Pipe out the mixture into small, even rounds, about 2 cm/¾ in diameter onto a baking sheet lined with greaseproof paper. Pipe the macaroons in staggered rows, about 2.5 cm/1 in apart.

· TO COOK ·

Method 1: Preheat the oven to 180°C/350°F/gas 4. Leave the macaroons at room temperature for about 15 minutes, until a light crust forms, then bake for 10 minutes, leaving the oven door slightly ajar (about 2.5 cm/1 in) to allow the steam to escape from the oven.

Method 2: Preheat the oven to 220-230°C/425-450°F/ gas 7-8. After piping, bake the macaroons immediately in the preheated oven for 2 or 3 minutes, then quickly transfer them to another oven heated to 180°C/350°F/gas 4 and bake for a

1

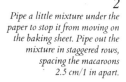

1

Fill the piping bag with the prepared macaroon mixture.

2

Pipe a little mixture under the paper to stop it from moving on the baking sheet. Pipe out the mixture in staggered rows, spacing the macaroons 2.5 cm/1 in apart.

2

3

When the macaroons are cooked, pour a little cold water between the greaseproof paper and the baking sheet.

4

After 2 or 3 minutes, lift the macaroons off the paper and press the underside with your fingers to make a small indentation.

4

5

5

Spread the underside of the macaroons with redcurrant jelly or the filling of your choice.

6

Sandwich the macaroons together in pairs and leave to cool on a wire rack.

6

further 6 minutes, leaving the oven door slightly ajar.

Whichever method you use, place an empty baking sheet under the sheet containing the macaroons to protect the bottoms and prevent them from burning. As soon as the macaroons are cooked, run a little cold water between the greaseproof paper and the baking sheet which will detach the macaroons. After 2 or 3 minutes, lift off the macaroons with your fingers and gently stick them together in pairs.

If you like, you can use a palette knife to smear on a little redcurrant jelly, chocolate *ganache* etc. before sticking them together.

Leave to cool on a wire rack.

· STORAGE ·

Packed in an airtight container, the macaroons will freeze very well.

TEA AND PICNIC CAKES

*In the hamper are Cake au citron (page 211) and
Cake marbré (page 210). On the hamper are
Cake aux fruits confits (page 209) and Cake au
vin de fruits (page 212).*

CHAPTER
· 5 ·

TEA AND
PICNIC CAKES

*T*hese cakes, which can all be made well in advance, are ideal for afternoon tea and, because they are easily transportable, perfect for picnics. Serve them with a red fruit *coulis*, fruit compote or jam, or with chilled fresh fruits; this will enhance the flavour and make the cakes even more appetizing.

Our own favourite is the delicately scented lemon cake, the recipe for which was given to us by our friend and colleague from Paris, Denis Ruffel.

C A K E A U X F R U I T S C O N F I T S
(Fruit cake)

· INGREDIENTS ·

125 g/4 oz butter, plus
30 g/1 oz for greasing

125 g/4 oz sugar

1 × 70 g/size 1 egg, at
room temperature
(20°C/68°F)

1 egg yolk

125 g/4 oz moist candied
fruits, diced

60 g/2 oz raisins

Few drops vanilla
essence, lemon juice or
orange blossom water

5 g/2 tsp baking
powder

150 g/5 oz flour

1 tbsp full-flavoured
rum

50 g/2 oz apricot jam,
sieved

30 g/1 oz flaked almonds
or 6 glacé cherries,
halved

Serves 6

Preparation time: 25
minutes, plus 20 minutes
chilling

Cooking time: 40 minutes

· PREPARATION ·

Preheat the oven to 240°C/475°F/gas 10.

In a bowl, cream together the butter and sugar until soft. Beat in the warmed whole egg, then the yolk. If the mixture separates, stand the bowl in a bain-marie for a few seconds, beating all the time. Using a spatula, stir in the candied fruits, raisins and the flavouring of your choice.

Sift together the flour and baking powder. Fold into the mixture, using a spatula. Cover the bowl with clingfilm or a plate and leave in the fridge for 20 minutes.

· TO COOK ·

Brush the inside of the loaf tin with butter and line it with the paper which should come 2-3 cm/about 1 in above the top of the tin. Pour the cake mixture into the tin, taking care not to drop any onto the paper.

Bake in the preheated oven for 7 minutes, then lower the temperature to 180°C/350°F/gas 5 and cook for a further 33 minutes. To check when the cake is ready, insert a skewer or the point of a very fine knife into the centre; it should come out clean.

· TO DECORATE ·

As soon as the cake comes out of the oven, sprinkle over the rum. Leave the cake in the tin for 10-15 minutes, then unmould it onto a wire rack.

Cut the paper into zigzags all round the cake, leaving the paper slightly higher than the top of the cake.

Brush the top with warmed apricot jam and decorate with the almonds or halved glacé cherries.

· TO SERVE ·

It is always best to serve a cake at least 12 hours after it has been baked and always at room temperature. Serve it thinly sliced, on its own or with a *crème anglaise* or some home-made jam.

· STORAGE ·

You can freeze this cake for up to a week. Sprinkle over the rum, but do not coat with the apricot jam. Leave the cake to cool slightly, then wrap it in clingfilm while still tepid and freeze.

Twenty-four hours before you want to eat it, place the cake in the fridge for 12 hours, then leave at room temperature for 12 hours before coating and decorating.

· EQUIPMENT ·

1 bowl

1 loaf tin,
23 × 9 cm/9 × 3½ in,
7 cm/2¼ in deep,
19 × 6.5 cm/7½ × 2½ in at
the base

Thick white or greaseproof
paper

Wire rack

PICTURE PAGES 206-7

CAKE MARBRE
(Marble cake)

PICTURE PAGES 206-7

· INGREDIENTS ·

240 g/8 oz softened butter, plus 30 g/1 oz for greasing

300 g/10 oz icing sugar, sifted

6 × 50 g/size 5 eggs, at room temperature (20°C/68°F)

280 g/10 oz flour

5 g/2 tsp baking powder

40 g/1½ oz cocoa powder, sifted, or 40 g/ 1½ oz plain chocolate, melted

60 g/2 oz moist candied orange peel, finely diced

Serves 10-12

Preparation time: 30 minutes, plus 20 minutes chilling

Cooking time: 1 hour for the large cake, 15 minutes for the small cakes

· EQUIPMENT ·

2 mixing bowls

1 loaf tin, 22 × 9 cm/ 8½ × 3½ in, 8 cm/3 in deep, 19 × 7 cm/7½ × 2¾ in at the base

6 small brioche moulds, 8 cm/3¼ in at the top, 4 cm/1½ in at the base, 3 cm/1¼ in deep, or 6 fluted tartlet tins

Thick white or greaseproof paper

Wire rack

This cake is similar to a classic pound cake. For a different flavour, replace the cocoa powder or melted chocolate with instant coffee powder. It is also nice to add some dried fruits, like stoned apricots or prunes. Add them to the unflavoured mixture.

· PREPARATION ·

Preheat the oven to 220°C/425°F/gas 8.

In a bowl, lightly whisk together the softened butter and icing sugar until pale. Do not overwork.

Separate the eggs and set aside the whites.

Add the yolks, one at a time, to the butter and sugar, stirring well to mix thoroughly.

Sift together the flour and baking powder, then fold into the mixture with a spatula. Stop mixing as soon as the mixture is homogenous.

Beat the egg whites until soft peaks form, then, using a spatula, fold them gently into the mixture.

Pour one-third of the mixture into a bowl. Stir in the cocoa powder or melted chocolate.

Stir the diced orange peel into the remaining mixture.

Cover the bowls with clingfilm or plates and refrigerate for about 20 minutes.

· TO COOK ·

Brush the inside of the tin and moulds with butter. Line the large tin (but not the small moulds) with the paper, which should come 2-3 cm/about 1 in above the top of the tin.

Spoon the 2 mixtures alternately into the moulds to show the 2 distinct colours, or drop them in rivulets to give a marbled effect. Take care not to drop any mixture onto the paper.

Bake in the preheated oven for 7 minutes, then reduce the temperature to 190°C/375°F/gas 6 and cook the small cakes for a further 8 minutes. (The large cake will need about 53 minutes.) To check when the cakes are ready, insert a skewer or the point of a very fine knife into the centre; it should come out clean.

· TO DECORATE ·

Remove from the oven and unmould immediately. Place on a wire rack. For the large cake, either cut the paper into zigzags all round the cake, leaving the paper slightly higher than the top of the cake, or simply remove it altogether.

· TO SERVE ·

It is best to serve a cake at least 12 hours after it has been baked. Serve at room temperature, thinly sliced. Sprinkle the top with a little icing sugar if you like.

· STORAGE ·

To freeze the cake for up to a week, let it cool slightly, then wrap in clingfilm while still tepid and freeze.

A day before you want to serve it, place the cake in the fridge for 12 hours then leave at room temperature for a further 12 hours.

CAKE AU CITRON
(Lemon cake)

· INGREDIENTS ·

Zest of 1 large lemon, finely grated

2 × 70 g/size 1 eggs or 3 × 50 g/size 5 eggs, at room temperature (20°C/68°F)

Pinch of salt

175 g/6 oz sugar

75 ml/3 fl oz double cream

140 g/4½ oz flour

2.5 g/1 tsp baking powder

50 g/2 oz butter, melted and cooled

20 ml/1 fl oz full-flavoured rum, plus 1 tbsp

30 g/1 oz butter, for greasing

75 g/3 oz apricot jam, sieved

For the icing:

80 g/3 oz icing sugar, sifted

Juice of 1 lemon

Serves 6

Preparation time: 15 minutes

Cooking time: 40 minutes

· EQUIPMENT ·

1 mixing bowl

1 loaf tin, 23 × 9 cm/9 × 3½ in, 7 cm/2¾ in deep, 19 × 6.5 cm/7½ × 2½ in at the base

Thick white or greaseproof paper

Wire rack

PICTURE PAGES 206-7

This excellent recipe was given to us by our friend and fellow *pâtissier*, Denis Ruffel. It is so delicate and delicious that once you have tasted a slice, you will not be able to resist another, then a third. . .

· PREPARATION ·

Preheat the oven to 200°C/400°F/gas 7

In a bowl, whisk together the lemon zest, eggs, salt and sugar. Do not overwork.

Stir in the cream, then sift together the flour and baking powder and fold in. Finally, add the cooled melted butter and 20 ml/1 fl oz rum.

· TO COOK ·

Brush the inside of the loaf tin with butter and line it with the paper, which should come 2-3 cm/about 1 in above the top of the tin.

Pour the mixture into the tin, taking care not to drop any onto the paper.

Bake in the preheated oven for 7 minutes, then lower the temperature to 180°C/350°F/gas 5 and cook for a further 33 minutes. To check when the cake is ready, insert a skewer or the point of a very fine knife into the centre; it should come out clean.

· TO ICE ·

Unmould the cake as soon as it comes out of the oven. Place it on a wire rack set over a shallow dish and remove the paper. Sprinkle over the remaining rum.

Increase the oven temperature to 250°C/500°F/gas 10.

When the cake is cold, brush the top and sides with

warmed apricot jam. In a bowl, make the icing with the lemon juice and icing sugar exactly as you would with water. Spread the icing over the cake; any excess will be caught in the dish.

Place immediately in the very hot oven for about 15 seconds to 'set' the icing.

· TO SERVE ·

Unlike most cakes, this lemon cake can be served on the day it is made, as soon as it has cooled, although it is equally good 2 or 3 days later.

Eat this light cake on its own, or served with a chocolate mousse or *Oeufs à la neige* (see page 105). Serve it very thinly sliced.

· STORAGE ·

The cake will freeze very well for up to a week; sprinkle it with the rum, but do not glaze with the jam. Wrap in clingfilm and freeze while still slightly warm.

One day before you want to eat it, place the cake in the fridge for 12 hours, then for 12 hours at room temperature before coating with jam and icing.

CAKE AU VIN DE FRUITS
(Cake with fruit wine)

· INGREDIENTS ·

30 g/1 oz butter, for greasing

2 eggs, at room temperature (20°C/68°F)

130 g/4 oz sugar

100 g/3½ oz moist mixed crystallized fruits, diced

80 g/3 oz raisins

80 g/3 oz sultanas

80 g/3 oz glacé cherries

450 ml/16 fl oz fruit wine (eg, plum or cherry)

340 g/11 oz flour

10 g/4 tsp baking powder

This cake contains no fats, which makes it perfect for people on a fat-free diet and makes it firmer and more compact than a classic cake — its texture is more like that of a malt loaf.

· PREPARATION ·

Preheat the oven to 240°C/475°F/gas 10.

In a bowl, whisk together the eggs and sugar until pale. With a spatula, fold in the diced crystallized fruits, the raisins, sultanas and cherries. Stir in the fruit wine.

Sift together the flour and baking powder, then, with a spatula, fold them into the cake mixture. As soon as they are thoroughly blended, stop mixing. Do not overwork the mixture. Cover the bowl with clingfilm or a plate and refrigerate for about 20 minutes.

· TO COOK ·

Brush the insides of the tin and moulds with butter. Line the large tin (but not the small moulds) with white or greaseproof paper, which should come 2-3cm/about 1 in above the top of the tin.

Pour two-thirds of the cake mixture into the large tin,

· EQUIPMENT ·

1 mixing bowl

1 loaf tin, 23 × 9 cm/ 9 × 3½in, 7 cm/2¼ in deep, 19 × 6.5 cm/7½ × 2½ in at the base

6 small brioche moulds, 8 cm/3¼ in at the top, 4 cm/1½ in at the base, 3 cm/1¼ in deep

Thick white or greaseproof paper

Wire rack

PICTURE PAGES 206-7

Serves 12

Preparation time: 15 minutes, plus 20 minutes chilling

Cooking time: 1 hour for the large cake, 15 minutes for the small cakes

taking care not to drop any onto the paper, and divide the rest between the small moulds.

Bake in the preheated oven for 7 minutes, then lower the temperature to 180°C/350°F/gas 5 and cook the small cakes for a further 8 minutes. (The large cake will need about 53 minutes.) To check when the cakes are ready, insert a skewer or the point of a very fine knife into the centre; it should come out clean.

· TO DECORATE ·

Leave the cakes in the moulds for 10–15 minutes, then unmould onto a wire rack.

For the large cake, either cut the paper into zigzags all round the cake, leaving the paper slightly higher than the top of the cake, or simply remove it altogether.

· TO SERVE ·

It is best not to serve a cake for at least 12 hours after it has been baked. Serve it at room temperature, thinly sliced, on its own or with fresh unsalted farm butter, if available.

· STORAGE ·

It will freeze well for up to a week. Leave to cool slightly, then wrap it in clingfilm while still tepid and freeze.

A full day before you want to eat it, place the cake in the fridge for 12 hours, then leave at room temperature for a further 12 hours.

CHAPTER
· 6 ·

DECORATION
AND
PRESENTATION

*T*his chapter is intended to inspire everyone to try his hand at creating different decorations. Whichever method you use — piping, painting with food colouring or cocoa, *pastillage* or almond paste, or working with sugar in various forms — poured, blown, pulled, spun etc — it only requires a little application to produce an impressive result which will amaze those new to the art.

COOKING AND WORKING WITH SUGAR

*E*ven an amateur with no previous experience can be creative with sugar: just follow our methods and the recipes in this chapter and you will find it less difficult than you feared. Remember that when we took our first steps in this direction we were just sixteen years old.

By following all these rules, even total beginners can launch themselves into the art of working with sugar. Start by working with poured or pulled sugar before embarking on blown sugar, which is always more complex. If you want to create a big, important piece in blown sugar, it is better for two people to work together — one to blow and the other to fashion the decorative piece.

Beginners should space out their sugar-working sessions. Once or twice a week is quite enough; the skin on your hands must become accustomed to the heat, which can cause blisters, particularly on the fingertips.

· COOKING ·

It takes only a few simple gestures to weigh the sugar, moisten it with water and add cream of tartar or glucose. The pan, all clad in copper, set over direct heat, gentle at first, then fierce, is now entrusted with this boiling, seething mass until it becomes 'hard crack'. And while it cooks, your nimble fingertips, dipped into icy water, will guard against the formation of crystals on the inside of the pan.

· COOLING ·

As the sugar is gently poured onto a lightly oiled marble, the outer edges will spread; fold them back inwards with a palette knife or metal scraper four or five times. By now, you can risk it with your fingertips.

· CONTACT ·

At last you can hold the sugar with your fingers — but not for long, because it is still extremely hot. As it makes contact with the marble, keep stretching the sugar and folding it back on itself; it will still feel very hot, but not unbearable. Now your fingers can hold the mass without making contact with the marble. After two or three minutes, hand and sugar are finally and completely united; they seem to have attained precisely the same temperature. The sugar bends, takes on a satin sheen. Suddenly it sings, it makes a slight cracking sound, it talks to you. Proud, beautiful, docile, it is now ready to be shaped into flowers, leaves, animals, what you will. This is the *pâtissier-confiseur's* highest form of artistic expression.

W O R K I N G   W I T H   S U G A R

It is absolutely vital to study closely the following rules and advice before embarking on our recipes.

· IMPORTANT RULES ·

• You should never attempt to cook sugar in a damp atmosphere (ie, when the humidity is high). The sugar will 'sweat' when you try to work it and, once pulled, it will lose its glossy brilliance.

• You must never work in a draught. Sugar loves heat and dryness and if subjected to a draught will be unmalleable and difficult to mould.

• Scrupulous cleanliness — both personal and material — is essential. All equipment and working areas must be spotless. The sugar pan should be washed with coarse salt and vinegar, then rinsed with fresh water and drained but not dried. Your marble slab, utensils, hands and nails must be immaculately clean.

Assuming that you have abided by these three cardinal rules, there are certain other important factors governing your choice of equipment and ingredients.

· EQUIPMENT ·

• Choose a pan made of untinned copper, which conducts heat rapidly and holds it well.

• Never use a wooden spatula; it may look clean, but wood absorbs flavours and grease and could ruin the sugar; the only exception is for *sucre rocher*.

• Always pour the water into the pan before the sugar, so that it dissolves more easily. Stir with a skimmer until the sugar has dissolved completely, then stop just before it begins to cook.

· INGREDIENTS ·

• The amount of glucose you add to the sugar and water will vary depending on the effect you wish to achieve. You can add 10-20 per cent more glucose to *sucre soufflé*, which will become more malleable; raise the cooking temperature by 1° or 2°C (about 25°F).

• A sugar thermometer graduating from 70°C/158°F to 200°C/392°F is indispensable for the amateur. Once you are practised in the art, you can gauge the exact stage the sugar has reached simply by looking and testing with your fingers (see table opposite). Plunge them into iced water, then into the sugar, then back into the water; you will not need a thermometer.

• The precise cooking temperature varies according to the weight of sugar being cooked. Where our recipes are for 1 kg (2 lb 2 oz) of sugar, you may prefer to prepare only half that quantity; reduce the temperature by 1° or 2° C (about 25°F). If you are doubling the quantities, increase the temperature by 1° or 2°C.

· TECHNIQUE ·

• As soon as the sugar begins to boil, cover the pan with a lid with a small hole in it; this will enable you to keep the thermometer vertical and will prevent it from burning on the sides of the pan. It will also be easier to read the temperature, since there will be less steam and condensation; alternatively, partially cover the pan with a lid. This will become saturated with condensation and droplets of water will drip down the sides of the pan into the sugar. This process is very important; it not only cleans the pan, but also prevents the sugar from solidifying.

• It is important when cooking sugar that the flame does not lick up the sides of the pan, or the sugar, which cooks faster at the edge, will become yellowish in colour.

If you want to colour the sugar, it is advisable to use powdered food colourings. The colours are brighter and more vibrant than liquid colourings.

Before using, dilute them in a few drops of 90° proof alcohol or Cognac or Armagnac. Add the colourings to the boiling sugar when it reaches 140°C/284°F. If you prefer, you can add the colouring to the sugar as soon as you pour it onto the marble slab. Pour a very few drops into the centre of the sugar mass.

It is very important to note, however, that colour must always be added to *sucre coulé* while it is cooking. Remember that it should be as transparent as glass, so be careful not to overdo the colouring. Pastel colours look much more attractive

• Once sugar has reached the desired temperature, you must on no account take the thermometer out of the boiling liquid and plunge it into iced water. The sudden drop in temperature (from about 150°C/302°F to freezing) will play havoc with the temperature gauge, even if it doesn't actually break it.

• As soon as the sugar on the marble becomes satiny, it should be transferred to a special, very thick and heat-resistant plastic sheet.

• So that the sugar retains its heat and remains pliable, place it under an infra-red or radiant heat lamp. If you don't possess one, roll the sugar into a ball and place it on a sieve or baking sheet. Heat the oven to 100°-120°C/212°-248°F and work the sugar at the opening of the oven, with the door half-open.

• For a perfect result when working with *sucre coulé*, use a small gas jet to eliminate any air bubbles while you pour the sugar.

• Once you have made your sugar ornaments, place them in an airtight container which you have carefully prepared beforehand. Line the bottom with a dehydrating compound, such as silica gel, carbide or quicklime, covered with aluminium foil. Seal the container tightly and put in a dry place; your sugar decorations will keep for several weeks before you use them. This allows you to create really imposing competition pieces, which may have taken several months to prepare — or simply to make smaller decorations for a family celebration.

TEMPERATURES FOR SUGAR BOILING

°C	°F	Sugar stage	Method of testing
100	212	small gloss or thread	Take a little sugar syrup between your thumb and index finger and stretch them apart. Short threads will form.
104	219	large gloss or thread	Test as above; longer, stronger threads will form.
106	220	small pearl	The sugar boils in the pan and forms small, pearl-like balls.
109	228	large pearl	The 'pearls' are better formed and separated.
112	234	small soufflé	Dip a skimmer into the sugar syrup and blow across the holes; small sugar balls will be blown off.
114	237	large soufflé	Test as above; the sugar will form larger bubbles.
118	244	small ball	Dip your finger into cold water, then into the sugar syrup. Plunge immediately into cold water; the sugar will slide off your finger and be soft enough to roll into a ball.
120	248	medium ball	The sugar balls are harder and more resistant.
124	255	large ball	As medium ball.
135	275	light crack	Dip your finger into cold water, then into the sugar syrup. Plunge into cold water; a sliver of sugar will fall off your finger.
144	291	crack	Test as above; a larger piece of sugar will slide off your finger.
152	306	hard crack	Test as above; the sugar will slide off your finger and shatter when it touches the water.

SUCRE COULE
(Poured sugar)

· INGREDIENTS ·

1 kg/2 lb 2 oz beet sugar
or cane sugar cubes

400 ml/14 fl oz water

250 g/9 oz glucose

Food colourings, as
appropriate

1 tbsp peanut oil or pure
vaseline, for greasing

Royal icing
(see page 236) (optional)

Pinch of cornflour

Preparation time: about 20
minutes

Cooking time: about 25
minutes

Models made from *sucre coulé* are quite stunning — like stained glass windows. Place them on a platter with a special dessert for an occasion, or feature them on a buffet or at a banquet.

Although these models are not difficult to make, they do require a great deal of application and, above all, time.

· OUTLINING THE MODEL AND ITS BASE ·

The model and base must be prepared with the utmost care and attention. First of all, draw and cut out templates of your chosen model and its base, using either pliable or rigid paper. The base must be sufficiently large and well-proportioned to give the model a very stable support. It can be any shape — oval, round, rectangular etc.

When the templates are ready, on a wooden or formica surface, lightly dusted with cornflour, roll out the modelling paste to a thickness of between 5–7 mm/$\frac{1}{4}$–$\frac{1}{3}$ in, depending on the size of your model. The larger the model, the thicker the paste should be to make it more solid.

Place the template on the paste and, using the point of a small knife, cut around the edges. Remove the template, then the cut-out model. Take great care not to spoil the edges, which must be very smooth.

Using another piece of modelling paste, prepare the base in the same way. Lay a sheet of foil on the marble slab or baking sheet, taking care not to crumple it. Carefully place the prepared modelling paste on the foil. Use the templates to check that the edges have not stretched.

With a small brush, grease the inside edges of the paste with oil or melted vaseline. The paste is now ready for the sugar.

At this point you can, if you wish, pipe out some decorations in royal icing. This will add interest and life to your model. Use a paper cone or piping bag fitted with a 2 mm/$\frac{1}{16}$ in nozzle.

If you are adding this decoration, leave the piped icing to dry on the foil for at least 4 hours before pouring the sugar, otherwise it will swell and disintegrate when it comes into contact with the hot sugar.

· PREPARATION AND COOKING ·

Pour the water into the pan, then add the sugar. Stir gently with a small skimmer. When the sugar has dissolved slightly, set the pan over a gentle heat and stir until the sugar has dissolved completely.

Once it begins to bubble, it will throw out a kind of white

· EQUIPMENT ·

Copper sugar pan

Sugar thermometer

Marble slab or an absolutely
smooth, flat work surface or
baking sheet

Small paintbrush

Aluminium foil

Modelling paste, plasticine
or confectioners' rulers, or a
metal strip which is pliable
enough to be bent into any
shape

Gas jet (optional)

PICTURE PAGES 230–1

Continued overleaf

1

1

On a surface lightly dusted with cornflour, roll out the modelling paste or plasticine to a thickness of 5–7 mm/¼–⅔ in, using wooden rulers to measure the thickness accurately.

2

2

Place the templates on the plasticine and cut round them with a sharp knife, keeping the knife vertical. Carefully lift out the plasticine shapes.

3

3

Lay the prepared plasticine on smooth foil. Use the templates to check that the edges have not stretched. Oil the inner edges of the plasticine.

4

4

Cook the sugar and add colourings. Stand the pan on a wooden trivet for 1½ minutes to cool the sugar and burst the air bubbles. Pour into the model and base.

5

5

Make 1 cut in the plasticine and lift it away from the sugar models when set. Gently scrape away any plasticine which sticks with a sharp knife.

6

6

Leave the model and base to cool for several hours, then pipe on any decoration in royal icing. When the icing is dry, assemble the model and base.

foam. Skim this carefully off the surface until it is completely clean, taking care to rinse the skimmer well each time in a bowl of very clean water.

Use your fingertips to brush down the inside of the pan, dipping them into cold water each time, or use a perfectly clean pastry brush dipped into cold water. This will prevent the unmelted sugar from sticking to the sides of the pan and crystallizing. The crystals might also fall back into the boiling sugar and cause it to recrystallize. It can also cause the sugar to lose its transparency once it has been poured.

Add the glucose and partially cover the pan with a very clean lid. Cook the sugar over high heat.

Place the thermometer in the sugar; add any colourings when the temperature reaches about 140°C/284°F. When it reaches 156°C/312°F, take the pan off the heat.

Stand the pan on a wooden trivet for 1½ minutes so that the sugar cools very slightly before pouring, and to allow most of the small air bubbles to escape.

· POURING THE SUGAR ·

Pour the sugar in a regular, continuous stream into the cut-out template in the modelling paste until it reaches the top of the paste. Should any air bubbles appear, and you want a completely smooth surface, gently blow them away immediately with a gas jet wherever they appear, or prick them quickly with the point of a very fine knife, wiping the knife carefully each time.

Leave to cool for about 20 minutes; the edges of the sugar should have begun to harden. Lift off the modelling paste; having been oiled, it will peel away easily. If any should stick, gently scrape it away with the point of a knife. Leave the model to cool completely for 3 or 4 hours. You can then carefully peel off the foil and attach the model to the base.

To attach the model, dip the very bottom, for one second only, into some hard crack sugar, then immediately stick it onto the base; or, using a small spoon or paper cone, pipe a fine line of hard crack sugar round the perimeter of the base and quickly set the model on top. In either case, hold it down for 2 or 3 minutes, so that it sticks firmly to the base.

· NOTES ·

You can use a pliable metal strip or confectioners' rulers instead of modelling paste; oil the inside edges before pouring in the sugar.

To keep your models transparent and brilliant, spray a thin film of clear varnish over the models and bases as soon as they are cold. This will also protect them from damp, dust and fingerprints etc. and will preserve them for several days.

S U C R E   F I L E
(Spun sugar)

· INGREDIENTS ·

250 g/9 oz sugar

90 ml/3½ fl oz water

65 g/2½ oz glucose

1 tbsp peanut oil *or* pure
vaseline, for greasing

Preparation time: 5 minutes

Cooking time: about 15
minutes

Spun sugar, which is so easy to make, is chiefly used for decoration. Its delicate, brilliant quality gives a festive air to *pièces montées* or *Soufflé glacé aux fraises* (page 178), iced desserts and sorbets and to our *Igloo Douillet* (see page 108). Since it is supple and pliable, spun sugar can be bent into all sorts of attractive shapes.

· PREPARATION AND COOKING ·

Pour the water into the pan, then add the sugar. Stir gently with a small skimmer. As soon as the sugar has dissolved slightly, set the pan over a gentle heat and stir until the sugar has dissolved completely and begins to boil.

Once it starts to bubble, it will throw out a kind of white foam. Skim this off the surface several times, using a skimmer, taking care to rinse it well each time in a bowl of very clean water.

Use your fingertips to clean the inside of the pan, dipping them into cold water each time, or use a scrupulously clean pastry brush dipped in cold water. This will prevent the unmelted sugar from sticking to the sides of the pan and crystallizing. The crystals might fall back into the boiling sugar and cause it to recrystallize.

Add the glucose, partially cover the pan with a very clean lid and cook the sugar over high heat.

Place the thermometer in the sugar. When the temperature reaches 152°C/305°F, take the pan off the heat and rest it on a wooden board for 2 minutes to cool and thicken.

If the sugar is too hot, it will fall in little drops, but will not spin; if it is too cold, it will be very difficult to spin.

· PREPARING THE WORK AREA ·

Lay several sheets of greaseproof paper on the floor to protect it. Balance a lightly oiled broom handle across two chairs or stools, or use an oiled rolling pin, holding one end carefully in your hand.

· SPINNING THE SUGAR ·

Dip the prongs of the forks or whisk into the sugar and flick them rapidly backwards and forwards above the rolling pin or broom handle. The sugar will run down and spin into fine threads on both sides. Continue to 'throw' the sugar in this way until the broom handle or rolling pin is moderately well covered. Do not overfill it with too many threads. Collect up

· EQUIPMENT ·

Copper sugar pan

Sugar thermometer

2 forks or a small balloon
whisk, with the rounded
ends cut off

4 sheets of greaseproof paper

Rolling pin or broom
handle

all the sugar threads (or 'Angel's hair') and place on a lightly oiled baking tray, if you are going to use them within an hour. To keep it for any length of time, pack in an airtight container lined with silica gel, quicklime or carbide covered with foil. It can be stored for up to 2 days.

· NOTES ·

Spun sugar very easily picks up moisture from the atmosphere and softens, so if you have to work in a humid atmosphere for any reason, leave sugar spinning until another day.

Spun sugar is also used to make the stamens of sugar flowers. Gently roll a handful into a sausage shape about 2 cm/1 in diameter. Squeeze in the base to 4-5 mm/about ¼ in diameter and, with a heated knife, cut off about 3-4 cm/1½ in, taking care that the other end remains open. Dip the open end into crystallized sugar, tinted pink, yellow, or whatever colour you like. Repeat the process as often as necessary. You can keep the finished stamens in an airtight box containing a dehydrating compound.

SUCRE ROCHER
(Rock sugar)

· INGREDIENTS ·

500 g/1 lb 1 oz beet sugar
or cane sugar cubes
200 ml/7 fl oz water
1 tbsp Royal icing (see page 236)
Food colourings (optional)

Preparation time: 5 minutes
Cooking time: about 20 minutes

· EQUIPMENT ·

Copper sugar pan, large enough to hold 3 times the given quantities
Sugar thermometer
Aluminium foil
1 soufflé dish or bowl

PICTURE PAGE 230

Unlike other sugars, *sucre rocher* keeps very well exposed to the air, and it is very simple to make. It adds an unusual decorative touch, and can be embellished with flowers made from pulled sugar. As its name implies, *sucre rocher* can be used to give a very attractive rocky effect.

· PREPARATION AND COOKING ·

Preheat the oven to 120°C/250°F/gas 1. Line the soufflé dish or bowl with foil. Pour the water into the pan, then add the sugar and stir gently with a small skimmer. When the sugar has dissolved slightly, set the pan over a gentle heat and stir until the sugar has dissolved completely and begins to boil.

Once it begins to bubble, it will throw out a kind of white foam. Skim this off the surface several times, using a skimmer, taking care to rinse it well each time in a bowl of very clean water.

Use your fingertips to clean the inside of the pan, dipping them into cold water each time, or use a pristine clean pastry brush dipped into cold water. This will prevent the unmelted sugar from sticking to the sides of the pan and crystallizing. The crystals might fall back into the boiling sugar and make it grainy or cause it to recrystallize.

Partially cover the pan with a very clean lid and cook the

sugar over high heat. Place the thermometer in the sugar; add any colourings when the temperature reaches about 120°C/248°F. When it reaches 138°C/280°F, take the pan off the heat and, with a scrupulously clean wooden spatula, very quickly stir in the royal icing. Mix well, but do not overwork. The sugar will now rise and almost double in volume (hence the need for a large pan!) Do not stir while the sugar is rising. It will fall and then rise again. As it begins to rise for the second time, quickly pour it into the prepared dish, where it will finish rising.

· DRYING THE 'SUCRE ROCHER' ·

As soon as the sugar is in the dish, place it immediately in the preheated oven for 10 minutes, so that it does not fall again and will harden. Put the sugar, still in the dish, in a dry place and leave it for about 12 hours.

· FINISHING ·

After 12 hours, turn the sugar out of the dish and remove the foil. With a serrated knife, cut off the crumbly outer crust.

Depending on what you intend to make, cut the sugar with a fretsaw, or break it into pieces by tapping it lightly with the back of a large knife. You can also file it down if you want a fairly flat, smooth surface.

The sugar is now ready to use.

· DECORATION ·

Colour this sugar during cooking for a pretty, smooth effect. If, however, you want to give your imagination full rein and are aiming for subtle reflections and highlighted reliefs, it is best to use an atomizer or spray. Spray-on colours are added after the model is completely finished.

Assemble and stick together various pieces with a little royal icing. You must leave the finished model to dry for at least 12 hours.

If you want a lighter, more crumbly sugar, add a touch more royal icing.

SUCRE SOUFFLE
(Blown sugar)

· INGREDIENTS ·

1 kg/2 lb 2 oz beet sugar
or cane sugar cubes

400 ml/14 fl oz water

250 g/9 oz glucose

1 tbsp peanut oil *or* pure
vaseline, for greasing

Food colourings, as
appropriate (optional)

*Preparation time: 5 minutes,
plus making the shapes*
*Cooking time: about 25
minutes*

· PREPARATION ·

Pour the water into the pan, then add the sugar. Stir with a skimmer. As soon as the sugar has dissolved a little, set the pan over a gentle heat and stir until the sugar has dissolved completely and begins to boil.

Once it starts to bubble, it will throw out a kind of white foam. Skim this off the surface until completely clean, rinsing the skimmer well in a bowl of very clean water each time.

Use your fingertips to clean the inside of the pan, dipping them into cold water each time, or use a scrupulously clean pastry brush dipped in cold water.

Add the glucose, partially cover the pan with a very clean lid and cook the sugar over high heat.

Insert the sugar thermometer and cook until the temperature reaches 150°C/302°F. Take the pan off the heat and stand it on a wooden trivet for 30 seconds. During the cooking process, up to 140°C/284°F, the sugar will discolour a little and should take on a slightly yellow tint. This will provide the ideal base colour for painting the models and will help in obtaining the deeper and more vivid colours.

· COOLING THE SUGAR ·

Pour the sugar onto a spotlessly clean oiled marble slab or the tefal sheet. Use a lightly oiled palette knife or metal scraper to fold the edges back on themselves 3 or 4 times, until they have almost stopped spreading.

· 'SATINIZING' THE SUGAR ·

Leaving the sugar on the marble, fold the mass back onto itself with your fingertips or the palette knife. Start to pull it 5 or 6 times. The sugar should now be cool enough to handle. Place one hand on one end of the mass and pull it out, then fold it back on itself. Do this 20-30 times, alternating the direction each time, until the sugar becomes very glossy and smooth. Place the sugar on the plastic sheet under the lamp, or stand it in a sieve or on a baking sheet just inside the open oven, which you have preheated to 120°C/250°F/gas 1.

· BLOWING THE SUGAR ·

Now the sugar is satinized, cut off a ball large enough to make your desired shape. This ball should be at a uniform temperature, still warm and firm but malleable.

Dig your thumb into the centre to make a cavity. Heat the end of an aluminium tube or the nozzle of the pump so that

· EQUIPMENT ·

Copper sugar pan

Sugar thermometer

Marble slab or *a tefal sheet,
60 × 40 cm/24 × 16 in*

Palette knife or *metal
scraper*

Sugar lamp

Thick, heatproof plastic sheet
or *a sieve* or *baking sheet*

Aluminium tubes or *a
sugar-blowing pump*

Small electric fan

Foam rubber mat

Small paintbrushes

PICTURE PAGES 230-1

the sugar will stick to it, then insert it halfway into the cavity. With your fingertips, firmly press the edges of the sugar around the end of the tube or nozzle so that it sticks.

Blow in air gently and regularly, so that the sugar ball swells; make sure that the thickness remains constant and even throughout the operation. Use your hands to support the swelling bubble and, with your fingertips, begin to form your shapes. Blow constantly while you do this, just enough to maintain the air pressure inside the sugar ball.

When you have achieved your desired size and shape, mark the shape as you wish; for example, roll it over a grater or hard bristle brush, or mark it with the back of a large knife to look like a peach. To imitate the bloom on a peach skin, just roll the blown and painted sugar peach in a plate of cornflour. To make an animal's paws or tail, cut out the shape with scissors.

Place the finished object in front of a small fan or in a relatively cold place. Never put it directly onto a flat surface, or it will lose its shape. Heat the blade of a small knife over a gas flame, then carefully cut the sugar cord between the model and the tube or nozzle. Place the sugar model on a piece of foam rubber so that it does not break.

· NOTES ·

If you wish, you can paint the finished models with food colouring — give your artistic imagination full rein! All kinds of fruits and animals can be created in sugar, some very simple, others more complex.

Once the sugar is satinized, it can be divided into 4 with a large knife. Use only 1 piece for the *sucre soufflé;* the others may be kept until needed in an airtight container lined with quicklime, carbide or silica gel covered with foil. Then you need only reheat them under a lamp or at the opening of an oven preheated to 120°C/250°F, turning from time to time, so that the sugar softens evenly as it warms.

If you want to keep a high gloss on the finished sugar pieces, spray each one with an aerosol lacquer. This will also protect them from quick deterioration.

SUCRE TIRE
(Pulled sugar)

· INGREDIENTS ·

1 kg/2 lb 2 oz beet sugar
or cane sugar cubes

500 ml/18 fl oz water

1.5 g/scant ½ tsp
cream of tartar

1 tbsp peanut oil or pure
vaseline, for greasing

Food colourings
(optional)

Preparation time: 5 minutes,
plus making the decoration

Cooking time: about 25
minutes

· PREPARATION AND COOKING ·

Pour the water into the pan, then add the sugar and cream of tartar. Stir with a skimmer. When the sugar has dissolved a little, set the pan over a gentle heat and stir until the sugar has dissolved completely and is beginning to boil.

Once the sugar begins to bubble, it will throw out a kind of white foam. Skim this off the surface until completely clean, taking care to rinse the skimmer well in a bowl of very clean water each time.

Use your fingertips to clean the inside of the pan, dipping them into cold water each time, or use a scrupulously clean pastry brush dipped into cold water. This will prevent the unmelted sugar from sticking to the sides of the pan and crystallizing. The crystals might fall back into the boiling sugar and become granular and the grains may show when the sugar is pulled.

Partially cover the pan with a very clean lid and cook the sugar over high heat.

Place the thermometer in the sugar; add any colourings

· EQUIPMENT ·

Copper sugar pan

Sugar thermometer

Marble slab or tefal sheet,
60 × 40 cm/24 × 16 in

Palette knife or metal
scraper

Thick, heatproof plastic sheet
or a sieve or small baking
sheet

Sugar lamp

A set of modelling sticks and
pastry-cutters on which to
rest the flowers

Gas jet or small spirit lamp
for sticking together leaves
and petals

PICTURE PAGES 230-1

1
Pour the cooked sugar on to a spotlessly clean oiled marble slab and with a palette knife fold the hot sugar mass back on to itself.

2
With your fingertips start to pull the sugar 5 or 6 times.

3
When it has cooled sufficiently, place a hand on one end of the sugar and pull it out. Fold it back on itself and repeat 35–40 times until very glossy and smooth ('satinized').

4
Cut the satinized sugar into 6 or 8 pieces. Work with only 1 piece at a time; store the rest in an airtight container with a dehumidifying agent.

5

Place the satinized sugar under a
sugar lamp and begin to pull and
mould it into the desired shape.

6

Break off small pieces of the sugar
to form flower petals. eg: for roses
or carnations.

7

Use sugar tinted with different
food colourings during the
cooking stage to make petals,
leaves etc.

8

As you finish each petal or leaf,
rest it on a pastry cutter so as not
to spoil the shape while you are
moulding the next one. You will
need at least 27 petals to make a
perfect rose.

9

To finish, use your fingertips to
mould the petals into elaborate
flower shapes.

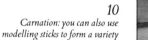

10

Carnation: you can also use
modelling sticks to form a variety
of leaf and petal shapes.

11

Heat the ends of the petals with a
gas jet before assembling the
finished flower.

12

Add extra texture to the petals by
marking them with the bristles of
a brush.

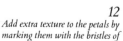

when the temperature reaches about 140°C/284°F. When it reaches 156°C/312°F, take the pan off the heat and stand it on a trivet for 30 seconds, or plunge the base into iced water for 5 seconds.

· COOLING THE SUGAR ·

Pour the sugar onto a spotlessly clean oiled or greased marble slab, or onto the tefal sheet. Use a lightly oiled palette knife or metal scraper to fold the edges back on themselves 3 or 4 times, until they have almost stopped spreading.

· 'SATINIZING' THE SUGAR ·

Leaving the sugar on the marble, fold the mass back onto itself with your fingertips or the palette knife. Start to pull it 5 or 6 times.

By now, the heat of the sugar will be more bearable and you can hold it in your hands and begin the satinizing process properly. Place one hand on one end of the mass and pull it out, then fold it back on itself. Do this 35 or 40 times, alternating the direction each time, until the sugar becomes very glossy and smooth. It will make cracking sounds, known as 'singing.' It is now ready for moulding.

Place the sugar on the plastic sheet under the lamp, or stand it on a sieve or baking sheet inside the opening of the oven, which you have preheated to 120°C/250°F/gas 1. Now cut off a ball large enough for the shape you want; work with only 1 piece at a time, pulling and moulding the sugar into the desired shape.

· NOTES ·

Once the sugar mass has become satiny, it can be cut into 6 or 8 pieces with a cook's knife. The unused pieces, once they have cooled, can be kept until needed in an airtight box lined with silica gel, carbide or quicklime covered with aluminium foil. Then you need only reheat them under the lamp, or at the opening of the preheated oven, turning from time to time so that the sugar softens evenly as it warms.

A tefal sheet is less effective than a marble slab for cooling cooked sugar. If you haven't got a marble, it is better to cook a smaller quantity of sugar.

PRESENTATION

Decorations must always be neat and very simple. They must never dominate or take over the dessert. Their rôle is to delight the eye and titillate the tastebuds; sometimes, they serve to highlight a special occasion, such as a christening or birthday.

Some decorative motifs can be prepared hours or even days in advance. Store them well away from any heat or damp. These embellishments (called *décors rapportés*) are made separately and added to the dessert or *pièce montée* just before serving. They add a more sophisticated touch than the *décors appliqués*, which are applied directly to the dessert at the last moment.

PATE A CHOUX A DECOR
(Decorative choux paste)

· INGREDIENTS ·

35 g/1½ oz butter, cut into small pieces
50 ml/2 fl oz water
50 ml/2 fl oz milk
Pinch of salt
60 g/2 oz flour
2 × 50-55 g/size 5 eggs

Makes about 300 g/10 oz

Preparation time: 20 minutes

Cooking time: 6-10 minutes, depending on the size of the decorations

You can use these decorations to complement various desserts and sorbets.

· PREPARATION ·

Preheat the oven to 160°C/320°F/gas 4.

Cooking the paste: Cook exactly as for *Pâte à choux*, (see page 54) but stir in the flour with a wire whisk instead of a spatula and dry out the paste, using a spatula, for only 30 seconds.

Beat in the eggs, one at a time, then pass the paste through a very fine sieve, rubbing it through with a plastic scraper into a bowl. Set aside.

Piping the paste: Line a baking sheet with baking parchment or buttered greaseproof paper and pipe out the paste into your desired shape — chequerboard, pine trees, fish net, seashell etc.

Bake in the preheated oven for 6-10 minutes. For shells or any raised shapes, pipe them out flat, bake and, as soon as they come out of the oven, mould them around a spherical mould, or whatever shape is appropriate. Leave to cool on the mould.

· STORAGE ·

Pâte à choux will keep very well for a week in a dry, airtight container.

· EQUIPMENT ·

1 saucepan
1 fine sieve
Piping bag with a plain 2-3 mm/¹⁄₁₆-⅛ in nozzle, or a paper cone
Greaseproof paper or baking parchment
1 baking sheet

MAIN PICTURE *Floral presentation in pulled sugar*
LEFT, TOP TO BOTTOM *Madame Fish: poured
sugar over royal icing piped on to paper; Rabbit:
poured sugar with decoration piped in royal
icing; Pink flamingo: pastillage; Cottage:
pastillage.*

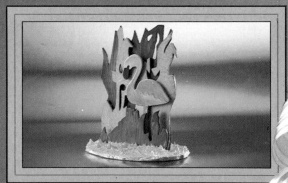

RIGHT, TOP TO BOTTOM *Fruit bowl: bunch of
grapes and vine leaf, pear, apple, lemon and
banana in blown sugar; Penguin waiter in blown
sugar; Fish in blown sugar on rock sugar, with a
poured sugar base; Sugar cubes and rock sugar.*

RIGHT *'Stained glass window', Village in a
landscape: design piped on to paper and dried.*

PASTILLAGE
(Gum sugar paste)

Making *pastillage* does not require much experience, but you do need nimble fingers for cutting out and moulding. In culinary competitions, one often sees models which have taken thousands of hours to prepare — cathedrals, temples, Eiffel Towers etc. Sometimes, *pastillage* is made with gum arabic instead of gelatine which is why it is called 'gum' sugar paste.

· PREPARATION ·

Place the sifted icing sugar and starch on a wooden surface and make a well in the centre. Pour in the lukewarm water.

Put the egg white in a bain-marie and heat gently, stirring with your fingertips, so that it does not coagulate. Remove from the bain-marie and stir in the well-drained gelatine until completely dissolved. Still stirring with your fingertips, pour this mixture into the well, add the lemon juice and knead together, gradually drawing the icing sugar and starch into the centre. You should have a firm but malleable paste. If it seems too soft, add a little more icing sugar; if it seems too firm, add a drop of lukewarm water.

Immediately wrap the *pastillage* in a sheet of polythene so that it does not dry out or crack.

· SHAPING ·

If possible, this should be done on a very smooth, clean wooden table, dusted with arrowroot.

Roll out the *pastillage* to the appropriate size, shape and thickness for the model; use a template to help you if you like.

· DRYING ·

Immediately place the shaped model on a very smooth baking sheet lightly dusted with icing sugar and leave to dry at room temperature for 24-48 hours. Once the top is dry, turn the model over so that the bottom also dries. The drier the *pastillage*, the more solid the model will be.

For a really smooth finish like porcelain, polish the surface with very fine glasspaper.

· TO SERVE ·

You can make several pieces to fashion one larger model (eg, our little house, page 230). Stick the pieces together with royal icing (see page 236), piped out with a paper cone.

Pastillage painted with food colouring looks very attractive and artistic on a buffet table; it is also very simple to do. If you like, you can also colour the *pastillage* during kneading.

· STORAGE ·

Pastillage will not keep for long; it will dry out and crack. For best results, shape it immediately after kneading. It will, however, keep for up to 24 hours in the fridge if you wrap it well in polythene.

N O U G A T I N E

· INGREDIENTS ·

480 g/1 lb flaked almonds

660 g/1 lb 6 oz sugar

60 g/2 oz butter (optional)

2 tbsp peanut oil

Makes 1.2 kg/2 lb 12 oz
Preparation time: 25 minutes

Little *nougatine* shapes (squares, lozenges etc) make a delightful accompaniment to coffee. Serve them with other petits fours. Dip one side in chocolate for a perfect finishing touch.

· PREPARATION ·

Preheat the oven to 180°C/350°F/gas 5.

Have ready all the cutters and implements you will need for shaping the *nougatine*.

· TO COOK ·

Spread the flaked almonds over a baking sheet and place in the preheated oven until very lightly browned. Put the sugar in the pan, set over low heat and cook until melted and light golden, stirring gently and continuously with a spatula, then stir in the almonds.

Stir over low heat for 1 minute, then add the butter if you are using it; it will give the *nougatine* an extra sheen but is not essential. Mix until the butter is completely absorbed.

Pour the mixture onto a lightly oiled baking sheet.

· SHAPING THE NOUGATINE ·

Place the baking sheet near the warm oven, keeping the oven door half open; if it is not placed near a source of heat, the *nougatine* will become difficult to work. Work with only 1 piece at a time, using the appropriate size for the shape you want. Roll out each piece on a lightly oiled, warmed baking sheet, or on a plastic board or lightly oiled marble. You must work very quickly, since the *nougatine* quickly becomes brittle.

Roll it to an appropriate thickness to the desired shape, but never thicker than 5 mm/¼ in.

Quickly cut out the shapes with the cutters, or the blade or heel of a knife. If you are moulding the *nougatine*, do this very fast, so that it follows the shape and contours of the mould. Do not unmould before the *nougatine* is completely cold.

· EQUIPMENT ·

1 baking sheet

1 baking sheet or a plastic or marble board

1 sugar pan

Weighted or hardwood rolling pin

Pastry cutters, flan rings or a chopping knife, depending on the desired shape

Sugar lamp (optional)

Continued on page 236

Cat (120 g/4 oz pink almond paste).

Owl (120 g/4 oz green almond paste).

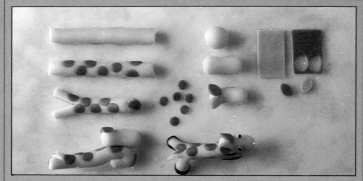

Spotted dog (105 g/3½ oz untinted and 15 g/½ oz light brown almond paste). Marzipan is tinted with liquid food colouring. The eyes are Royal icing, pupils, ears and feet are dipped in chocolate.

MODELLING IN MARZIPAN AND ALMOND PASTE

Rose (40-50 g/1½ oz red almond paste).

Marzipan seals, tinted and painted a strong blue; base and icebergs are coloured poured sugar.

Marzipan pieces should be brushed with cocoa butter to protect against dust and fingerprints, and to give an attractive sheen.

If you have a sugar lamp, place just far enough from the *nougatine* to keep the whole mass warm while you mould individual pieces. Any small leftover pieces can be reheated in the oven and used again.

· STORAGE ·

Like all sugar-based confectionery, *nougatine* dislikes humidity, and therefore keeps for only a day or two in damp conditions.

· NOTES ·

You can use nibbed almonds instead of flaked, but they look less attractive.

Pieces of *nougatine* can be stuck together with hard crack sugar to make all sorts of artistic shapes and designs. To make a really classic *nougatine* sculpture, pipe out a pattern with royal icing.

GLACE ROYALE
(Royal icing)

· INGREDIENTS ·

50 g/2 oz egg whites
250 g/9 oz icing sugar, sifted
Juice of ¼ lemon, strained

Preparation time: 5 minutes

· EQUIPMENT ·

Electric mixer, with a paddle or a mixing bowl and wire whisk

· PREPARATION ·

Put the egg whites into the bowl and, beating at low speed, add the sifted sugar, a little at a time, then the lemon juice. Beat until the icing is firm and has risen slightly. It is ready if, when you turn the whisk, the icing forms a fine, straight point and holds its shape whichever way you turn the whisk.

If the icing is too thick, so that a point does not form, add a touch more egg white. If it is too liquid and the point flops over when you hold it upwards, add a little more icing sugar.

· STORAGE ·

Royal icing keeps very well in an airtight plastic container or in a bowl covered with a damp cloth, which will prevent it from drying out and forming a crust. It will keep in the fridge for several days, although it is better to use it immediately.

· NOTES ·

Use a palette knife to spread the icing thinly on pastry matchsticks (see page 198) to serve with coffee, or pipe it into all sorts of decorative shapes using a piping bag. You can also use it to assemble *sucre rocher* creations (see page 222).

Royal icing can be tinted with a little food colouring to brighten up petits fours and decorations.

Inspiration for the shapes of letters and words in Royal icing (opposite page) can be drawn from many sources. Book jackets and food packaging are readily available and encompass both traditional and contemporary motifs. Examples here include English and Roman scripts, bookface, Art deco and fantasy designs.

A series of decorative borders in Royal icing add the finishing touches to such desserts as Le Fraisier (page 114) and Croquembouche (page 126).

Bowl, moulded from ice, filled with flowers and
foliage (page 241)

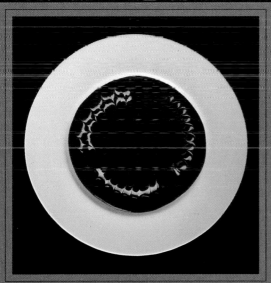

FEATHERING

A decorative motif that relies for effect on contrasting colours, a steady hand, and a very finely pointed knife or cocktail stick. Combinations of Melba sauce, melted chocolate, double cream, caramel sauce and chocolate sauce decorate a variety of bases: ABOVE LEFT *Melba sauce, and* RIGHT *Caramel sauce (page 64).* BELOW LEFT *Chocolate sauce (page 67), and* RIGHT *Peach coulis (page 71).*

PATE A DECOR
(Decorative cornets)

· INGREDIENTS ·
60 g/2 oz flour
60 g/2 oz icing sugar
1 white from a 70 g/ size 1 egg or 1½ whites from 2 × 50 g/size 5 eggs

In our restaurants we like to present the sorbets in these enchanting cornets, but take care because, like all delicate and elegant objects, they are very fragile.

This mixture can also be used for piping all sorts of decorative shapes — pine trees, fences, little houses or birds, using a very small nozzle.

· EQUIPMENT ·
1 template with diagram
Piping bag or paper cones, fitted with a plain 2 mm/¹⁄₁₆ in nozzle
Baking sheet
Baking parchment or greaseproof paper

1

Butter and flour a baking sheet. Press the template, design side downwards, on to the baking sheet to impress the design on the flour. Leave space between each impression.

2

Pipe the mixture around the edge of the design, then make a mark in the centre and pipe 2 V-shapes on either side, then 2 inverted V-shapes. Also pipe serpentines for the bases.

1

2

3

Add more water to the mixture to make a thick liquid paste. With a small palette knife, fill in the bases of the cornets with this paste.

4

Bake for 2-3 minutes, then carefully bend the mixture into cornet shapes.

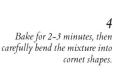

3

4

5

Carefully place the cornets inside dariole moulds, lattice side down, and leave to harden.

6

Dip the bases of the cornets into hard crack sugar and gently stick them on to the solid part of the serpentine 'feet'.

5

6

Makes 8–10 cornets

Preparation time: 25 minutes

Cooking time: 3 minutes

· PREPARATION ·

Preheat the oven to 220°C/425°F/gas 8.

The mixture: Sift the flour and icing sugar into a bowl. Add the egg white and work together with a spatula until completely amalgamated. Cover the bowl with a damp cloth and refrigerate for at least 30 minutes before using the mixture. This resting time is essential, but you can make the mixture in advance and keep it in the fridge, covered with clingfilm, for up to 24 hours.

· TO COOK ·

Pipe out the mixture onto a baking sheet lined with baking parchment or buttered greaseproof paper. Depending on the size and shape of your model, bake in the preheated oven for 3–5 minutes.

You will need to add enough cold water to the mixture to make a thick liquid paste before piping the bases.

COUPE EN GLACE MOULEE
(How to mould a bowl out of ice)

Put some ice cubes in the larger bowl, then place the smaller bowl on top. Pour some iced water into the gap between the bowls, then put in some brightly coloured flowers and foliage and add more ice cubes, making sure that they hold down the flowers and foliage and prevent them from rising to the surface.

Continue until the space between the bowls is filled. Now weigh down the smaller bowl to stop it from floating and to keep it at the correct height. Freeze for 6–24 hours until solid.

To unmould, remove the weights from the smaller bowl and pour in a little lukewarm water (no hotter than 30°C/86°F). Remove the smaller bowl after 1 or 2 minutes.

Dip the bottom of the larger bowl into lukewarm water and carefully unmould it. You now have a bowl made of ice in which to serve fruit sorbets in their skin — pineapple, for example — or scoops of ice cream. If you are serving ice cream, first line the bowl with foil. If you like, you can stick the bowl onto a stand also moulded from ice; use finely crushed ice to attach the bowl to the stand. The edge of the bowl can be decorated in a zig-zag pattern by marking with the back of a knife dipped in boiling water between each cut.

Just before serving, place the bowl on a napkin to absorb the moisture as it melts. It will last at room temperature for about 30 minutes or more, depending on the size.

· EQUIPMENT ·

2 freezerproof hemispherical moulds, 1 two-thirds smaller than the other

Ice cubes

Flowers and foliage

PICTURE PAGE 238

C O P E A U X D E C H O C O L A T
(Chocolate curls)

Chocolate curls make an attractive decoration for many desserts, including *Oeufs à la neige* (page 105). They can be made with either plain or white chocolate or, for an unusual 2-tone effect, you can combine them. Spread some dark chocolate on the slab and just before it sets comb it with a pastry comb. Coat with a thin layer of white chocolate. Once this has hardened, proceed as for Step 2 (below).

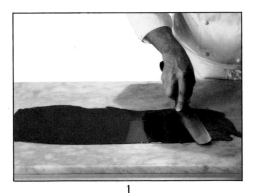

1
Pour the melted chocolate on to a chilled, dry marble slab. Spread it thinly backwards and forwards and from side to side, with a palette knife, until the chocolate sets.

1

2
With a large knife at a 30° angle, push the chocolate away from you, gradually straightening the knife until it is at 90° to the slab. The sharper the angle, the smaller the curls.

2

3
To make petals pull a plain 10 cm/4 in pastry cutter across the chocolate towards you.

3

4
Dip the base of each petal into melted chocolate and place one petal on top of the other to form a flower.

4

GLOSSARY OF PATISSERIE TERMS

Abaisser:
To roll out pastry.

Abricoter:
To apply a thin, even layer or coating of apricot jam, redcurrant jelly, etc with a brush.

Appareil:
The mixture of ingredients used in the preparation of a dish (eg, *appareil à soufflé*: soufflé mixture).

Apprêt:
The time needed for a leavened mixture to rise and ferment between the preparation and the baking.

Beurrer:
To brush the inside of a mould, or a baking sheet, with melted or softened butter. It also means placing the butter in puff pastry dough before rolling out.

Beurre clarifié (clarified butter):
To clarify, heat the butter very gently until it comes to the boil. Ladle the clear butter through a muslin-lined sieve leaving the milky deposit in the bottom of the pan.

Beurre noisette:
Bring some butter to the boil. When it stops foaming and just before it begins to colour, it gives off a wonderful, nutty scent.

Beurre pommade (softened butter):
Remove the butter from the fridge and leave in a warm place until softened.

Blanchir:
To whisk egg yolks and sugar vigorously together until light and foamy. (In pastry-making, this term has a different meaning from 'blanching' in cookery.)

Bloquer:
The point at which a chocolate coating becomes too thick to spread and then solidifies.

Carameliser:
To coat the inside of a mould with caramelized sugar; or to flavour a sauce or cream with caramelized sugar or liquid caramel.

Chemiser:
To line or coat the inside of a mould with a thick or thin layer of mixture (eg, a *bombe*), or with greaseproof paper.

Chiqueter:
To mark out the rim or edges of pastry dough (such as a *galette des rois*), by indenting diagonally with the blade of a knife; this ensures that the dough will rise uniformly and gives an attractive, tasteful decorative effect.

Concasser:
To pound or chop roughly.

Corser:
To give body to a dough or mixture so that it can be worked until it becomes firm and elastic.

Coucher or **dresser:**
To pipe choux pastry into various shapes using a forcing bag and nozzle (eg, choux buns or *éclairs*).

Cracher:
To cut or mark out incisions in puff pastry using a sharp knife; this is done, for example, with a *Pithiviers* so that it will develop properly during cooking.

Cuire à blanc (bake blind):
To bake pastry shells, flan cases, etc without a filling; the empty case is lined with greaseproof paper and filled with metal, ceramic or dried beans before baking.

Dessecher:
To evaporate moisture from a preparation (choux pastry, apple purée etc) by stirring over gentle heat.

Détailler:
To cut out pastry shapes with a pastry cutter (eg, tartlet cases or *fleurons*); or to divide a piece of dough into even-sized pieces (eg, bread dough).

Détrempe:
A dough mixture of flour, water, salt and sometimes, fat; sugar and butter are also added for croissants.

Dorer (to glaze):
To brush dough with beaten egg or eggwash made from egg yolk and milk before baking; this must be done very lightly.

Emincer:
To cut into very fine slices.

Enrober:
To cover a cake, sweet or petits fours completely with fondant, chocolate, icing, caramel, etc.

Fariner:
To dust a work surface with flour before rolling out pastry dough so that it will not stick; or to flour a greased mould lightly.

Foisonner:
To beat a mixture until it increases in volume (eg, ice cream).

Foncer:
To line a mould with pastry.

Fouetter:
To beat a fairly liquid mixture either in a machine or by hand.

Fraiser or **fraser:**
To work pastry ingredients with the palm of your hand to ensure that they are thoroughly mixed (eg, *pâte sucrée, pâte sablée* and shortcrust).

Glacer (to glaze):
To sprinkle a puff pastry dessert with icing sugar before putting it in a very hot oven for a few seconds to caramelize the sugar; or to ice a dessert or small choux pastries with a thin coating of fondant.

Macérer:
To steep dried, candied or fresh fruits in syrup, alcohol or liqueur so that they soak up the liquid and absorb its flavour and aroma.

Marbrer:
Fondant icing, decorated and marked with lines to look like marbling.

Masquer:
To use a palette knife to spread a smooth, even layer of cream over a dessert before adding the final decoration or icing.

Masse:
A mixture of several ingredients which will form the basis of a more elaborate dish (similar to *appareil*).

Meringuer:
To add a little sugar to fresh egg whites to strengthen the albumen and prevent them from breaking down; or to place a meringue-topped dessert in a very hot oven to give it an attractive colour.

Monder:
To skin almonds, walnuts, pistachios, etc and certain fresh fruits (eg, peaches) by pouring over boiling water for a few seconds, then refreshing in cold water.

Napper:
To cook until thick enough to coat a wooden spoon; *napper* denotes that a *crème anglaise* has reached the desired consistency; or to coat as in *abricoter*.

Paton:
A block of puff pastry during its preparation; any piece of dough of the correct size to use for a given recipe.

Pincer:
To pinch up the edges of a tart using your fingers or a pastry crimper.

Pointage:
The time between kneading a leavened dough and the first rising (the biological interaction of the yeast and sugar).

Pousse:
The development of a leavened dough caused by fermentation — the rising between kneading and baking.

Puncher:
To brush a *génoise* or sponge with alcohol-flavoured syrup.

Rognures:
The pastry trimmings left over from cutting out larger shapes. These may be used as flan cases or to make *mille-feuilles*.

Rompre (knock back):
With a lightly floured hand, lift up your risen dough and quickly flip it up 2 or 3 times; this will bring it back to its original volume.

Sabler:
To rub fat into flour with your fingertips until the mixture has a granular texture resembling fine breadcrumbs.

Sangler:
To pack a mixture of ice and salt around a mould filled with a *bombe* or other mixture to freeze it quickly.

Tabler:
To cool a chocolate coating once it has melted, while still keeping it at the right spreading consistency. This is done by working it on a marble slab with a palette knife or triangular scraper so that it does not harden and become lumpy (see also *bloquer*).

Travailler:
To beat a mixture with a whisk or spatula to make it smooth and homogenous.

Vanner:
To stir a sauce or cream occasionally while it is cooling, using a spatula. This prevents a skin from forming and the mixture from separating.

Zester:
To grate the rind of an orange or lemon with a cheese grater, or finely pare the zest with a zester, taking care to leave behind the bitter white pith.

· CONVERSION TABLES ·

Approximate equivalents		Liquid measurements	
Metric	Imperial	Metric	Imperial
15 g	½ oz	25 ml	1 fl oz
25–30 g	1 oz	50 ml	2 fl oz
40 g	1½ oz	100 ml	3½ fl oz
50–60 g	2 oz	125 ml	4 fl oz
75 g	2½ oz	150 ml	5 fl oz
100 g	3½ oz	200 ml	7 fl oz
125 g	4 oz	250 ml	9 fl oz
150 g	5 oz	275 ml	10 fl oz (½ pt)
200 g	7 oz	300 ml	11 fl oz
225 g	8 oz (½ lb)	350 ml	12 fl oz
300 g	10 oz	400 ml	14 fl oz
350 g	12 oz	450 ml	16 fl oz
400 g	13 oz	500 ml	18 fl oz
450 g	16 oz (1 lb)	575 ml	1 pt
500 g	17 oz	850 ml	1½ pt
900 g	2 lb	1 lt	1¾ pt
1 kg	2 lb 2 oz	2 lt	2½ pt

· USEFUL MEASUREMENTS ·

1 level tablespoon (15 ml) contains:

Caster sugar	15 g/½ oz
Flour	10 g/⅓ oz
Salt	20 g/⅔ oz
Cocoa powder	10 g/⅓ oz
Cornflour, potato flour, baking powder or semolina	7 g/¼ oz
Icing sugar	10 g/⅓ oz

There are 3 level teaspoons to 1 level tablespoon

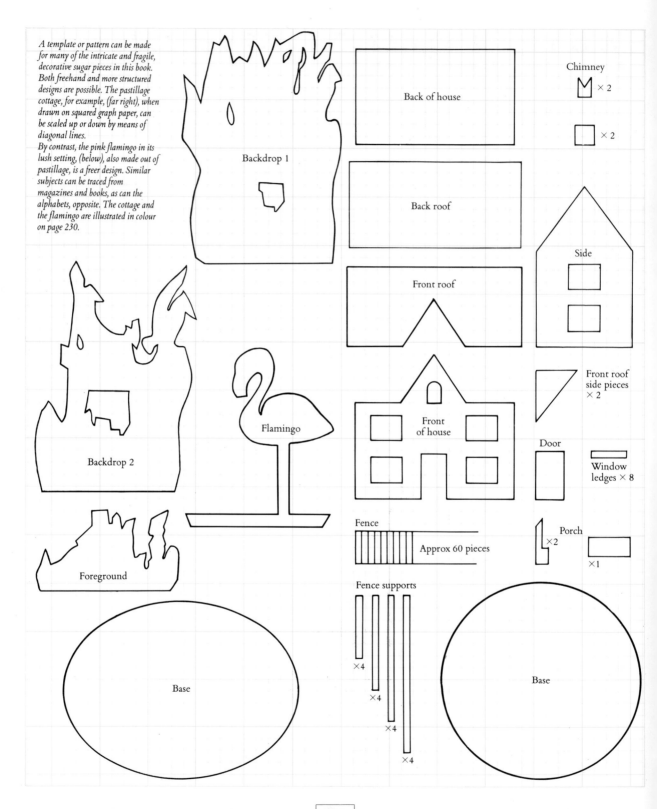

A template or pattern can be made for many of the intricate and fragile, decorative sugar pieces in this book. Both freehand and more structured designs are possible. The pastillage cottage, for example, (far right), when drawn on squared graph paper, can be scaled up or down by means of diagonal lines.

By contrast, the pink flamingo in its lush setting, (below), also made out of pastillage, is a freer design. Similar subjects can be traced from magazines and books, as can the alphabets, opposite. The cottage and the flamingo are illustrated in colour on page 230.

Backdrop 1

Back of house

Back roof

Front roof

Chimney
× 2

× 2

Side

Front roof side pieces × 2

Door

Window ledges × 8

Backdrop 2

Flamingo

Front of house

Foreground

Fence
Approx 60 pieces

Porch
× 2

× 1

Fence supports
× 4
× 4
× 4
× 4

Base

Base

AA ABBCD DEEF F
GHHITJKKLLMM
MNNOPPQRRR ST
1234567890
UUVVWWXXYYZ

ABCDEFGHIJKLM
NOP2RITUVWXYZ
1234567890

ABCDEFGHIJKLMN
OPQRSTUVWXYZ
1234567890

INDEX

'*Patisserie: An affair of the heart*'

MICHEL AND ALBERT ROUX

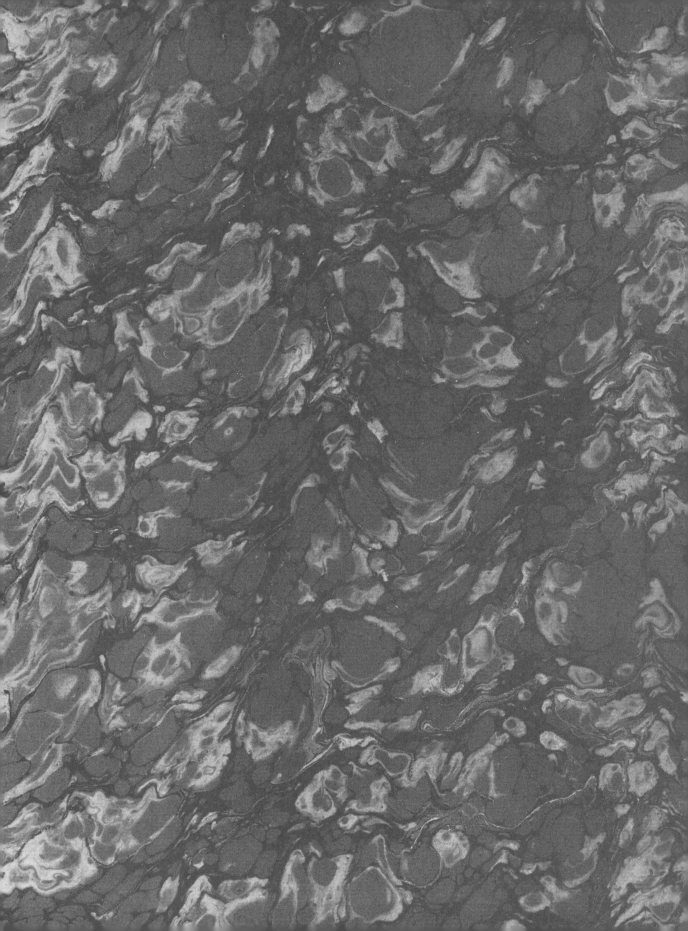